# Building Your Best Voice

# Building Your Best Voice

## HENRY N. JACOBI

PRENTICE-HALL, INC.
Englewood Cliffs, New Jersey 07632

Building Your Best Voice
by Henry N. Jacobi
Copyright © 1982 by Henry N. Jacobi

Printed in the United States of America

Prentice-Hall International, Inc., London
Prentice-Hall of Australia, Pty. Ltd., Sydney
Prentice-Hall of Canada Inc., Toronto
Prentice-Hall of India Private Ltd., New Delhi
Prentice-Hall of Japan, Inc., Tokyo
Prentice-Hall of Southeast Asia Pt. Ltd.,
Singapore
Whitehall Books Limited, Wellington, New Zealand
Editora Prentice-Hall do, Brasil LTDA., Rio de
Janeiro

10 9 8 7 6 5 4 3 2 1

ISBN 0-13-086587-7 (PBK.)

ISBN 0-13-086595-8

Library of Congress Cataloging in Publication
Data
Jacobi, Henry N.,
    Building your best voice.
    Includes index.
    1. Voice cultures.  I. Title
PN4162.J3  1982    808.5    82-0027
ISBN 0-13-086595-8          AACR2
ISBN 0-13-086587-7 (pbk.)

To Tanya, my wife.
To Jeffrey, my son, who I hope
will carry on my work.

With Love

# CONTENTS

# ACKNOWLEDGMENTS

This is to thank my students for their help in
constructing this book which could never have
been done without their contributions.

Special thanks to Albert Kay of Albert Kay
Associates, Concert Artists Management, New York
City, for his good taste and judgment.

# FOREWORD by Tony Randall

I can imagine an actor being introduced to this
approach to the vocal problem asking a few typical questions: "Why do actors need what is generally known as singers' training? If my speech
is clear and I can be heard, if I know how to
'project,' isn't that good enough? Modern plays
don't demand Shakespearean voices." Let me answer as well as I can from my own experience.
When I was about fifteen I decided to become an
actor and badgered my parents until they let me
study. My teacher drilled me in articulation. I
was lucky in having but few really bad faults to
be corrected. He had a deep, beautiful voice and
I imitated him. People began to tell me I had a
beautiful voice. I went to college and majored
in speech. Every morning for a year we had an
hour's drill in consonants and vowels. We
learned how to pronounce frequently mispro-
nounced words. We made records at the beginning
and end of the term and my speech had improved.
The teachers and students admired my voice. I
had added to it a tremolo copied from an actor I
admired. Then I went to dramatic school and two
more years of excellent speech training. Upon

graduation I was offered a position teaching voice and speech. Everyone considered me an authority, especially my pupils. During all this time I had been doing a great deal of acting, of course. This, the real test of my voice, gave me plenty to worry about. I knew that because my articulation was clean and well tutored I could be understood. People liked my voice because it had a naturally pleasant quality and it sounded deep, but it was my secret that I forced it to be deep. However, if I spoke that deep on stage in a large auditorium I couldn't be heard. Furthermore, when I raised my voice it no longer sounded good; it lost its quality. If the scene demanded power, I could only yell; I could not raise my voice without its becoming raucous and strained. After a performance I frequently had a sore throat. I had no idea what to do about it and I stubbornly believed that I had a well-trained voice and that I knew a lot about the subject. After all, in college we had even gone into the physics of sound, the science of acoustics. We had studied phonetics and practiced drills with a device in our mouths that kept the upper and lower teeth an inch apart. About this time I spent a summer in stock with an actor whose prime interest was singing. His voice amazed me. It had a boom and ring to it that I could not duplicate no matter how hard I tried to imitate him. On stage with him I had to shout to equal his normal vocal level. In big scenes he could roar like a bull without effort and without fatigue and without losing his mellifluous quality. Even choked up with a cold he had more voice than I at my best. How to attain such power and freedom and quality? I think my development began with that question. In time my search led me to the author of this book.

Now it's true that the modern media---movies, radio, TV---require very little from the actor vocally, or perhaps any other way. Even the stage does not absolutely demand vocal opu-

lence. To this argument I can only answer that
anyone with an ounce of artistic drive will not
be satisfied to meet only the minimum standards,
to leave himself so unfulfilled.

   I see one other question: Will developing
your tone give you a beautiful voice? That's
very hard to answer. What is beautiful? Beauty
sometimes is the gift of God. But let it content
you that you can bring what you have to a state
of fullness and health and real serviceability.

# Building Your Best Voice

# INTRODUCTION: THE BIRTH OF A VOCAL PRINCIPLE

Books on voice are said to be boring. I reluc-
tantly agree. No book by itself can do the job
of a teacher and show anyone how to speak or
sing well---or for that matter how to act or
dance. The written word alone cannot produce a
realization of creative experience, nor can it
serve to adjust and correct the living human instrument, with its subtleties and complexities.
Only the act of making sounds and dealing with
human sounds can do that. Only the insight of a
teacher can spot the basis of vocal problems.
Only the ingenuity of a teacher can help to introduce the remedial, technical exercises that
provide a definite solution to these problems so
that each student can fulfill the individual requirements of the moment.

This is, of course, easier said than done.
In the first place, what standards of judgment
shall be applied to selecting the proper
training for a particular student? Second, what
is to be considered the correct sound for a
voice student to produce? How is it to be
achieved? Who produces it? Who teaches it? These
are simple questions, yet no one has as yet been

able to find simple answers, and it is doubtful
whether anyone ever will.

Let us consider the case of a young student
who has been inspired and beguiled by art and
artists. As a singer, he is a psychological
puzzle. He sings because he wants to sing, because he must sing. It is often not vanity, but
the urge of the soul to speak in a language beyond the commonplace that drives him. Even people whose personalities seem dry and reserved
often glow with warmth and imagination when they
sing. They speak the language of the inner
voice.

However, this same young student has little
judgment regarding to whom he should entrust his
vocal abilities. Through recommendation or accident he selects a teacher. He lavishes all his
devotion upon this teacher who he thinks is the
right one for him. All too often he is capti-
vated by the momentary popularity, publicity and
connections of the teacher or by the accomplishment of the teacher as a singer. Being trusting,
he must depend upon his teacher and bear faithful allegiance to him.

The teacher, in turn, must depend upon his
own wisdom and experience and, on occasion, upon
recommended textbooks. As a member of the profession, I recognize with admiration all those
teachers who have been contributing to the solution of the vocal problem, and I admire all
those vocalists whose good vocal production
gives us an example and a goal. However, there
can be no doubt that a veritable chaos of opinions reigns today in the field of voice teaching. One training method opposes another, and
there are deep rivalries at play in the profession. This situation seems to create a necessity
for a fresh examination of the entire subject.
It is my hope that the new material presented in
this book and the analysis of the whole voice
training problem undertaken in this book, with
the intent to show the practical side of voice

study, may help to clear some aspects of vocal technique from further controversy.

My own 40 years of teaching have taught me that every effort to confine voice teaching to fixed patterns or to constrict vocalism to a single form is against nature and contrary to everything that is valid in human functioning. This raises the question: Can rule books on voice be helpful in voice training?

Many rule books have mechanical prescriptions and fixed exercises identical for all. At first, some of these books may very well find popular acclaim, because most people want to be told to perform some physical act. There are also standard courses and preformulated voice production methods for sale, and some vocal exercises are now available on phonograph records. One may ask, however, how many of these survive the test of time and use.

There is uncertainty connected with the outcome of any vocal exercise. To find a technique that works is always a problem. With each aspect of voice production, exploratory steps must first be taken to obtain reactions from the vocal instrument before any final outline can be drafted and specific technical devices be safely and successfully applied. If not viewed as tentative, any doctrine on vocal technique can easily mislead us from a clear view of the facts and principles.

It seems to me, however, that there is a strong need now for a clear statement of principles of voice development, principles that are applicable to every voice, principles with which to lay the foundation for a genuine, rational way of voice training, principles that will give a rock-bottom basis from which to develop any voice to the height of its possibilities.

It is for that purpose that I have written this book. No one will close the final pages and burst forth into perfect sounds. This book will not tell anyone how to teach himself or her-

self. It is not an attempt to make a voice
teacher out of every reader. In fact, it may
leave the reader believing that voice teaching
requires as much skill as any other specialty
concerned with human development. If it does, it
will have achieved much of its aim.

It is my hope, however, that the issues clarified in this book may give the layperson an
insight into the field of voice and what is involved in the training of the voice, that they
may help the voice student to make a choice of
training on a sounder basis, that they may guide
the already trained singer and speaker into new
channels of concentration and that, perhaps,
they may assist some teachers in their earnest
task to improve the voices of their students.

Particularly the beginning voice teacher
rarely receives much professional preparation in
vocal pedagogy. There is no apprenticeship.
There are no tryouts for voice teaching positions. It is in the light of his own, often
limited experience that he ventures into the
field of voice teaching and struggles with the
problems that arise, as best he can.

The greater portion of this book will be devoted to the most urgent and most frequent problems that have come up in the course of my work
as a teacher. As a practitioner who began to
teach voice at the age of 18 and who has been
specializing in training the speaking and
singing voice ever since, I believe I have encountered all the major problems of the vocal
field across the board. It is my pleasure therefore to present in this book my own work notes
regarding these problems, as well as the remarks
of students in dealing with these problems,
which I have collected throughout my years of
voice teaching and lecturing, both here and
abroad.

As I have dealt with vocal problems, cross-
references to other fields of endeavor have suggested themselves. By comparing the use of the

voice with other functions in life and by inter-
weaving vocal experiences with everyday experiences, I have sought to open a new perspective
in the field of voice.

I believe that the human being in his functioning is basically universal. Hence, the principles that govern the development of the human
being in his functioning are universal, too.
Practitioners in all fields who deal with the
human being's use of her psychophysical mechanism will come across the same basic problems,
even though in each field---as for instance in
voice, dance and acting---we express ourselves
differently and with different instruments.

I also believe that vocal education is a
process in which priority should be given to
reason and logic rather than to dogma, pet
theory or method. Further, I believe that what
is true about the voice is learned best when it
is geared to human understanding rather than
limited to shop talk and scientific abstrac-
tions. Where possible, I have used illustrative
examples and nontechnical language so as to give
the old, tired vocal terms and warmed-over
theories a rest, and to give the readers a com-
prehensible picture of vocal matters and conditions.

I have used a question-and-answer format, as
it lends itself most naturally to the student-
teacher situation. Before entering upon the dis-
cussion, however, I must acquaint the reader
with the special background against which I have
formulated these answers. Teachers are not born
with a spontaneous knowledge of their fields,
but are themselves influenced along special
paths. The wise student should want to be informed about his teacher's background and
training.

The voice teaching approach to which I ad-
here dates back to Mueller-Brunow of Leipzig
(Germany) who, in the late nineteenth century

introduced the <u>basic tone</u> principle to the field of voice training. He was not its originator, for earlier, in 1864, Friedrich Schmitt was already teaching what he called the "Schmitt-Tone." Schmitt, a voice teacher at the Royal Conservatory in Munich, was recognized by Richard Wagner as a master of voice building and an authority in the field of singing. However, it remained for Mueller-Brunow to develop a dynamic and revolutionary concept of the basis for voice teaching, by carrying the basic tone principle to its fullest formulation.

Proponents of the basic tone principle do not so much purport to found a new school over and against other vocal schools or to provide a new technique over and against other vocal techniques; they seek, rather, to create an understanding of what good speakers and singers do when they sound good. This endeavor should yield a foundation upon which all vocal techniques can be based.

It is a simple fact, yet one often overlooked: In speech and singing the artist expresses himself through the medium of sound. He is judged by the way he sounds and he is paid for the way he sounds. Hence, the sound is the thing.

With this in mind, basic tone study differs perhaps from other vocal methods. It starts with the search for all that is best in the sounds we can make and works back, step by step, to the place where work is needed in order to produce and perfect the best sound effect.

It starts with the search for organic unity and overall balance and works back, step by step, to the place where it is necessary to begin in order to obtain and perfect the balanced contribution of all vocal organs in action.

Because it deals immediately with the total vocal process rather than piecemeal work, basic tone study does not require standard breathing exercises, diaphragm exercises or posture and relaxation exercises.

Because it is concerned with the health and growth of the voice rather than with musicianship, coaching and the study of repertoire, basic tone study does not require the use of standard musical exercises, arpeggio, scale work or song and aria study.

Because it does without all these measures, which are today in worldwide use, basic tone study shortens the learning process and simplifies voice training methods.

For teachers like myself who were brought up in and follow this tradition, Mueller-Brunow perhaps stands in the same relation to us as does Stanislavsky to modern teachers of the internal approach to acting. It is natural that there should be innovations and variations as the span of time increases between the masters and their disciples, but the fundamental concepts are still looked to for guidance and inspiration.

It would be simpler, I suppose, to refer the reader to Mueller-Brunow's book, <u>Voice Culture or Singing Lessons</u> (1889), except that this work has never been translated into English. I shall therefore in the following pages try to present as concisely as possible what I consider the major concepts upon which his theories were founded.

The material that follows is my own free translation and adaptation of parts of Mueller-Brunow's book.

God has endowed every human being with natural organs for singing. All people receive the same basic vocal apparatus from nature. It is a misconception that someone who has no good voice cannot gain one. Every normal and healthy person wants to sing---if he has singing in his soul.

For a long time scientists have tried to throw some light upon the mystery of the good voice. They have compared the larynxes of different singers with those of nonsingers and have found no basic physical difference. The "secret" of the good and beautiful voice apparently does not exist only in the physical and mechanical process of the vibrating vocal cords (action of the breath on the vocal cords).

The first natural tone of the human being is a grunt or scream. The subsequent use of the voice only for speaking often creates bad habits. Climate, bodily structure and mental concepts also influence the vocal instrument. If human beings were not affected by growing culture and music and if, in addition, a harmonious production of sounds had not become an urge, our singing would be more comparable to the screaming of a primitive human.

But given a primitive human with the brain power of a present-day person, the teacher of voice would be able to guide that individual's organs into the right way of singing more rapidly than those of some civilized person, since he would be saved the extra work of freeing the tone before developing it. Though all people have been endowed by nature with the same basic apparatus, everyone has a body and nerve structure peculiarly his or her own. Each human being is unique. It is the individual, with unique vocal possibilities, who is the primary factor, and any voice training must be adapted to the individual from the beginning---or from the degree of development he has then reached to the point where the technical demands of speech and singing can be met with ease.

Every vocal instrument consists of moveable parts, some visible and some invisible. The visible parts could be educated mechanically by comparisons and examples, with pictures and words. The invisible parts can be controlled only by our feelings and impressions, both physical and mental. Mental feeling is also partly determined from the outside---for the vocalist, mainly through the ear.

There is no need to remodel God's tools, only to develop and use them most efficiently.

Every singer has a range and position uniquely his or her own. The root of singing is voice development. It means finding the basis of the voice. It means increasing the productivity of the voice. It is the study of attacking and sustaining the tone in a way that will allow the whole singing organism to be fully active and that will hold the entire vocal organism under control. Pure tone-building aims for the greatest possible utilization and equalization of all ranges of which each individual voice is capable.

To study the basic tone means to discover and develop new sound directions and dimensions. Musical exercises and coaching will not achieve this. The practice of correct tone production is necessary; hence the term tone building. Tone building is the root of the art of singing, and the ear for pure tone can be developed.

Everything nature has provided---throat, larynx, head and chest---can be made to "sing." If one is to accomplish this, first all obstacles and obstructions caused by habits of language, dialect, speech and mental attitude must be worked away. This liberation can be achieved with the basic tone. This means searching for that vocal tone that comes most freely and fully to the individual, according to his particular voice structure, range and build, rather than according to the habits he may have built up. It is the sound, no matter what the vowel or the pitch, that streams unfettered from his mouth. It is the sound that makes the singer free and comfortable.

The "secret" of how to build one's best voice consists of catching and controlling the tone, developing its concentration, resonance, roundness and suppleness by the proper use of all controllable parts of the vocal instrument.

The singer's ear allows the tone to sink in. His feeling absorbs it. His memory keeps an impression of it in order to reproduce and compare it. Experiencing correctly produced tones educates the memory, ear and feeling and enables the singer to repeat those tones.

A correct tone is like the sound of a detonated cannon. It pierces the atmosphere and finds an echo in the air waves. An incorrect tone---the strong tone of flat quality, made by throat pressure, tightening or gasping, or the soft tone made by narrowing the throat and cutting off sound---can be compared to an arrow shot from a wet bow string.

Nature should be given its rights. Life and vibrant power are demanded of the whole body, not just of the throat and larynx, as one often hears in lifeless singing. The whole upper part of the body must vibrate, so that the human being is like a sounding column.

The teacher of voice who lacks appreciation of the natural endowments of his students and their peculiarities runs the risk of viewing the human being as a mechanical instrument or puppet which can be operated from the outside. Many methods of instruction do just that. First, the student's exterior actions must satisfy the commands of the teacher; tongue, cheeks, lips or jaw are to be moved in arbitrary patterns. Second, with the invisible inner organ, the student has to produce the tones that satisfy the taste of the teacher and at the same time his or her own taste, which has become little more than a copy of the teacher's. At the same time, however, the inner apparatus goes its own way.

If a student is industrious, he will, with the help of his memory, produce the tones that please the teacher. Whether or not these tones are correctly produced, neither student nor teacher can determine, because the teacher who works from the outside to the inside works in a superficial rather than profound way and does not really understand the difference between a free and an unfree tone. Because the student believes the teacher and wants to be conscientious, he forces himself to accept everything, sometimes against his own convictions; and neither teacher nor student suspects that near the unfree one exists a free, big, broad road---unused.

The unfree mechanism also obeys the will, for it is governed by the habits that have existed through the years. The voice remains stuck in the constrictions that bad habits have imposed. In consequence, the tone is more and more narrowed into a position from which it cannot escape. Since the production is not effortless, the voice depends mainly on force and brutal strength. Such strength in the vocal mechanism often gives out rapidly. Then neighboring organs not meant to be used in singing are employed as a substitute or compensation. Instrument failure results.

In correct functioning, any kind of violence must be avoided. The voice must learn to obey with ease, in proportion to the existing condition of strength.

The voice of the fundamentally well-trained singer should be able to continue developing and growing; the voice with poor preparation is apt to deteriorate rapidly. Badly trained singers whose voices have lost their youthful vibrant power may try forcibly to narrow the throat, to help form a tone. However, even though an especially strong body structure can perhaps take the pull and push, such voices usually end up capable of mere bellowing. Some resulting chronic or acute disorder of the main throat parts may forbid even this work.

Then, too, it often happens that some singers have in their voice range certain tones that do not obey them properly. By desperate narrowing, pushing and using tricks, the singer tries to overcome the defect. Such unnatural manipulations serve only to throw the whole vocal instrument out of gear. Unfortunately, the basic defect is still there, waiting to infect adjacent tones.

On the other hand, a teacher who has asked the main question---how does a correctly pro- duced tone sound?---will in the answer to that question find the completion of vocal studies. He will not build his method according to the habits and experiences of his own or anybody else's body, but according to the law of nature as represented in each case. If the student can produce the tone with desired roundness, sup- pleness and concentration, he needs only to hold on to the tone and learn to articulate through it without interfering with it.

The teacher of this principle turns first of all to the mind of the pupil. It is up to the teacher to use intelligence and skill to make the purpose of any vocal exercise as clear as possible. If the singer has a practical under- standing of pure tone, she can, after five or six months, travel the right road by herself. An experienced teacher will be sensitive to the whole singing organism of his student, her voice structure and fundamental composition, after hearing only a few tones. When completely in- experienced voice students devote themselves to the study of this principle, it is desirable for the teacher to work with them until their voices have attained freedom. A wise student will not be in a hurry. Many who have worked in this way for a number of years still continue to develop vocally.

Under favorable conditions, the basic tone of the individual voice will be found after a few months of work. Still the voice may not yet be set into the new groove. The development of new sound channels takes up most of the time during the period of further study. The speed of this development depends greatly on the flex- ibility of the student's vocal instrument and the ability of the teacher to uncover the true nature  of the pupil's voice. One test of a teacher is the skill with which he coaxes the sound waves of the student into maximum vibration points.

Sometimes an untrained vocal mechanism, unaccustomed to such processes, will resist a singer. Miracles can be achieved with sufficient will power. The muscles and sinews that are subordinated to the will gradually learn to obey. The vocal organism thus develops a new capacity, which in time becomes a habit.

On the other hand, sometimes a student with an ear for correct vocal production can, through his own efforts, build up his voice alone better than with the help of a vocal instructor. A teacher whose ear lacks sensitivity cannot fully understand the nature of the student's gift and will not know how to do justice to the natural equipment or talent of the student. With such "born singers," an intelligent teacher need only awaken consciousness of the voice and set musical taste on the right road.

A singer who works according to the principle of the basic tone hardly ever gets hoarse from singing. He can, of course, become hoarse, like anyone else, when heated organs are exposed to sudden cold and tissues become inflamed. However, if his body is given decent and reasonable care, excessive precautions are unnecessary. If the vocal instrument is kept in good working order and is not misused, the risk of throat trouble will be minimized. One can easily understand that illness occurs less frequently when the organism is strengthened than when it is weakened in its natural activity. With correct tone production, singing strength is evenly distributed. Through practice it can be built up so that it will meet any reasonable vocal demand. This type of production proves to be especially healthful because in some cases it is able to support nature and work away a chronic throat ailment.

In addition, a singer who has perfected the basic tone principle throughout his range should not know technical difficulties. A full developed organism will obey any reasonable technical demand. The singer can then control his tone and produce it, soft or loud, fast or slow, legato or staccato.

The advantages of natural voice building are, of course, beneficial not only to singers, but to actors, lecturers, clergy, lawyers, even army officers---anyone whose profession demands vocal projection. As a matter of fact, many regular army men have seemingly chronic throat trouble. Medical treatment helps them only for the moment. The trouble has been brought about by barking orders under all weather conditions, under hardships and at various temperatures, giving more tone than the vibrations of the vocal cords will comfortably allow. Many an enlisted man would be grateful to the army sergeant who interested himself in voice culture.

As for the teachers who are guided by the basic tone principle, one instructor may favor a certain maneuver while another may find a different one more advantageous. However, the goal is always the same. Contemporary teachers should aim for a broadened viewpoint, which accepts each maneuver for what it has to offer in achieving the aim of basic tone teaching: to develop the individual voice in the most natural and effective way. As long as a teacher concentrates upon natural voice training, the risk of misleading a student is greatly minimized.

In the hearing lies the solution. He is the master teacher who, with a searching ear, can diagnose and perfect the essential qualities, can educate the ear of the student to recognize and remember them, and can educate the memory to reproduce them.

A singer, too, must know the abilities, possibilities and peculiarities of his instrument. He should control his vocal tools as a musician masters his instrument. The highest goal in art is to equal the elemental force of nature. Artistic efforts will complement a prepared vocal organism. If the proper technical foundation has not been laid, premature emphasis on artistic efforts will tend to upset an unprepared voice. It goes without saying, of course, that better singers, teachers and physiologists have always been aware of some proper basic tone function. Many try it, and whatever part of it they accept benefits them. Richard Wagner acknowledged its importance when he commended Professor Schmitt, who broke the ground for this concept.

"Art is joyous," Mueller-Brunow reminded us in Voice Culture or Singing Lessons (1889). "But the road of the artist requires seriousness and endurance. Singing is breath, sound waves, resonance hearing, feeling and music. The total effect of these factors on the living organs appointed by nature for singing is influenced by many conditions of culture, language and taste. Without a teaching principle to guide us, we will find the road uncertain, hazardous and, at best, accidental. I feel it is my solemn duty to stress the existence of a regular, dependable way of voice building, and to enlighten the doubtful and console the discouraged, and to refute the claim that good voices are only accidents."

Against this background, and in keeping with the ideas presented above, I shall endeavor in the following section to deal with the more specific problems that arise during basic vocal training that teachers like myself follow.

# THE VOICE STUDENT ASKS
# AND THE AUTHOR ANSWERS

A survey of the questions most frequently asked by voice students and the answers given during 40 years of teaching by the author.

# THE GOALS: WHAT WE WANT TO ATTAIN

**Q.** What qualities of voice do we want to develop?

**A.** Freedom, form, substance, flexibility.

The voice is a living wind instrument. Its tone is present in all normal persons. In order to fulfill the requirements of vocal art, the existing tone must be produced with freedom and fullness. Hence, to develop or build voice we must learn to produce the tone so that it sounds free, round, ringing and even-flowing.

Free---in contrast to a hampered tone, free from all the deficiencies that prevent control, strength and ease of tone.

Round---in contrast, for example, to a spread or narrow tone.

Ringing---in contrast, for example, to a dull or muffled or breathy tone.

Even---in contrast to unsteady; flowing---in contrast to a stiff, inflexible tone.

Freedom in vocal production, as in every aspect of our lives, is a necessity. Without it

19

we are enslaved. With it we can grow. Of all the
four components, freedom should therefore enjoy
the priority. Of the other three qualities---
roundness, ring and even-flow---none should have
priority; all three are equally essential, and
the order in which they are quoted here and in
which they appear in vocal development is of no
consequence. When we speak of the combination of
these three, we shall simply refer to them as
"qualities."

---

**Q.   Is there a simple definition of what a voice
must learn to accomplish?**

**A.   With some few exceptions, singing adds up to
the production of a phrase and series of
phrases.**

---

Whether in opera or the simplest folk song, each
phrase consists of text sung in one breath (just
as in a play each sentence consists of text spoken in one breath). For example, in "The Star-
Spangled Banner," "Oh say" is a phrase. Or, if a
person chooses to sing, "Oh say can you see" in
one breath, then that is a phrase.

A phrase consists of the production of
tones, syllables and/or words. These must be
attacked, sustained, ended and connected. The
capability to do this must exist throughout the
voice range.

Hence, to prepare for the art of phrase
singing, we must learn to produce in one breath,
with freedom and "qualities," the tones, syllables and words, so as to attack, sustain, end,
and connect them throughout the range.

In this way, all functions concerned in
vocal production will be developed in a definite
sequence of steps dealing with the health and
growth of the voice. The vocal instrument will
learn, through the use of graded vocal exercises, to meet the demands of vocal production.

Q.    That's all right for a singer, but does an
      actor need the same thing?
A.    Indeed. There is no basic difference in
      voice development. There is, however, a dif-
      ference between speech and singing in the
      way the developed voice is used.

While the actor depends more on tone color for
speech, the singer depends more on pitch, duration and volume of tone for singing. We meet
singers who carry over into their ordinary
speech drawn-out vowels, unnecessary loudness
and range, making themselves unbecomingly conspicuous. On the other hand, the musical comedy
actor who lacks the necessary range, volume and
sustaining power often sounds pale and "speechy"
in his singing.

The belief that the speaking and singing
voice are two different voices is widespread. It
is obvious, though, that each of us has only one
vocal instrument. Fundamentally, the production
of vocal sound is always the same. Whether we
employ the vocal instrument for speech, sing-
song, chanting, everyday singing or artistic
purposes, our vocal organs are governed by the
same basic laws.

The vocal instrument can reach its greatest
vitality and endurance more through singing than
through speech because the demands put upon the
voice in singing are by far greater than those
in speaking. Hence, in the development of the
vocal instrument, the singing voice leads the
speaking voice.

It is interesting to note that Constantin
Stanislavsky, in his book Building a Character,
describes how he attained the full utilization
of his speaking voice through the systematic
development of his singing voice. He also points
out how he worked from the sung tone to the spoken tone. This development is often omitted by

singers. When they neglect to incorporate the
support and resonance of their singing voice
into their speaking voice, they may find it
difficult to project their speaking voice. This
difficulty is often quite obvious in musical
comedy performers.

Some actors and speakers are afraid of the
term "singing voice." They take for granted that
a musical foundation is necessary for this type
of work. To be sure, a musical foundation can be
of importance for the purpose of improving
speech. For example, the tone deaf actor is usually incapable of fully expressing the nuances
of his emotional range, because he lacks variety
of vocal range. Since he hits the same note all
night long, his voice lulls the audience to
sleep. Ear training and the study of harmony can
enhance his effort to overcome vocal monotony
and to gain a more musical sound in the spoken
word.

In some cases, the inability to sing on key
is due mainly to a lack of confidence and experience. The mental and vocal controls are not
together. Body and brain were not given enough
opportunity to collaborate and become efficient
in singing. Once the individual is given a
chance through voice training, the pitch problem
may gradually subside and the grasp of pitch
eventually become normal without any special
course in ear training.

It is even possible to develop tone without
being able to carry a tune. It is not the tune
but the development of the vocal mechanism in
its production of tone that we are seeking.
Singing (that is, tone exercises) serves the
actor or speaker primarily as the means of getting the instrument into shape, so that the
voice can follow the feeling without undue
effort and the artist can use himself to the
fullest and express himself in the best way
possible.

We do not want to sing the lines of a play.
When the lines of a straight play sound as if

they were sung, the actor is putting voice before feeling, which is a mistake in order. A
similar wrong reveals itself when an actor or
actress sounds "voicy," "actressy" or "voice-
vain."

Some old-timers occasionally fall into
sing-song or they speak with a tremor. As a
rule, such melodramatic speech is no longer
acceptable as an adequate means of expression in
the theatre. We have become immune to the emotional appeal of a tremor actor. Time has condemned him as lacking in genuine significance,
although we may perhaps become susceptible to
him again at some future turn of the drama spi-
ral. Since the art of acting now shows a marked
trend toward realism, economy and simplifica-
tion, a melodramatic approach strikes us as
odd. Of course, even the tremor and other oddi-
ties of an actor may sometimes come to his aid,
as for instance when the part calls for a
"shaking with rage" or when he portrays eccen-
tric or grotesque people with an offbeat kind of
voice.

Some actors are afraid that the study of
voice will give them a phony or "put on" sort of
speech. Phoniness comes from an attempt to force
an artificial quality. This is true in voice,
acting, dancing and every other form of human
expression.

The way in which we should study depends
upon the purpose of study. For the purpose of
radio acting,[1] it was expedient to direct the
study of voice to some extent toward "put-on"
speech. This was particularly true when it came
to the various vocal sound effects that the
nature of radio acting required. The business of
characterization in radio acting frequently lent
itself to vocal tricks and the use of vocal imperfections. That sort of voice production, when
maintained for a great length of time or when
carried over into everyday speech, may later
prove to be antagonistic or even destructive to
a person's individuality. Voice culture, in con-

trast, depends upon the development of greater perfection. When studying voice culture, the individual works to free and form his or her existing tone and to make it more flexible and substantial. This study encourages rather than suppresses the individuality of the voice and directs it toward ideal rather than artificial ends.

The theatre is still a place where an audience can be gripped by the resounding tones of an actor expressing joy, pain, grief, horror, fear and other emotions. The present-day actor, however, is often incapable of the bare business of "noise making." He has not had much opportunity. His income is probably largely derived from television, movie, radio and night club engagements. There the microphone does it for him. Or he may even shy away from it because he feels that a stigma is attached to it. He associates power of voice with lack of reality in acting. Particularly the American "method actor" does not always dare to fill out the spoken word with enough dynamic impact and expansion. As a result, he stands so squarely within the law that he sounds too true to be good. It is easy to understand, therefore, why the audience often finds it very difficult even to hear him.

A shortcoming we notice in many actors' voices is the inability to sustain and control volume and pitch. Rather than using depth of tone for emotional scenes and dramatic climaxes, the undeveloped voice depends upon mounting pitch and gets squeaky. No wonder so many actors suddenly lose the vocal character of their role in a play. During the heat of emotion the thinness of their voice traps them. At the spectacular moments of a play, when the audience is eager to capture the full thrill and excitement, a letdown occurs. The seething passions which flare through the lines are lost because some of the actors suddenly begin to sound like their own immature selves. The exaltation is debunked by the sudden impact of vocal impotence.

Worse still, when a performance calls, for example, for anger and excitement, the untrained voice of an actor may become angry and excited as well, and begin to sound strained, raucous or rasping. These trends incorporate themselves into the actor's work and in time will settle into permanent habits. In order to portray anger and excitement, the actor automatically strains his voice. Much of his verbalization in acting then will be based on unhealthy tone and will be tied to vocal abuse.

A medium that exposes vocal flaws quite clearly and puts the voice to a severe test is Shakespearean drama. Under the weighty task imposed on the voice by every performance, a lack of appropriate vocal freedom, strength and range frequently gets the actor into trouble. A typical reaction of a young American actor who played his first leading part in a Shakespearean play was this: "I was ineffective because of my voice. I tried to compensate with my acting, but in vain; the other actors drowned me out."

Some actors, sensing a vague need for a certain something in their speech, fall into a clipped diction, reminiscent of the British. Or they begin to sound precious. Both effects clash with their personalities.

In the absence of systematic tone development, old-fashioned elocution ideas are sometimes used by speech teachers in drama schools. Elocution is concerned with style of speech. Style must be dictated by the varying needs of a particular dramatic undertaking. It follows that style of speech is the concern of the drama department and should be subordinated to the dramatic requirements of the moment. The vocal tone of a performance that is bound by scholastic notions of style becomes monotonous, the performance lifeless and the performer a crashing vocal bore.

The voice or speech teacher who is concerned with more than the development of tone or articulation is liable to interfere with the drama teacher and will confuse the acting student. In his book <u>Building a Character</u>, Constantin Stanislavsky points out that an actor should study voice and diction with separate instructors.

The main reasons for the general low level of vocal development in young actors are: (1) a lack of thorough training in how to make and sustain a wealth of free vocal "noise"; (2) an improper order of procedure, that is, the premature application of articulation to an immature instrument; (3) a lack of specialized training, that is, the unfortunate mixing of "voice, diction and line reading" in classes taught by one teacher. Students are made to concentrate on so many objectives and goals at the same time that their trains of thought are derailed. When they begin their "Roll on Thou deep and dark blue ocean," confusion, sweat, tenseness and disappointment result.

Without the full development of his vocal possibilities the employment potential of an actor is limited. The demands of the American theatre have changed. Acting and singing are no longer simply related but have become correlated professions. Nowadays, agents, producers and directors frequently ask an actor, "Can you put over a song?" The time of the singing actor has come.

Voice lessons in our time should be adapted so that they do more than just improve the speaking voice of an actor. There is a practical dividend for the actor whose voice has been trained in speaking and singing, simultaneously, through vocal exercises. He has obtained a foundation which may enable him to expand into musicals.

---

## Notes

---

[1] A medium rather extinct because of the popularity of TV.

# 2

# VOICE AND SPEECH

---

**Q.** Are tone and articulation two separate functions?

**A.** Of course they are separate. There can be a tone without conscious articulation, as is illustrated by a yawn, a laugh, a cry or even hemming and hawing. The latter are verbalizations of mental pauses. There can be articulation without tone, as is illustrated by an unvoiced stage whisper.

---

These are the opposite extremes of the two functions. Each can be developed to a high degree without the other. In the art of speaking or singing they must, of course, be brought together.

It is agreed that the tone is the sound. For the purpose of speaking or singing, articulation is applied to the tone. We might compare the tone form to a dressmaker's dress form. Unadorned, it is simply a figure. The articulation, which in this illustration can be likened to a

27

dress, will enhance a plain figure, but it must be made to the measurement of the individual.

It is from the study of a figure that a dress designer conceives a style, takes measurements and chooses the materials and colors so that the dress will be made to suit and complement that figure. It is highly improbable that a creation would first be finished and a figure sought to match and fit the measurement of that dress.

Consider some of the "voice and speech" lessons that are offered to the budding actor. The student is taught to improve rather than to alter the speech habits of long standing. This method can be effective in glossing over tone imperfections, just as a clever designer can, through camouflage, hide imperfections in an individual figure. However, this is not developing tone any more than a dress does anything but cover or minimize faults in a figure. Voice and speech lessons that do not consider tone development do not build up the vocal instrument. Neither do they develop the freedom, quality and carrying power of tone.

Many actors and singers tend to overlook the fact that lips, lower teeth, jaw, tongue and soft palate are influential in tone production and receive definite training through tone development. These moveable parts also perform a second function, namely, articulation. It is a mistake to consider these parts for articulation only.

Of the two functions---tone and articulation---which in the end we wish to blend, the function of tone is more complex and requires longer training. Articulation agents, when used specifically for the purpose of diction, are simpler in their application and require less long-range development. The improvement of tone is an organic development that involves the coordination of the entire vocal instrument. The improvement of diction is a more localized and mechanical task.

First the organic, then the mechanics---that must be the order of training procedure. A reversal of this order can easily lead a beginner to tighten. The more pedantic the approach to diction and the more arbitrary the pattern in which the lips, jaw, tongue or palate are set or exercised for diction, the greater the danger of tensing will be.

This does not mean that the organic development of tone production must be completed before the localized mechanics of diction can be successfully applied to it. Nevertheless, it is only when a student either is endowed with natural, free tone production or has developed a reasonable degree of tone freedom that he or she is able to fit the words to the proper sound and that his or her voice is in condition both to sound well and pronounce well.

The fact that diction requires less long-range development than does tone study does not mean that the study of speech should not be pursued for a good length of time. On the contrary, there is always room for improvement. Many of our leading actors who have studied speech still continue to do so. Their performance testifies to the value of good speech and to the beneficial results of speech study.

There is an additional aspect which prompts us to stress that, generally speaking, voice study is a more encompassing project than diction. Voice training must help the student to prepare for ordinary vocal risks as well as for vocal survival. The study of speech is directed more toward aesthetics, precision, clarity and intelligibility.

Of course, the speech teacher, like the voice teacher, may get a desperate call from an actor who has suddenly become aware of shortcomings and who feels that a lack of study of voice or speech has limited his or her career. Yet the voice teacher will get even more desperate calls. "Something went wrong with my voice during the matinee today, and I can't go on with the evening performance unless you help me" is but one of many vocal S.O.S. calls to the voice teacher.

---

**Q.   How and when do speech habits affect the voice?**
**A.   Speech habits tend to affect vocal freedom from the day the young mind discovers it can consciously make tone.**

---

Let us look at the voice before speech habits have made their appearance. The voice of a baby, with its strength and endurance, is a powerhouse of natural, uninhibited vocal production. It is interesting to note that, being unaware of any language or understanding, babies make no effort toward any definite vowel or speech formation. Their purpose is to make sound and they perform magnificently.

Sometimes an infant will wail for hours at night without any noticeable signs of fatigue, just as a dog will tirelessly bark at the moon for hours. A dog can do this throughout his life. A child, on the other hand, maintains this ability only as long as he or she is unconscious of tone. Even the presence of bad speech habits does not seem to interfere, until that fateful day when a conscious effort to produce tone is made by a youngster.

It is when the intellect thus begins to assert itself that inhibitions begin to enter the child's vocal life. The conscious effort to make sound, so often incorrect, is not directed at tone alone but incorporates and often over-emphasizes articulation. At this point, speech habits upset the apple cart.

From infancy on, our purpose in speech is to make ourselves understood. The way of learning is by imitation. In this way, we accept without question and imitate the voice placement, coloring, dialect, colloquialism and pronunciation of our elders. All these become part and parcel of our way of speech, and inevitably we incorporate them unconsciously but firmly into our tone production.

In the various dialects of the American language, it seems that one consonant partic- ularly sets its trap against tone, and that is the unrolled R, as in the words drawer, raw, and quarrel.

In the everyday pronunciation of these words, the R consonant is formed in a way and sustained to a degree that makes it no longer merely a consonant. It crowds itself into a vowel and narrows or distorts the vowel sound.

The peculiar influence of the R in American speech is made remarkably clear to us by the reaction of people abroad to our way of talk- ing. We need only overhear a foreigner imitating us to realize how our voices fall upon his ear. He looks for the trait that is most outstanding in an American voice and then stresses the pre- dominance of this trait and tries to produce most of the speech sounds in terms of this very trait. A parody results, and it is often based exclusively on the American unrolled R (as, for example, in the slogan, "I am an Amerrrrican").

It is sometimes assumed that good or well- trained speaking voices do not suffer from speech habits. This is an erroneous notion. Even the finest speaking voices, as for instance that of the late President Roosevelt, are not free from speech habits. Admittedly, these are per- haps not perceptible to those who share his mother tongue, because the most conspicuous national habits are sometimes the ones the nation itself is least conscious of. When he addressed the French troops in the American invasion of Africa during World War II, Pre- sident Roosevelt's French glaringly revealed those habits. His delivery was full of those typical impurities which the American speech framework or accent imposes upon the French language. And the rest of us, who have not perfected our speech to the extent to which President Roosevelt had, are known throughout the world by this accent.

Of course, when we try to speak Italian or any other foreign language, our American accent will be just as noticeable. At the same time, the Frenchman or Italian who tries to speak English can be recognized by the French or Italian character traits in his voice. It is obvious, then, that in speaking the mother tongue every voice is stamped in a definite way, and every person, trapped by fate and society, is more or less the victim of powerful effects of habit.

In addition to habits of language and dialect, there are other tendencies that we acquire in daily vocal use or that we carry over into the speech process. Although these habits are usually not consciously felt, they influence vocal behavior in numerous ways from childhood on. For example, there are people whose minds go faster than their speech. In their unconscious aim for speed, they try to pack into one breath as much as possible or perhaps even a little more than is comfortable. Not only do they over-extend the length of their sentences but they also tend to rush them. Overtension and gasping result.

Another case is that of the child who, as a result of being told never to wake the baby next door, unconsciously acquires a half-whispering tone. Breathiness results.

Another example is the young girl whose mother criticizes "that awful voice of hers" and so plants the seeds of a vocal inferiority complex; or the child, who, afraid of not pleasing with her own tone, develops a protective speech coloration that results in superimposed, unnatural or distorted manner of voice production.

Also we have the girl who goes to one of the

socially prominent colleges, where she learns to behave according to the code society dictates, with an overemphasis on reserved conduct, on keeping the emotions intact. Before long her verbal pattern begins to reflect her attitude. The girl begins to sound the way a "nice girl" is supposed to sound. (Or the girl tries not to sound the way a "nice girl" is not supposed to sound.) The transition from innate to learned behavior is sharply highlighted in a stickler for etiquette, whose voice keeps appearing under social disguise---for instance, a "goody-goody bore" or the so-called "society drawl," with elongated vowels and the transforming of regular vowels into diphthongs. A lack of directness in voice, speech and spontaneous self-expression results.

On the other hand, there is the youngster who, during the formative years, joins the gang. The gang, of course, believes that it is bad form to be graceful but good to be crude and rude. The order of the day is, "Let's all play it rough together." The game is to violate the code and weaken the attachments to the estab-lished culture. The lingo of the gutter, which may even be one of the criteria for acceptance into a gang, is symptomatic of lack of culture. A deliberate corruption of what a sensitive per-son is or was takes place, throwing a wrench into his psychological pattern. As a result of such peer pressure, his voice, which perhaps naturally revealed a pleasant personality, is turned into an unpleasant "lower male" type.

Also, there is the person who finds it dif-ficult to adjust to aging. To compensate for her vanishing youth, she develops a little girl's speech. A thin, high-pitched and shallow voice production results.

Finally, let us mention the person with a shrill and high-pitched voice, developed through competition with other members of his family, most of whom shout at the top of their lungs.

Psychological aspects lead to physical results. In everyday speech, the effects of physical and psychological influences may not necessarily stand out. We can get away with them, particularly when we compare ourselves to others and to the mediocre standard speech that exists in most countries. But the individual who aspires to the higher ideals of art, who seeks to fulfill her vocation as an artist whose tool-in-trade is voice, may well find the sound of her voice entangled in a mesh of bad speech habits, inhibitions and interferences.

The mistake frequently made in voice teaching is to accept the sound with its bad influences and to polish it, rather than first sifting away the slag in order to reach the rich gold.

# ITALIAN LANGUAGE AND VOCAL TRADITION

---

**Q.** Is it easier to sing well in Italian than in other languages?

**A.** Yes. More features of the Italian language help the voice, and less interfere.

---

There are hardly any features of Italian that tend to pull the voice out of its favorable position. In Italian there is no H consonant, which tends to interrupt a natural flow and which, when overdone, can throw the entire vocal process out of gear.

All these features are basic speech tendencies. Singers whose mother tongue is Italian therefore have less to overcome in this respect. On the other hand, singers whose mother tongue is not Italian should not anticipate that singing in Italian or living in Italy will free them from established, ingrained language interferences.

35

---

**Q.   Isn't the H consonant frequently used in It-
      alian singing?**
**A.   Yes, it is used in singing, but not in
      speech.**

---

In articulation, the uncontrolled application of
breath used in pronouncing the H can easily upset vocal production. Such uncontrolled use of
the H in established speech, when carried over
to singing, will have a more damaging effect.

The Italian singer, however, never having
used the H in his speech, and therefore not
having incorporated its bad effects into his
vocal production, is not usually harmed by it.
He will often add a controlled H to his vocal
process later, chiefly to help the tone. For
example, the tenor Rodolfo in the Boheme aria
"Che gelida manina," sings a high C in the
phrase, "la speranza." On the one syllable
"spe," he must sing an A flat and from there
connect to a high C. In most cases we find him
singing two E vowels and preceding the second
vowel, on which the high C is sung, by an H
consonant---thus: "Spe-he..."

This is a fine point, but it is important.
The H is comparable to medicine, which, taken in
small, controlled doses, benefits, but which,
taken in large, uncontrolled doses, harms.

Once the H has been controlled and subordinated to the tone, it can, of course, be
safely used for singing in any language.

The use of the added controlled H for the
purpose of aiding tone is possible in any language. It is a technical device which should be
employed when it can improve the tonal qualities.

In addition to its technical use, the H can
also be added for artistic or interpretive purposes, to embellish a vocal piece. In such a
case the use of the added H must be dictated by

the style of the composition and by individual
taste.

Sometimes a singer may want to add the H̲ as
well as some other vocal fixtures in an effort
to create Italian style in her singing. It is a
well-known fact that Italian vocal music lends
itself more readily to liberties, embroidery and
ornamentation than, for instance, German vocal
literature. Singers who perform at the Bayreuth
Festival[1] will confirm that the use of the added
H̲, of "sobbing," as well as of the portamento or
sliding from one note to another, is considered
questionable if not v̲e̲r̲b̲o̲t̲e̲n̲ in Wagnerian opera
---though even guardians of Wagnerian purity all
over the world need not always be so orthodox in
these matters. A little bit goes a long way.
Thus, in style it is a matter of the subtle
versus the obvious; it is a matter of finding
the right degree for the appropriate composition. However, the obvious and indulgent use of
extra fixtures in singing is neither good nor
Italian, but merely a cheap style, used everywhere by singers with poor taste.

Too much of the H̲ or any other extra vocal
fixture for the purpose of embellishment, defeats its purpose. The singer who is guilty of
overembellishment may have to purge his interpretation of the barnacles that have accumulated; otherwise his singing may turn out to be
more of a parody than a true means of vocal
expression.

---

**Q.  Do you teach the bel canto method?**
**A.  No. Bel canto is not a method.**

---

A method for anything is an accepted series of
steps leading toward a known goal. Compare the
methods of ten vocal instructors who advertise
"Teacher of bel canto." You will find no common
principles, no agreed-upon goal, only ten sepa-

rate points of view, each claiming to have its own cure-alls, but each above all zealously waving the flag of bel canto.

It follows that the expression "bel canto" has about as many meanings as the number of experts who claim to teach it.

Let us try to explain this magic expression, to which so many succumb in awe. It is sometimes used in the historical sense, to describe a period of vocal music in which the melodic line is decisive. The meaning of bel canto, then, is something like "beautiful melody singing." Bellini's operas are often mentioned as examples of the so-called bel canto period. Other than that, we need only translate the two words in order to understand them. They simply mean "beautiful singing." Certainly any singing teacher would be foolish to deny that she is trying to teach exactly that.

In addition, there are those who believe that beauty, as a norm, reflects some functional excellence. In line with this belief, vocal beauty reflects some excellence of the vocal function. Since those voices that sound best also function best, there is good reason to share this belief. Be that as it may, as far as what method of singing bel canto is, this view keeps us guessing as much as before. Any voice teacher again will tell us that she is trying to teach just that: how to sing well---which is the same thing as how to function well vocally. So, since we are all striving to sing well or beautifully, we are all on the highway toward bel canto.

It is a beautiful expression but as a method it suggests much and signifies little. Many professional men have something on their shingle to enhance their name: Dr. of this or Professor of that, or possibly a string of initials after the name. This all serves to establish their authority. Who then is to blame the voice teacher if, on her shingle, she adds "Teacher of bel canto?"

Like the honorary Southern Colonel, she likes the title; it has flavor. It has an impact on the student. It makes him feel he is with the vocal "in-group." His teacher has found and will pass on to him the secret of the past. As a result, he too will soon be able to reenter the Golden Age.

---

Q.  Is there a special Italian voice teaching method?

A.  There is no such thing as an Italian method of singing, no more than there is a German, French or Russian method of voice training. There is, however, an Italian style of singing. In the same sense, there are German, French and Russian styles, in music, painting, literature, architecture and other art forms.

---

There is no fixed method of voice training. The problems of each voice should dictate the method used.

Only principles are universal. Methods must be devised and practiced individually. The challenge in solving voice problems is to find the tools that fit the needs and are thus appropriate.

The supposition that a special Italian method exists is common because it was in Italy that singing first became recognized as an art. Singing was used in the glorification of the Church service and was developed to a high degree for that purpose. The first voice teachers of modern history were therefore Italian. As the Church's influence spread, singing was introduced outside Italy, wherever the Church existed. As the theatre, which was originally a by-product of the Church, gradually became independent, so did singing eventually come to stand on its own merits as an established art. When the power of the

Church waned, singing remained and, coordinating itself with local minstrelsy, became secular.

Singing, and especially opera, became the pastime of the Italian nation, much as baseball became the pastime of the Americans and bull-fights of Spaniards. Singing, in Italy, pre-served itself as a highly respected part of the national heritage.[2]

Despite the development of native music and style by each country, traditions have persist-ed. Even today in America we find most of our printed music marked in Italian: "andante," "presto," "piano," "forte" and so on. In the field of voice, the Italian words "falsetto," "soprano," "mezzo-soprano," for instance, are not even translated into English.

Until quite recently, many non-Italian singers went so far as to Italianize their names. The tenor Edward Johnson, for instance, who in his later years was manager of the Metropolitan Opera, was also known under the stage name Eduardo de Giovanni.

As the art of singing progressed and became recognized in other countries, and as singers came to be judged more by their talents alone, the tradition of Italian superiority faded. In recent years, for instance, the Scandinavian countries have produced a relatively large number of singers of international reputation who have been prominent in the Italian, German and French styles. America, of course, is becom-ing an increasingly rich source of vocalists of all styles. The import of European artists is noticeably decreasing. Furthermore, many Ameri-cans are successfully making their marks on stages abroad.

In our gradual drifting away from tradition, there has been a tendency to overlook the most important reason for the old Italian vocal as-cendency, namely gradual and timely ripening. In Italy the study of tone and tone development were practiced as preliminary vocal disciplines.

Moreover, students remained in the studio until ripeness was reached. Great singers of the past such as Caffarelli, Rubini and Farinelli worked with their teachers an hour or more almost daily, for eight to ten years. In just eight years, which was then considered a normal preparatory period, a student would receive perhaps 2,500 hours of vocal training.

Indeed, no secrets, miracles or tricks led to those days of vocal glory, but attitude did. The attitude toward the study of voice that has come down to us from the old Italian masters and their disciples is that of patience.

Fine wine cannot be brought to its peak of maturity by the use of chemicals or short-cuts. It is the same with the voice. No durable vocal product has ever been rushed onto the vocal market. Only careful development can prepare the voice for its mature function. There is indeed no substitute for gradual ripening. The same is evident in the preparation of instrumentalists who spend a good many years of disciplined study in learning technique. The average standard of performance in this group of artists has steadily risen to an all-time high, simply because of their serious attitude, patience and willingness to ripen gradually.

The requirements for such a standard are the same the world over, in all arts: time, constructive work and, above all, a dedicated spirit and the perseverance to come as close to faultlessness as one can. How long it will take depends upon our gifts, capacity, capability and our goal. Generally speaking, it takes as long to sing well as it takes to unfold. Each student proceeds toward the goal as directly as the obstacles permit.

Q.  How does voice training these days compare
with the old Italian school?

A.  Not very favorably. Nowadays a four-year
course of approximately forty weeks each
year, with two half-hour voice lessons week-
ly, is the usual procedure. In four years
the student receives an average of 160 hours
of voice lessons. However, many of these few
and precious hours are not used for technical work on the vocal instrument but are
spent on coaching and program building.

It is clear then, by comparison with the olden
days, that the time and effort spent on voice
study have been sharply curtailed. In addition,
the learning process has undergone a significant
change. Pure, unadulterated tone study and tone
development have been more or less abandoned,
and a singing-coaching-musicianship lesson has
become routine.

The main reason for this change is the pro-
liferation of education as a whole, vocal education included. The number of experts and specialists in the field of voice teaching no
longer sufficed for the number of persons aspiring to study voice. This opened the door for
coaches, accompanists and sight-singing teachers, who originally worked with singers only in
their own field as musicians but who later in
some cases also taught some voice to fill the
gap.

Since the study of singing, coaching and
musicianship is now so intermixed, offered under
the title "vocal instruction," the whole issue
is somewhat clouded and the purpose and emphasis
of the study are vague. To cut through the
vagueness and confusion, to make the right
choice and to find what he needs are tough tasks
for a student in search of a teacher, particularly for the novice who is not quite sure of

what he has and what he needs. Whatever a voice lesson consists of, in a commercial setup or rat race, the teacher with the best business brain and the hardest-hitting salesmanship is likely to catch the greatest number of students, regardless of his specialty, and perhaps regardless of his degree of teaching skill. Indeed, excellence and success are not always synonymous, especially in the arts.

Because art reflects its time as well as its sponsorship, even our greatest music schools and universities are not always able to escape commercial influence, pressure and routine. Furthermore, since one tends to maintain the customary, every new music school will probably follow the same route.

While generous school budgets could allow ample time for patient work and study, major portions of a voice student's courses are devoted to less essential pursuits. As a result, the student may attain a thorough knowledge of some related subject while sacrificing time that should be devoted to voice production. The net result is that the student does not acquire an adequate technical foundation which would enable him to apply the related information he has obtained.

A typical complaint of a young singer who has undergone such training is: "I didn't have enough time and opportunity to concentrate on my voice, because I had to cover so much repertoire. I am nowhere and not ready for anything." We must realize that the singer in America who is not fully ready is in trouble. She finds no place where she can perform, where she can make mistakes and thereby learn, as she might abroad. In Europe small stages serve as showcases for talent in need of experience. In America, for the beginner the struggle can be overwhelming. Particularly in the operatic and concert field it is often a case of do or die. There is rarely a second chance.

The young singer who has completed her courses at a music school but finds that her study has not equipped her for the career she would like to pursue may wonder whether her own lack of vocal competence may not be the fault of the teacher. It is well-known that voice teachers have become targets of sharp criticism, some of it informed and intelligent, but some of it spiteful. Much of it has been expressed in broad, sweeping terms, which have unfairly indicted a large segment of teachers, a great many of whom have earned their reputations through a consistent record of good teaching over the years.

To judge a teacher fairly, one must also consider teaching conditions. For instance, the voice teacher of our young singer from music school may be excellent and may have a real sense of vocation. If so, he is not "routine-minded" and will have his own quarrel with the music school system. There is nothing new, let alone unique, in his discontent. He is pressed for time and he has to spread himself thin. Coaching and teaching repertoire, both of which many a voice teacher is required to do, often so much absorb his attention that he and his students must cope with vocal difficulties in the face of much uncertainty. Techniques have to be more or less smuggled in. Work on tone and tone development is minimal.

Of course, a teacher will not always feel free to express his views and criticisms openly. Because of his loyalty to the school, he will tend to refrain from exposing unfavorable conditions. Only occasionally will he bemoan the fact that teaching is no longer a proud profession and that the teacher has lost his grip, a situation that is in the nature of the times.

In particular will he feel regret if the policy of the school is not to aim at building for a student's vocal future but to exploit the talent of a student to its own critical needs.

This happens when the immature voice of a student is cast for mature assignments in school performances. Another unfortunate situation exists when a voice lesson is used to rehearse the repertory requirements of those students who have to display themselves prematurely in school recitals and sometimes even in the singing of grand opera.

We can see there is much to be said about voice teaching and learning conditions in music schools. But the new student in a voice department does not really know what is in store for him and has no clear picture as to what vocal training he will and will not get. He and his parents are impressed by the reputation of the school and all its facilities. Innocent and inexperienced, the student believes he will get everything he needs in school, but that is not always so.

While the intricate and highly demanding art of vocalism may be recognized by a school as a requirement from the musical point of view, it has not been fully treated as a technical necessity. In spite of good intentions, responsibility toward vocal technique is something that a great many music schools have neglected. As a result, a number of voice students find it necessary to look for outside help in voice production.

In essence, the problem of vocal education in the music schools comes down to a few simple questions. Are the vocal health, the vocal production and the vocal development of the vocal student the concern of the music school? If so, who teaches vocal production, and what does the curriculum consist of? If not, is the prospective student told by the music school that he will not receive adequate technical groundwork there but must get it elsewhere?

It is a simple fact, yet it is often overlooked; singing is primarily the art of tonal delivery. It is making of vocal sound a strong lyric or dramatic experience. To teach singing is primarily to try to provide the conditions that promote good vocal sound. These are the essentials. A singing school is a place where these essentials should be practiced.

Thorough and alert voice teachers recognize the shortcomings of the vocal assembly-line system so typical of many music schools. Among such teachers one finds the true teacher with the moral and intellectual authority to challenge the routine and to bring reforms in the music school system. It is the artistic conscience of such teachers that forms a connecting link between the great vocal past and the vocal present, between the old Italian masters and the real vocal masters of our day. It is to this group of elect teachers that we must look for genuine voice teaching.

## Notes

[1]A special theatre in the Franconian part of Germany for the production of Wagnerian operas, founded and operated formerly by Richard Wagner himself, and now by members of his family.

[2]Recent reports from Italy point to a decline of interest in opera by the younger generation.

# VOCAL SCIENCE, MECHANICS AND SENSE PERCEPTION

Q. How much have new scientific discoveries simplified and speeded the process of vocal development?
A. Not much. The objectivity of scientific facts and descriptions and the subjectivity of personal experience are the two sides of a single vocal coin. A wide gap divides scientific vocal theory and actual voice practice.

Physiology describes muscular activity; acoustics analyze sound phenomena which occur in tone production. Though their explanations are not always final and exhaustive, both sciences have unearthed a great number of interesting facts and swept away a mass of futile speculation. However valuable the information both sciences supply, when it is applied to vocal technique, the outcome is somewhat inconclusive, if not unhappy. The reason is that when experts evaluate and describe vocal technique, the theories used and the conclusions reached are highly con-

47

troversial. Lack of agreement, and even heated scientific debates, result mainly from differences in methods of scientific study and, even more, from differences in the interpretation of the data obtained.

The apt vocal scholar who turns to vocal science in the hope of finding a practical aid to the study of vocal technique will soon discover that scientific investigation can also lead to a failing. What well-meaning investigators (with their long, learned treatises and involved references) have concluded as to breath control, posture, voice placement and so on is often so complicated in application that the solution is more confusing than the problem.

It is perhaps not very difficult to turn a voice lesson into an anatomy course and to impress the vocal beginner by surveying practically every organ in his body, giving him "the great anatomical rundown," and showing him charts of the various body structures. It is perhaps also not too difficult to create a muscle theory for voice production, but it is certainly difficult to put one's finger on it. Therefore, it is hard to predict whether or not the theory works when it is put to practical use. Sometimes the assumptions upon which a vocal theory is based are far-fetched, or fictitious. Many ambitious vocal theories have been built on shaky ground. Be that as it may, scientific statements about voice production that do not correspond to the laws of nature or common sense and that cannot be traced to definite experience are of no value to the singer or speaker who studies to master his craft. They may have value as a contribution of a special kind to the literature of scientific vocal research.

One must remember that the scientist can measure the whole voice only as accurately as he can hear it; he can judge it only as well as he understands it. No scientific data compiled from the study of all aspects of the human voice can account for its totality. Vocal lilt, verve or warmth, for instance, are important vocal properties that cannot be pinned down within the bounds of vocal science.

In the act of voice production something is made of the voice-producing parts which cannot be truly grasped by a separate analysis of each part. Indeed, the appreciation of a voice takes place on quite a different level from a scientific knowledge of specific things about the voice. For, no matter how interesting and theoretically true it is that a voice is composed of such and such elements and acts by such and such mechanisms, the crux of the matter is always this: here is someone who sings or speaks and the sound she makes comes forth with all its manifold properties. How now to recognize the vocal condition she is in? What to do about it? How to achieve completeness and satisfaction with the voice? These are the key questions. No scientific data compiled from the study of all aspects of the human voice can give the answers to these questions. Hence, no scientific data can lead universally and without question to an indisputable conclusion as to what correct voice teaching is.

Physiological and acoustical research does provide us with a great deal of information about the underlying causes of vocal functioning and thus broadens our knowledge of vocal theory. We learn more about the "why" of our development, but the "how" is a different matter. The doctor or the psychiatrist, with all his research and scientific training, is not a better athlete, dancer or vocalist than any other person who has no particular knowledge of the body and brain. The dancer may study anatomy or even study X-rays of his legs and other parts of his body, but none of this will help him to attain beauty in dancing any more than will the study of anatomy and acoustics help the vocalist to attain vocal beauty. The swimmer may make a study of the body and water, but will such a study simplify or speed the learning of how to swim? Furthermore, will the acquisition of knowledge that cannot be converted into any practical ability merely complicate the learning process and increase the difficulties of achieving the ends?

Learning the "how" depends greatly upon the "feel." We really don't know what to try for before we know how it feels. We may begin to know what is right by the way it feels. Only by doing can we establish a feel and by trying can we improve it, so that we reach a state of well-being and the activity always feels good or right in some degree.

Control, coordination and balance in voice, as in dancing and sports, come through experience and exercise. The correctness of these in voice is confirmed by the quality of the resulting product---the tone.

Physiological and acoustical research can assist us by explaining what artistic taste dictates, but we should not expect such clarification to help much in body work and coordination. We don't arrive at it just by knowing what it is. We can't really grasp it until it happens or takes hold. Singing, like swimming, can be "explained" and "understood," but in spite of the fact that both of these functions can be quite clear intellectually, performance remains a problem for body and brain. To acquire a new skill is a matter of conditioning, and to perfect a new skill is a matter of ripeness. This stage in the voice is reached and can be exploited only when technical preparations have advanced to the point where they make ripeness both possible and exploitable.

With the help of research, too, a teacher can find out whether the terminology he uses in his teaching is scientific or unscientific, whatever that knowledge may be worth. One can

use scientific terms that are meaningless in
voice training because they cannot be traced to
definite experience. On the other hand, one may
use unscientific terms that are of value because
they can be applied to the know-how and, as suggestions, produce results.

Some authors and teachers seem to think that
the more scientific the language and the more
technical the jargon they use, the more respect
they will command. Other voice experts, appalled
at the confusion of vocal terms and theories
that haunt vocal literature and vocal studios,
try to reduce voice study to precise scientific
processes. This striving for vocal blueprinting
or for the presentation of scientific process
rather than for a human experience is apt to ex-
clude from voice study most of the points helpful to voice training. In voice training, as in
learning to ride a bicycle, the learner goes
through processes, many of which may be scientifically defined but which he himself cannot
define or pin down. To try to teach technique by
pointing out these processes is useless.

The controls of vocal activity function
largely below the level of consciousness. That
is why personal experience is remote from and so
much at variance with the scientific process.
That is why vocal science is separated from vocal work or know-how, and the grand field of
voice study is often parcelled out into a wide
range of sciences which do not communicate to a
layperson.

The use of the word "scientific" in the
teaching of an art form is questionable. The
purpose of science is to establish facts. However, the voice student cannot derive sufficient
benefit from mere facts; he goes to a voice
teacher for advice. Finding the next step that
will lead to his personal development is the
crucial problem that confronts both student and
teacher. Science cannot provide a solution to
this problem, for as soon as science separates

facts, gives personal advice or tries to show correct steps, it is no longer science and loses its own peculiar value.

Also, science is almost always universal. In contrast, art, a conception of beauty, varies even geographically. One's conception of beauty is dependent upon that intangible thing known as "taste." This, in turn, is subject to many variables.

The vocal tone that we may defend as true or most beautiful might not always sound so good to a foreign audience. In Italy, for example, the use of the so-called chest voice in pronounced or extreme form is often highly encouraged in the female voice on the lower notes, even by sopranos. In contrast, German and Scandinavian opera divas tend to produce the same lower notes more lightly and more with a mixed or so-called head voice. They thus shy away from so much "masculinity." They also try to avoid making a sharp separation between the head and chest voice, except for occasional and very special effects. In Italy, as well as in Russia, a more metallic sound is often preferred in the female voice. Americans are apt to criticize that metallic sound. Of course, their taste is as valid as ours.

It may happen that one group will apply its scientific findings in order to predict woe to a female voice that produces very chesty sounds and that carries the chest voice way up the range. Another group, in contrast, may foretell trouble for a female voice that does not bear down heavily on the chest tones and does not carry the chest voice way up the range.

Singers in the Orient---for instance, members of the Chinese Opera---find our true tone as strange as we find theirs. Again, their taste is as valid as ours. Who is right? Who is wrong?

When we consider the controversies raised by authors of scientific vocal books, how can we determine who is scientifically correct?

This formula is the "truth" and that formula is the "truth." Which one is the greater truth? The one that fits into the whole perspective. Hence, the total truth will reveal itself only in the total tone of the individual and will vary with each case.

The vocalist in search of the truth who is impressed by the authentic aura that surrounds scientific theory and who accepts a particular formula in blind faith, without testing "truth" by its practical consequences, may come to false conclusions from false premises.

All of the foregoing is by no means intended to belittle the value of vocal research, nor is it meant to discourage the voice teacher who is interested in it. Full tribute must be paid to those who, through research, have increased our knowledge and clarified our understanding of the voice. This is only to show the pitfalls of a mechanistic approach. It is also a warning not to repeat the following mistakes that the claimants to scientific authority so often make in the field of voice teaching: (1) to overrate the value of vocal research to vocal training and to confuse breakthrough in vocal research with breakthrough in vocal teaching; (2) to attack the problems of vocalism, a fine art, with methods of science---making the voice satisfy graphs and prove itself on measuring instruments---or to view the living human organism as a collection of static mechanisms; (3) to reduce the whole teaching of an art to a mere set of mechanical rules, making people into robots.

The essence of vocalism is that it is a living thing and not a fixed set of rules, formulae, motions or actions. Being a fine art, vocalism is subject to the laws of creating. In the creative process, we must cope with the many unknowns and intangibles.

There can be no right vocal patterns for mass use. There are too many ifs. The right is so close to the wrong. The one pattern that all voices seem to have in common is that their problems, if not attended to in the course of training, become progressively worse. The voice then takes revenge exactly in the area where the shortcomings originated.

Voice training is body training. There are no short-cuts in body training. Development is organically determined. Voice training can only follow and perfect the path laid out by the organic. It can stretch the path but it cannot exceed it. It cannot dictate the path to the organic, nor can it make over the voice in line with any dogmatic theory, no matter how scientific or unscientific it may be. Any attempt to remake a voice is a tampering with the course of vocal nature. It is often done by transsexuals[1] and by those who have an unrealistic craving for an absolutely perfect voice, or who confuse an ideal voice with a possible voice.

The voice teaching approach that is truly right is the one that attempts to adjust to reality and seeks to explore the individual vocal mechanism rather than to rule it arbitrarily. Specific mechanical directions given to the controllable parts of the vocal instrument may be helpful in exploring possibilities and variations in tone but will be harmful when used for arbitrary control. Arbitrary mechanical control will lead to rigid and mechanized rather than to free and flexible musical sounds.

To sum up: The goal of the singer and speaker is to obtain vocal freedom and "qualities." The purpose is to use herself to the fullest and to express herself in the best way possible. The road to success cannot be a fixed scientific road, but must be compatible with the natural ability of the vocalist, considering the manifold, unique aspects that every voice possesses. Success must be the result of exploration and observation with one's goal in mind. When success is obtained, it then becomes the personal, individual "science" of the vocalist, which is sharpened and preserved by objective technical study. In the process of technical study, physiological and acoustical research can explain and specify.

"Scientific" is indeed an irreproachable, unassailable term under which many seek cover. It tends to become accepted as a credential. Its value is commonly exploited in advertisements of cigarettes, patent medicine and beauty preparations. A New York barber advertises "scientific haircuts."

Scientific discoveries and inventions are responsible for the development of engineering equipment that reproduces, measures, transmits and amplifies sound. The home recorder is a popular gadget. It gives the vocalist an opportunity to review his own past performance. It enables him to listen to himself as an outsider who stands back and looks more critically and objectively at his own efforts, at general effects and details. The vocalist who hears his voice played back for the first time is usually as much surprised as the television actor who sees his first tape. The reason is that to see or hear oneself as one is seen or heard from the outside is a novel experience for anyone and a painful experience for many. It is hard to sustain the shock of suddenly discovering shortcomings or imperfections in oneself of which one was previously unaware or uncritical. How often do we hear the performing artist complain: "I am embarrassed and ashamed. What I believed was happening didn't happen. The sounds I thought I was making, I didn't make at all. How could I have deceived myself so much?" To reduce the shock of the encounter with reality, it may be said that it is quite easy to horrify oneself, vocally. Reproduction is not the original; therefore the played-back voice differs from the real voice, high fidelity notwithstanding. The lucky possessor of a voice that records well can sometimes cash in on the peculiarities and imperfections of the recording machine, as a photogenic model exploits the peculiarities of the camera for professional purposes.

The use of a recording machine is sometimes overdone. Some students, in order to hear their voice and judge their production, tend to depend more upon this mechanical playback device than on their own sense perception. It must be emphasized that the principal purpose of voice training is to prepare the student for those fateful moments when he has to take the plunge and face the audience. No props can help him then; he is all on his own. Common sense should prevent one from falling prey to technical devices that cannot be used in performance.

Our latest technical progress has, through its amplification systems, to a high degree aided the vocal "have-nots," to the detriment of the "haves." Improved amplification methods have made it possible for the have-nots to compete successfully with the haves by basing the whole vocal technique on a whisper, by smoothing out and polishing the absolute minimum of a potential voice and by disregarding the natural amplifying possibilities of the human apparatus, leaving that function to the mechanical device. This situation has created an entirely new field in which record companies, commercially exploiting their main market of teenagers, aided by large publicity budgets, have blown small vocal talents into national figures. Alas, with electronics at work, the end of the twentieth century witnesses the assertion of "the little vocal man with the mike." He is the prototype of vocal degeneration.

Of course, we must not generalize and altogether condemn the use of the microphone in singing. On the contrary, this mechanical device deserves much praise, since it has proved time and again to be an aid to genuine vocal performance. Without it, many open-air spectacles

could not take place successfully. In nightclubs
where singers often have to compete with the
noise made by guests, waiters and bartenders,
the mike can be a blessing.

Not every singer, indeed, uses it to cover
up a lack of normal vocal carrying power. The
reason for using a microphone and the extent to
which it is used must always be considered.

Singers whose vocal technique starts and
ends with electrical amplification cannot be
considered legitimate vocalists. Their voices
arc not judged on their merits alone. They do
not reach their listeners in true form. Their
singing is turned into a product in which de-
ception has become quite strong. Whether the
help of engineering equipment justifies greater
fame and fortune for a crooner than for the
greatest internationally recognized artist is
something the taste of the general public alone
can determine.

---

**Q.  When are scientific explanations helpful in
     voice training?**
**A.  When they clarify what our senses can per-
     ceive.**

---

Unlike the scientist, who must study and analyze
all elements, the vocalist, as an artist, needs
to know only those elements that he can actually
control (voluntary functions), that he can practice and discipline and that contribute to the
fulfillment of his desired vocal end.

Some of our vocal functions are automatic or
involuntary. The vocal cords fall into this category. In speaking and singing, the action of
the vocal cords is, for all practical purposes,
outside our control. Involuntary vocal functions
can be adjusted and expanded only indirectly and
in conjunction with voluntary functions, through
vocal exercises.

Timing, in voice production, is the proper coordination of the voluntary function and the involuntary. It is impractical to analyze involuntary functions in voice training because the knowledge gained cannot be put to fruitful use. We must recognize the difference between useful and useless knowledge. We must, above all, learn to deal with the essential rather than the unessential. Hence, it is imperative that we use and build on the relevant aspects of vocal production while simplifying or omitting the rest. Otherwise we get sidetracked in the training process.

Because it deals with the involuntary, much of the material that purports to be important and fills the pages of books on voice and speech training is merely an elaboration on irrelevant theoretical detail. Abstraction is piled high upon abstraction. Granted that an analysis of such tedious detail may serve the medical student for the purpose of diagnosing and treating diseases of the larynx. However, just as brain research does not help a writer to improve writing technique, neither does analysis of the involuntary help the singer and speaker improve vocal technique. The voice student who is confronted with such material may well express his frustration and state, "I get the words, but they have no meaning whatsoever to me. I cannot even track down all the muscles that are described here." All of this goes to show that to analyze a muscular act is not necessarily the best way to improve it.

The vocalist can control production by hearing, feeling, sensing and memory (aural recall). The talent of a voice student, therefore, depends greatly on her sense perception, her sense impulse, involvement, and her reaction to her own sensory experience. There is no talented voice student without a good ear, just as there is no talented art student without a good eye.

A good ear and mediocre natural equipment can eventually make a better vocalist than can

good vocal equipment and a bad ear. There are
students whose voices, because of natural gifts,
are more advanced than their hearing is, but
they will rarely progress further until the ear
catches up and assists the voice in its development.

Equipment, or natural gift, of course, comprises ability. The ear is the principal means
of vocal perception. It is clear, then, that
everybody possesses a certain degree of ability
and perception. When perception equals ability
or is greater than ability, the student is
safe. But when ability is greater than perception, the student is in trouble. His work is
aimless and therefore rich in opportunity for
error. He is like the blind chicken that by
sheer accident finds food occasionally.

Granted, lucky accidents have always played
an important part in the history of discovery.
Thus, to stumble into a vocal revelation by accident is still better than to have no revelation at all. However, generally speaking, a
deficiency in the sense department is a severe
handicap to progress. To fight this handicap is
exceedingly difficult. To overcome the deficiency totally and absolutely is perhaps not always
possible, but one can always hope and try.

What the student must try for is to intensify his vocal life, to gain a heightened consciousness of his own voice and of the vocal
world around him. This process is part of the
development of perception. It runs parallel with
the development of the voice. In this process,
the student's senses are trained to grasp, absorb and remember the production of vocal sound
ever more sharply, precisely and vividly.

By the student's exploring the possibilities
and variations in his own tone production, his
sensory powers will steadily grow toward recognition of the essential qualities as they apply
to his own voice. In time, the vocalist establishes a "sense of sound," as the dancer establishes a "sense of movement." Eventually, the

voice student will arrive at a point at which he
will be able to compare features of his voice
with those of other vocalists. Once he has
reached this point, he can learn to deepen his
understanding of his own voice, by confronting
it with the experience of listening to other
voices and their way of functioning. Skill in
perceiving the vocal world and himself, in an
ever more meaningful light, can thus grow.

Let us now try to delve a bit further into
the spectrum of vocal perception. No speaker or
singer can hear himself as he is heard by others. Similarly, no actor can see himself. A
certain untrustworthiness in self-hearing and
self-seeing exists in varying degrees in every
person. Quite often the acting student as well
as voice student, particularly when untrained,
projects little of what he thinks he is projecting. In the study of acting as well as in
voice, the orientation is therefore difficult,
especially for the beginner.

The voice student hears himself and yet
hears something else. While he is making sounds,
he is in his own "bell tower," so to speak,
where the vibrations and reverberations bombard
his senses and get the best of him. In other
words, he hears his voice, produced by a human
vibrator and resonator, with the sensations that
affect his hearing from within---the inner ear.
Yet, at the same time, he hears the sound of his
voice as it strikes his ear from without---the
outer ear. Both the inner and outer ear of the
student are thus busy in the process of tone
production and both are being educated to become
cooperatively keener in the process of tone
study.

The outer ear is the means by which the student can recognize the qualities in the voices
of other singers. As his outer ear becomes
sharper and more accustomed to working in conjunction with his inner ear and vibratory sensations, his perception will steadily grow toward a recognition of the essential qualities as

these apply to the voices of other vocalists. Because of his sensory awareness, he will become increasingly able to analyze voices and to recognize and search for essential qualities and definite tone criteria in his own voice.

A voice student who wants to test the growth of his sensory powers can do so by listening to the same vocal recordings again and again throughout the years. He will find confirmation of sensory progress by discovering new vocal elements in those recordings as he plays them after lapses of time. The truth is that he would not have recognized these elements had they or similar vocal features not developed to some degree in his own voice. It follows that if a vocalist progresses, his concept of a voice is not the same as it was years before, even though the performance of that voice may have remained the same.

Eventually, an increased capacity for perception or a heightened experience of sensory awareness can develop into superior personal judgment. By means of the so-called inner voice or mirror, a performer can determine the connection between stimulus and result.

A small vocal deficiency often seems bigger inside than outside. When an inexperienced vocalist, for instance, is bothered by a slight head cold and feels a minute lack of vocal resonance---a circumstance perhaps hardly even noticeable to the audience---he is apt to compensate by overworking other parts of the vocal instrument. In contrast, an experienced artist, who already knows what not to bother with, will stay away from such unnecessary, extra efforts, which do not really compensate but further defeat her. Her inner voice enables a sensitive artist to measure the degree to which differences in production affect the reaction of an audience. The artist senses how her voice comes across, when she is favorably disposed or indisposed or when she feels something amiss in performance.[2]

Musicians who teach voice but who have not studied voice often fail to realize that hearing the voice internally (largely through bone conduction) is an integral part of singing. They lack the understanding of the peculiarities of human tone and treat a voice through the outer ear only, in a mechanical way, as if a voice were a ready-made instrument.

---

**Q.    Why can't I treat my voice like a ready-made instrument?**

**A.    The ready-made instrument is made exclusively for the purpose of producing music; the human body is not.**

---

The ready-made musical instrument is manufactured by experts. It is as mechanically perfect as can be. It is so constructed that it will accept all reasonable demands put upon it. It is controllable, though weather and other conditions may affect it. The human voice, by contrast, is not only far more sensitive, but also touchy.

Originally, the human body was not made to function as a musical instrument or as a speech mechanism. Both speech and singing have been superimposed on it in the process of human evolution and as part of civilization and culture.

Various human organs active in speaking and singing are utilized at different times for other than vocal purposes. Vocal organs are organized into different groups and positions for the achievement of several ends. It is easy to understand, therefore, why some activities that we perform as part of daily life make the vocal instrument more vulnerable than is a ready-made, manufactured instrument.

The closest parallel in the human voice to manufactured perfection is the rare "born singer," whose ear is good and whose vocal organs are healthy, flexible and in fortunate workable balance to each other. The vocal training of a "born singer" will take less time because nature gave him a head start. Unfortunately, the more nature has endowed him with gifts, the more he tends to take them for granted. The "have" usually has little understanding of the "have-not" and is impatient to push ahead.

In sports, a very promising baseball pitcher, who to the mind of the expert has every potential, is not allowed to play in the major leagues until he has been seasoned in the minor leagues. As long as he is inexperienced, he is not intimidated by the company of giants and is not called upon to face overpowering opposition and to overtax himself. In the same way, a boxing prospect is brought along gradually, learning the "hows" and "wherefores" against opponents who will test but not overwhelm him. Only in this manner does he build himself into a seasoned, knowledgeable fighter. If such a competitor takes on first-rate opponents prior to the seasoning preparation, depending for success solely on his natural gifts, his career is liable to become a flash in the pan. He will have squandered his capital without carefully investing it. Had it been invested with care, it would have drawn interest.

The exceptional voice, whether it is innate or the result of training, will usually obtain good engagements. If it is not produced with technical insight and know-how, the danger exists that the voice may not last. A cold, fatigue, emotional upsets, battle with nerves and the wear and tear of show business set their traps for the sensitive human wind instrument.[3]

When the natural work-balance of such a singer is impaired and the ease of automatic functioning is no longer available, he is at a loss; he has not learned how to help himself. When he feels that something is wrong, he is often unable to leave bad enough alone but, left to his own devices, does still more wrong. In consequence, his voice goes from bad to worse. In time the emergency cries out for an immediate corrective. Then, the belated and frenzied consulting of voice teachers starts. The singer hopes to find a teacher who "does it for him," or he expects a teacher to show him "the experiment" through which he can get back to normal in a hurry.

If a cure is to be accomplished, the "born singer" must learn to undo and redo. He must experience the process of formalized training that he had previously neglected. Similar to a beginner, he must content himself with study and work on a fundamental level, to gain a firm hold over his voice and to learn technique.

A redevelopment is difficult. It involves assisting the organism in restoring its natural powers and reviving the vocal abilities that had been operative in the past but that went astray or were used up by wear and tear. It is not always possible to make a clear distinction between vocal wear and vocal tear.

Unfortunately, at this advanced stage of his career, an artist will be reluctant to start more or less from scratch. He will be reluctant, too, to admit that he has utilized his voice in a possessive and exploitative way. That is because of his lack of comprehension of what to look for in his voice and what conditions promote good sound, and also because of his refusal to take a deeper interest in the principles that relate vocal forces to the forces of nature.

Above all, it is painful to see that one can no longer do the things that once came naturally. In the case of a recognized singer, redevelopment is even more difficult because of psychological barriers. Like a millionaire who in 1929 lost his capital overnight, he is frantic. In his struggle to get on his vocal feet again, he often falls into the hands of those who prey on people's helplessness, inferiority and vanity and promise the fastest of cures.

Nobody can recondition a voice in a short time. Finding a restoration of balance and perspective, an antidote to excesses, a reestablishment of confidence and assurance---these are processes that cannot be rushed upon the ailing voice.

The vocalist who tries for a miraculous comeback tries to achieve the impossible and may end up with an unexpected farewell performance. While his commanding presence can perhaps still hold the day, there is not much hope that present mercies would continue. True, his fans may still give him a rousing cheer for his pains. Yet, an uneasy and sad feeling prevails among the rest of the listeners. It is hard to witness the final act of the vanishing process in which an artist himself spoils the memory of what he was. His voice is no longer a responsive instrument. The techniques of vocalism no longer come to him freely and fully; the mechanism begins to fail him, the bloom of his sound is gone. All in all, his singing turns into a disappointment from which neither audience nor artist ever fully recovers.

From such a fall from vocal heights, the career of a singer cannot survive. This is often the point at which an artist turns to teaching. A new vocal instructor is born.

In the hope that his name will be a drawing card, some universities and music schools will be quite eager to add a celebrity to their staff. The list of distinguished voice teachers, skilled specialists and seasoned practitioners is thus augmented by a newcomer who is inexperienced in pedagogy and unfamiliar with voice teaching techniques.

Since the artist has to teach a subject in which he was not quite sure of himself, he is now in a predicament. (So are his students!) His own past vocal failures do not readily qualify him for future success in the teaching profession. The less the artist is temperamentally suited to this type of work, the greater will be the predicament and the more he will be forced to venture into the role of a teacher because of economic pressure.

But the case of the "born singer" is rare. The vast majority of aspiring singers must go through a gradual process of developing the vocal instrument. This process is intricate, and the mechanism involved is complex. It is in this process, with all its trials and tribulations, that true awareness and insight into the workings of the voice are gained and that we learn to do the many things that must be done to make a sound come out right.

The task is doubly difficult because, in producing the voice, each of us is instrument and player at the same time, and, in handling the voice, most of the factors we have to deal with and most of the forces that affect us are unseen. This goes to show how indirectly we know the vocal instrument with which we work. In fact, not only are the vocal organs and their activities invisible, but any interference with them are mostly invisible, too. Hence, in our aim to bring the vocal organs to productive use, we must often fight against many unseen foes, such as sluggishness, stiffness, tightness and tenseness. All of these, like bacteria, affect our inner vocal being and tend to lower our standard of functioning.

The very fact that so many events in the vocal mechanism are invisible has lent weight to the mistaken idea that the voice is merely an independent, locked-up mechanism whose sound production may be imitated and polished but not developed and expanded.

Often a singer, impressed by another singer's tone and eager to copy the externals, takes the first chance to look into his mouth and asks, "How did you do that?"

The answer to such a question cannot be given directly in a few words. Nature may have given him such a tone. If so, he usually does not know how to explain. His method of work may rely on aural imagery, or on muscular imagery or on resonance imagery, all of which to him are vague, sketchy and hazy.

On the other hand, if he developed the tone that he produces, then it is the result of a process. If the singer wanted to explain the gradual process of building up and to do justice to all the work he has put into his voice, he would have to write a book.

Moreover, we must remember that by looking into a singer's mouth or face we can see only visible parts. They reveal merely a fraction of the vocal instrument, which always works as a whole and mostly with unseen parts. It is naive to think that, through any manipulation of the visible, the invisible can be put into its proper place. It is a great disappointment to a singer when, upon imitating the visible elements of the model, he cannot duplicate that highly desirable and so badly wanted model tone.

In order to produce tones of vigor and quality, we must gradually develop organs that are usually unripe, raw and weak into a coordinated mechanism that must ripen and become strong. This is all the more difficult because we cannot practice on these organs separately during tone production. From the start of sound production, all organs of the vocal apparatus become active, often wildly fighting each other. Established ones may wrestle strongly with newly used or emergent ones. Competition for predominance of component parts may create a condition quite confusing to the beginner. He exclaims: "Sometimes I think my body is rebelling against me."

The trouble with voice production, and also its fascination, is that so much is happening at the same time and is perceived at the same time. To be able to control more than one thing at a time is a task. We are not equipped and we cannot expect to perform this task in voice production until we have gained a certain degree of technical knowledge and development.

Particularly in the first stage of voice study, we are steered in a direction quite unfamiliar to us in many respects. Not only is it new for us to use our vocal organs for the production of musical sounds, but it is also new and not easy for us to deal with the effect---the produced vocal sounds---and to control those sounds. They are momentary, like some scents. They rarely communicate themselves instantly and fully to the senses. The first sensations of fulfillment are fleeting.

All of this results in various uncertainties and imperfections, most of which can be overcome only gradually and by steady use and practice. Troubled by these, the student might complain: "I am at loose ends," or "It's like blind man's bluff," and he may wonder whether his teacher can do anything to get him out of the vacuum. Unfortunately, the teacher can't, provided, of course, he is working in an organic way and not just for tricks. What the teacher can do is to encourage the student to plug along, to open his senses without too much knowledge, and to wait it out. Thus, by opening himself to vocal work and experience, the student will bring these problems toward a solution, at least within his own understanding. In consequence, he will eventually have at his disposal the tools for a true understanding, which are the cumulative product of practice, use and experience.

Unfortunately, at this point some beginners may run out of patience and fail to see it through. Or, they may succumb to a study of tricks. The latter are plentiful on the vocal market. However, they give the beginner false hopes. A mastery of voice tricks does not lead to a mastery of voice culture.

Some of the voice tricks that are taught derive from impatience to come to grips with the physical forces in the system. Others result from haste to control the muscular and resonating processes that go on in the body of the producer. Still others come from a taste for gadgetry. In contrast, the organic way of learn-

ing depends upon self-assertion. First, muscles
and resonance forces must be given a chance to
establish and to regulate themselves. Thereafter, self-assertiveness is harnessed to the
task or directed toward the goal. The latter
consists of gaining ever more tone freedom and
"qualities."

Because it interferes with self-assertive
tendencies, with natural processes and with the
conditioning of reflexes, a teacher who follows
the organic way cannot jump to any particular
tangible body manipulations. He can neither set
arbitrary production rules nor superimpose upon
a student a correct method or pet theory of "how
to do it." This may disappoint many a student,
since many love to be told to do something to
the body or to promote some physical event. In
some cases, this may even be a plight; yet it
cannot be avoided. The uncertainties, the imperfections and the lack of control are the beginners' fate, and they affect each student in
different ways and degrees. The less perceptive
and more impatient the student, the greater the
degree. Often, many lessons have to go by before
he reaches a fuller understanding of the intricate vocal processes, and with that a higher
level of enlightenment.

---

Q.  What about the set of exercises one sees in
    print? Are they valuable for vocal develop-
    ment?
A.  Seldom. They may have some general value: to
    warm up the voice, give it a workout and
    test musicianship. But they can rarely serve
    any constructive, functional purpose, for it
    is highly improbable that fixed exercises
    for range, volume, vowels and tempi could
    suit specific vocal needs or cure individual
    vocal ills.

---

Printed as well as prerecorded standard vocal
exercises consist of a ready-made sequence of

notes to which strict adherence is virtually automatic. (Similarly, metronomes impose arbitrary successions on the time sense.) The few cases that respond well to such arbitrary mechanical prescriptions do so accidentally. Even if such practice does not strain a voice (which it often does, particularly at the start of voice study), it is as generalized as the prescription of an army doctor who, at sick call, makes no diagnosis but doles out aspirin to all.

High-quality vocal training cannot be mass-produced nor standardized. Instead, each case must be diagnosed individually, and the whole work plan based on that diagnosis. The wise voice teacher will not use the same exercises for all, but will devise specific exercises for each student and revise them to match individual development and needs.

As long as a speaker or singer is in the process of developing her voice, the exercises should support the demands of the growing mechanism. Growth of the voice depends upon those specific building processes that give rise to it. The success of voice training will accrue from the vocal diets served---the constructive force and impact of graded vocal exercises given to each student in the training process.

This is a point that we should not forget, because in some voice studios the routine for all students consists mainly of "warming up" and thereafter going into songs and arias. The students then depend upon their natural equipment. If they do not belong to the blessed few who are gifted to the extent where the inherent superiority of their vocal material survives all production hazards, the result can only be a groping around, without their ability being developed or their achievement aided.

Such treatment can be compared to the procedure of a ballet teacher who immediately takes his students into dance routines and omits all work at the barre and center. In dancing, one builds up strength, coordination and balance through such practice and later applies these to dance routines. Leaving natural gifts aside, one cannot expect to gain more from the dance routines than one has put in at the barre and center.

The same principle---first develop, then apply---goes for voice training. A grave mistake is committed by putting too much and too early emphasis on application at the expense of building. Trying to put a voice into finished form before the vocal raw material has been developed into a usable product will always prove futile.

## Notes

[1] A gender change does not affect the voice. After the required operation, transsexuals have a changed body, but not a changed voice. In order for them to gain a voice in harmony with their looks, adjustments in pitch and in vocal weight are desirable.

[2] Plane trips can upset the hearing capacity and blur the senses and judgment of a vocalist. Though these effects prevail merely temporarily, they may be most annoying while they last. It is therefore advisable for a performer to get to his point of destination early so that he may have time to recuperate and the balance between the voice and the hearing faculty can reestablish itself. Arriving by plane at the last moment and then immediately proceeding to perform may throw off even the most seasoned of vocalists.

[3] The "vocal jet-set" takes its toll. Singers who, in a brief span, perform in many different parts of the world constantly change time zones, which affects their sleep. Constant changes in diet, climate and altitude further tend to disrupt their being. Exhaustion is prone to accumulate. An artist often lacks the stamina to carry the role he is called upon to carry.

# 5 INSTRUCTOR AND STUDENT: TEACHING AND LEARNING CONCEPTS

---

**Q.** Can voice be taught by correction only?

**A.** No art can be created by correction alone. Imperfections must be eliminated before the entire vocal function may grow healthfully. This, however, is only the beginning. Art asks for a steady development and a continuous process of growth.

---

If the student belongs to the blessed few who stand at the threshold of vocal maturity, correction may be sufficient.

Unfortunately, even the immature vocalist often believes that there is just one small problem in her production, one little kink that holds her back. She is convinced that all she has to do is get that little kink ironed out, and she will be made. This is the student with the "success is just around the corner" or "I have arrived" attitude. She needs immediate encouragement in order to sustain her self-confidence. The thought of finding the use of her instrument, of searching out the values lying concealed in her voice and of waiting patiently until everything shapes into gear does not appeal to her. She constantly looks for a point of fixation---"the perfect thing to do." She tends to grasp at gimmicks and clichés and clings to them until she later discovers that much more than some minor adjustments are necessary before the finished product can freely and fully emerge. But gimmicks and clichés fail at the crucial moment and set their own arbitrary limits, which fall far short of the goal toward which the true artist aspires.

There is a widespread belief that a faulty voice is merely the result of self-inflicted bad treatment and that a vocal fault occurs only when a singer or speaker "makes" it sound badly. This is an oversimplification. Were it true, there would be many more fine voices around. Besides, voice and speech correction would be easier. Unfortunately, most of the trouble lies deeper and so does the remedy.

Granted, "scooping," for instance, is a fault that a singer can often avoid. This is particularly true when the scoop is merely a stylistic trait and, as such, a matter of taste or musicianship rather than vocal technique. The fault then is more annoying than dangerous. It attacks only the periphery but not the heart of voice production. It can be studied as a mannerism or affectation. Correction, as a rule, is therefore not difficult (though in some cases the unfortunate old pet dies hard, and to resist the temptation utterly and absolutely may not be easy). A singer who scoops tends to hit a note below the center of the pitch and then sneaks up to it. This is like driving a nail into the wall crookedly and then bringing it up to level. A double action results, starting with the imprecise. Gradually, this becomes more precise. In order to correct himself, the singer must learn to hear and feel the difference between the precise and the imprecise, and he must reduce the double action to a single one. To be sure, he must first make a conscious effort to control the listening experience when attacking a note. Later he need only set up a watchdog committee for himself to remind him not to scoop.

The habit that the scooper is trying to overcome is one that he himself has developed in the course of satisfying his own taste. A singer usually likes to scoop, but the audience usually does not like to hear it or before long gets tired of it. In contrast, many other vocal faults and problems have not been developed directly by our own tastes and desires but have crept in against our wishes and knowledge.

Let us examine in this connection some forms of singing off key. As we all know, even some famous singers are not always able to avoid this vocal anomaly.

When a singer starts to produce sound, he brings to the act a certain habitual use of his vocal organs. When he sharpens or flattens, the mechanism concerned with the control of the pitch may fail to function as he desires. Then something goes wrong. A discrepancy exists between what he wants to perform and the action he carries out. This may be due to the particular ends he has in mind. First, he wants to make the sound "methody," that is, according to the method he has been taught, employing arbitrary production rules that do not always agree with his voice. Second, he wants to make the sound beautiful; therefore, at the moment he uses his voice, he starts for that end directly and without considering what manner would be best to use for the purpose. It follows that as long as he is dominated by the habit of "method singing" or "beauty making," he will react to the stimuli by the same misdirected use and will continue to sing off key. Even after the pitch impurity has been pointed out to him, he will be unable---to his dismay---to set right what he knows to be wrong.

What is at the bottom of this singer's difficulty? The habitual use of his vocal organs
has always been accompanied by certain sensory
experiences, such as self-hearing. Through the
years, these have become quite familiar to him.
In fact, by their very familiarity, they have
come to sound right to him, and he derives considerable satisfaction from hearing them and re-
peating them. On the other hand, the use of his
voice singing on key would be a different, if
not an entirely contrary one. It would be associated with unfamiliar sensory experiences that
might not sound right---or perhaps even wrong.
But just these latter experiences are the ones
he might have to gain in order to learn to correct himself. To do so, he must be willing to
change the sensory appreciation of the use of
his voice. He must give up the "method singing"
or the "beauty making" and he must look for the
fundamentals: tone, freedom, flow, ring, roundness. By exploring these, and reaping the benefits from the novel procedure of consciously
using these, he may gain those tone qualities
that are associated with pure pitch.

Most of our vocal problems are deep-rooted
and of a highly complex nature. They are due to
structural and psychological characteristics
within our makeup. Both, in varying degrees and
combinations, strike the more vital centers of
our vocal being and affect our vocal work in
numerous unfortunate ways.

The possessor of a faulty voice usually does
not consciously "make" his voice sound faulty.
The fault is not due to his own violation; he is
the captive of processes he does not know how to
control. The interfering processes function unconsciously. While he is, for example, subject
to throatiness, he is to that extent unable to
produce his voice without throatiness.

When a voice is throaty or breathy or has a
wobble, it is fairly impossible to show the student how not to sound throaty, breathy or wob-

bly. There is no instant remedy. Correction is a step-by-step process in which the student must learn to change the balance of functions concerned with production, so that the disruptive forces that have dominated his production will dominate less and less, and the tone that has sounded faulty will come to sound less and less faulty.

When a voice sounds tight-throated, the student is sometimes advised to lie down on the floor and do breathing exercises or to perform calisthenics: to roll her head, shake her arms, and so on. Exercises of this sort may put her into a more relaxed mood or they may generally tone up or relax parts of the body. However, they will fail to provide the specific devices that could enforce a letup on the vocal constrictor. Since they do not get to the core of the problem, they will fail to accomplish their purpose, for even though the student diligently rolls her head, shakes her arms, lies down, and tries harder and harder to relax, she does not learn to "play" her instrument any better. Therefore, as soon as she is again confronted with the voice work, the unfree feeling from the throat recurs and so does the tight-throated sound.

Such general exercises and relaxation devices can actually become gimmicks and crutches, which compound the problem. They add to the discomfort of tenseness and self-consciousness. They are efforts spent on the wrong objective, turning the attention of the learner away from the most pressing vocal task directing her into areas within which no vocal processes take place.

Only in the act of voice production can the vocal instrument acquire action freedom, and only through that can we learn to let loose psychologically and free our mind in regard to voice. To relax the tenseness in vocal production is a vocal problem that has to be solved by

means of remedial vocal exercises and in the
process of vocalizing.

An inexperienced teacher will sometimes suggest to a student who has a throaty voice,
"Don't constrict so much---not so much tension."
This negative advice "not to constrict," "not to
tense up," is, under the circumstances, not a
good suggestion. To harp on problems before a
remedy is feasible tends to lead to frustration
and is bound to discourage the efforts of the
student. In an attempt to follow this negative
advice, the student tortures himself in vain.
The throaty element continually asserts itself
with great persistence. Even when the student
recognizes it as a fault, he cannot make a
direct effort toward eliminating it. In order
for him to control it, a positive development
must take place and the hindrance must be worked
away. But tenseness of the vocal organs cannot
be directly worked off. Only indirectly can
techniques be developed by which to induce the
necessary change in the malfunctioning parts of
the vocal instrument. To free the various muscles of tenseness, counter forces must be
brought into play. Other functions in other
zones, which can exert a conditioning influence
on the throaty tone, must be strengthened. The
more strength appears in the right places, the
more it will disappear from the wrong places.
Thus, through the process of strengthening, the
process of reducing tension is gradually brought
about. As a result, throatiness will gradually
be lessened and perhaps eventually overcome.

The teacher's job of balancing the component
parts of each voice into the best possible result is a complex one. As the tone improves, it
will sound more natural and simple to the lis-
tener, but it is usually not as easy as it
sounds. Voice---like dance---if correctly produced, is done so with little effort that shows.
However, the tuning and adjusting of the human
instrument are complex and subtle processes, and

a great deal of ingenuity must go into perfecting them. The means of training the vocal instrument, therefore, can no more be condensed into a few words and sold like a recipe than can the learning of the technique in any field of art.

Often, when two singers meet, one will rave about his teacher. In a few words the teacher's "method" will be explained. Almost invariably one will end up with that persuasive question, "Why don't you try it, too?" The technique thus advertised must make any thinking person suspicious. To explain his theories on the art of acting, Stanislavsky had to write books on the subject. Anyone who can explain a vocal method in a few words proves how little he knows about it. In fact, the student who is well taught will usually be unable to give a faithful account of the learning process, which is always multidimensional and defies short, quick and exact description.

There are those who try to be helpful. When they find out that we have a cold, they advise, "Take a laxative." Likewise the vocal coach who, upon hearing an imperfect tone, advises each voice student to "Raise your uvula" or "From the diaphragm." These suggestions are pushed as practical remedies for all vocal ills. Unfortunately, they cannot do any good, except by accident. The vocal instrument is not responsive to a push-button approach.

In order to tune and successfully adjust the voice, one must decide upon the parts that require attention, individually, after a careful diagnosis. To put it bluntly, this is a job for a "physician," not a "pharmacist."

Q.  **How do I recognize a good teacher?**
A.  **By his patience, sensitivity and objectivity.**

There is no successful builder, trainer or gardener without patience. There is no successful searching into the potentialities of the voice or the handling thereof without sensitivity. There is no truth in one's profession or art without objectivity.

Of the three points, objectivity seems to be the most neglected. One teacher may fall in love with his pupil's voice---and love makes for blindness. If a teacher has eyes and ears only for his student's talents but cannot recognize virtues in the products of other voice studios, he is a bigot devoid of objectivity. He indulges in "wishful hearing" as others indulge in wishful thinking.

Sometimes the approach of a voice teacher is, "Hear ye, students, I, the voice teacher, I am the only one"; that is the attitude of a fool. In art, as in science, no monopoly of the means of grace has ever been possible.

Art comes first, personal taste comes last. A teacher should develop the ability to inspire his students and give them confidence. Instead of a blind, emotional, slavish attitude toward the teacher, good training should build in a student a feeling of self-confidence. Instead of a blind, emotional, slavish attitude toward the teacher, good training should build in a student a feeling of self-confidence, which comes from increasing security in and devotion to one's art.

The student should become so well acquainted with his voice under all conditions that he will know how to proceed on his own. The uncertainties of vocalism should be changed into definite understanding and faith in control.

This is a point that we should remember, because some teachers often unconsciously foster a student's dependence upon them. Instead of gradually weaning the student, they fasten themselves on the student and seek to bind him closer and closer, and eventually try to run his personal life. Teaching for some then becomes an outlet for bossiness.

A good teacher usually likes to give a great deal of himself in a lesson. He tries to understand the student. He establishes a relationship of togetherness with the student. He identifies with the student. The faculty of projecting his own vocal self into the student's vocal skin enables him to think, "I know how you feel vocally; and since I know how you feel, I also know how to help you with your problem." Then, unfortunately, the teacher is sometimes tempted to go a little further and wants to possess the student.

If there are understanding and knowledge on the teacher's part, these will be reflected in the atmosphere of the studio. Where they do not exist, a student is prone to be "nerved up" in the learning process, and the uncertainties of vocalism will easily lead to hysteria or similar professional diseases.

A good teacher will seek to know rather than to treat a new student. If she immediately begins to treat him, she is clearly assuming that she knows the rights and wrongs of a complex situation, that she knows what needs adjusting and how to go about it. But she doesn't, and she never will unless she is first willing to do nothing but listen, learn to understand the student and his voice and then start with a fresh point of view.

A good teacher will heed the warning "Never disturb a student who works well." He will not flood the lesson with talk but will focus as much as possible on doing.

A good teacher will start with a simple concept and use the simplest means for the solution
of a problem. It is a symptom of our time that
many well-meaning teachers in the arts cannot
resist the temptation of giving corrective
training outside of the technical field where it
does not belong, where they have little professional expertise. A case in point is physical
instruction (how to get the kinks out) or the
lesson being turned into psychiatric treatment.

Let us stress here that most students in the
arts respond quite well to a technical approach.
The voice student and particularly the acting
student is far better off when he is able to use
his voice as a creative instrument in its own
right, when his voice functions independently of
events that take place at the same time and when
his voice does not first need a personal, emotional experience in order to come to life.[1]

Even in the case of emotionally troubled
people who have voice problems, it is usually
simpler, more direct and faster to cope with the
problems by dealing with the technical aspects
of the voice than delving into the emotional
undertow and trying to treat the pathological
modes of the case.

A good teacher will grade criticism according to the level of ripeness a student has
reached. She will not set performance standards
for development sessions. At an early period of
vocal study, one should be involved more with
process than completion. At that state of work-
in-progress, the end product is not the chief
concern and some failures are to be expected and
tolerated. Otherwise, the teaching is neither
indulgent nor kind and the danger exists that
the student will try to jump the gun and be
ahead of himself.

There is an unfortunate belief among many
people that it is not important to be selective
in choosing a voice teacher for the beginner.

Their attitude is, "Almost anyone will do just to get him started." In any art, however, the foundation is most important. Poor vocal work at the start is often the major cause for subsequent vocal deterioration. Better none than a poor voice teacher.

The gift for inventing terminology is one of the tests of a good teacher. In this connection the problem of defining terms in art must be stressed. This is particularly true in those fields of art concerned with ideas and sensations. In training the voice, the success of a teacher depends largely upon his ability to present the study material in terms that appeal to his student's imagination and sense of humor.

The art of voice teaching is a specialty. It requires two main gifts: pedagogical talent and tone instinct.

The tone instinct of the voice teacher depends first upon the degree of his sensitivity and susceptibility to human tone and its peculiarities. Second, it depends on his ability to analyze each voice correctly in its complexity. Third, it depends upon his good judgment of human tone. This judgment should help him in an important decision: How much can the student take? How much at a time can the student's voice be safely expanded and corrected? Generally speaking, gentle procedures and caution are advisable in the treatment of the voice. This very judgment must likewise help the teacher to determine whether the sounds his students make in the studio are substantial enough to carry in an auditorium.[2]

Tone instinct is an inborn gift. Through practice and experience we can improve it, but we cannot learn it or teach its fundamentals any more effectively than we can teach a person how to acquire sensitivity. A person without tone instinct lacks the essentials for the teaching of voice. Incapable of relying on sensory impressions, he will be forced to compensate by the use of tricks, imitations, fixed mechanical patterns and set generalizations.

A good teacher will love teaching. She will "see" voices grow and enjoy the gradual unfolding that takes place. She will observe with interest the minute changes that occur in the growing process. She will evaluate these changes. She will try to make the student interested in them.[3]

Because the voice does change its quality and texture rather slowly, the student himself may not always notice it when he is in the midst of vocal transition. The overall change that takes place in his own voice is to him often vividly perceptible only in retrospect.

The teacher, as a practitioner, will seek to put his own observations and vocal experiences into the framework of technical and psychological reason. To translate these observations and experiences into the particular case before him presents a never-ending challenge. In spite of occasional obvious similarities, no two voices are the same. Working with each student in an individual way will always bring new knowledge to the teacher. Teaching the individualistic way becomes a source of enlightenment which constantly renews itself.

However, how many teachers love or even enjoy the teaching of voice production? How many suffer voice teaching as a necessary evil?

Any pursuit in the arts is difficult. Most people realize that an artist is, generally speaking, in the midst of a constant struggle, which necessarily has disappointing aspects. Nevertheless, no matter how difficult the pursuit may be, if one derives joy from it and if one can help the individual to find joy, the studying need not be drudgery or mechanical, dry and empty. Often the truth hurts, but sometimes the truth is refreshing. In 1951 in the New York Times, Dr. Poell, a member of the Vienna Opera, was quoted as saying, "I shall never again forsake medicine. When my singing days are behind me, I will be spared the agony of teaching. My ears could never stand it."

Just as a good trainer is not necessarily a good performer, a good performer is not necessarily a good teacher. Just as one would not choose someone with an excellent reputation as a voice teacher and blindly sign her to fill engagements as a performer, neither should one choose a performer because of her reputation and blindly engage her to teach voice. Performing and teaching are two different professions. Success and preeminence in performing are not the same as success and preeminence in teaching.

Unfortunately, a performer-teacher may sometimes listen to her student with mixed emotions. This happens when the teacher is in competition with the student.

A performer might be an excellent teacher, but only when she possesses the qualifications of an excellent teacher. As long as a voice teacher is not chosen exclusively for her ability to teach voice, she is being judged by false standards, and the profession may pay dearly for the lack of discriminate judgment. There is another point that we should not forget: Each voice is composed of a jumble of unique characteristics and patterns of growth. Each voice must develop its own pattern of growth according to its own unique needs.

Most people know about the existence of high and low, large and small, bright and dark voices. In addition, some voices, because of their particular makeup, are essentially light. Others are necessarily robust. Most are in between. This applies to all voices, male and female, from the coloratura to the bass.

The teacher who recognizes this is wise. The one who has one method for all and has allowed his personal taste to dictate the basic balance he demands in all his pupils obviously can turn out only one balance in all. Thus, all voices, rather than being brought up within their own league, are put into the same weight class.

Take, for instance, the performer-teacher who is known as a wonderful interpreter. His voice is light and he is very lyric in leaning. His personality and artistry rather than vocal opulence make him outstanding as a performer. He must be considered more as a coach than a teacher of vocal production. This is so because under his guidance the course of study is much more directed toward the interpretive than the productional aspects of vocalism.

If he works with a student who can already sing, the performer-teacher may have genuinely valuable suggestions for artistic improvement. However, when he teaches students in need of technical development, their voices are usually not expanded. Instead, they are polished, put in a frame and exhibited in their immature stage. Then, true to form, they are thereafter fed on the light fare.

A young student with a heavy voice, upon entering this studio, might as well leave a part of his voice at the door. In the course of the training that lies ahead, he will be unable to grow to his full capacity. This studio, rather than uncovering and building up his potential, will go immediately into distilling what is already there. An underuse of the productive capabilities results, and with it a false delicacy. The voice is condemned to reserve or powerlessness in varying degrees. A typical shortcoming of such a voice is that it does not get loud enough, often enough, for long enough.

Add to this the unconscious desire of the star-teacher to breed his own kind and a situation arises in which some studios become factories, devoted mainly to turning out reasonable facsimiles of the master.

Just as the so-called "light teacher," because of his own experience and personal taste, unconsciously pinches down the potential of heavy voices, so will the "heavy teacher" (who likes to teach what he knows best and does best) tend to overload light voices. One thinks immediately of the illustrious heroic baritone who, knowing only one road, inspires all his baritones to essay the heroic road to Valhalla. Pity the poor pilgrim with a light voice falling by the wayside.

Let us quote Enrico Caruso (in the Musical Observer, November 1919, taken from the monthly musical record): "...there are actually as many methods as there are singers, and any particular method, even if accurately set forth, might be useless to the person who tried it.... The knowledge he has attained will be valuable to him only, for somebody else would produce the same note equally well, but in quite a different way.... This is what I really would reply to anyone putting the question to me---that my own particular way of singing, if I have any---is after all peculiarly suited to me only."

Indeed, each vocalist, because of his individual makeup, needs his individual method. The method should consist of the eternal search for the best possibility and the subsequent effort to improve that possibility. Since perfection in art is merely an ideal, each artist wanders along a road to which there is in fact no end unless by his own wish he will go on no more and thus comes to a halt.

The teacher's job is first that of a guide or scout whose task is to discover new and better ways of voice production and to communicate the nature and location of them to the student. Later, the teacher should act as a helper and still later as an adviser along the way of using and improving the student's best possibility.

Yet, one voice teaching approach forever advocates the "yawn," another "chewing," another "diaphragm tension," another the "mask." These devices are their stock-in-trade. Granted, at particular stages of vocal development the use of some of these devices may very well be of benefit for the purpose of tuning or adjusting individual needs of the moment. However, although these may occasionally provide one answer to a vocal problem, these devices are not the answer to the voice training problem.

Unfortunately, these devices are often overrated and devoured. No wonder! They are something to point to and aim for within the realm of description; voice production is, after all, quite elusive. Because they offer some tangible factor that will entice the beginner to work in a specific direction and because his hunger is for something tangible and specific, who can blame him when he wants to latch on to them? He may be inclined to believe that all he has to do is to master the technique of a "yawn" or the "mask" or "diaphragm tension" or "chewing" and he will have mastered the technique of voice production. In addition, at first there is also the Power of Believing. It may work because of its novelty, but before long the novelty wears off. Then the student discovers that even if these devices here and there produce results, they have no permanent value but in time outlive their usefulness or burn themselves out. They may degenerate into meaningless vocal clichés. As soon as they are antiquated, other devices will have to be found to replace them.

In very rare instances, some of these devices may fit, like "lucky pieces." Then, the vocalist may find it difficult to realize that there are limitations to the use of these devices. He becomes obsessed with such notions and believes in them fanatically. It may take him years to discover that good vocal tone will be the more complete the more parts of the body participate in making it good and that there are many more devices and productive areas that should contribute toward enriching his development but that so far have not had a chance to enter the picture.

More often, however, these devices are quite misleading. They make the student think, "If it's not coming from there, I'm on the wrong track," or the other way around, "If I am ever going to have it, it must come from there." But it may not want to come from there. Let us take, for instance, the case of a basso profundo. The sound of his voice comes forth with rolling richness. He may feel a lot of rumble or vibratory sensations way down in the chest. However, rather than using these sensations and building on them as part of an approach to the development of his voice, he is constantly advised to proceed in the other direction, to shoot the voice up into "the mask." He may then chase one false hope after another and wait forever for the occurrence of the improbable.

These suggestions, then, cannot serve as a means by which to establish a solid vocal technique, nor can any list of devices, however inclusive, be complete for that purpose. Vocal effort as a whole has no devices on which it can rely exclusively. Hence these devices are fruitful only as long as their one-sidedness is recognized and appreciated. It follows that basing one's entire system of voice teaching upon such devices results in a one-sided and inadequate vocal approach. Similarly, there are some dance instructors who pick up a few steps at a dance convention and then teach a complete course based upon them. There are also teachers of acting who select one aspect of an acting approach and harp upon that, applying it generally rather than specifically.

In summary, no one aspect or device will ever work along the whole training course and all devices within a technique should be related to specific individual needs alone. The teacher must therefore adapt himself to each student's individuality and not try to make each student conform to his own. By this we mean that during lesson time the teacher should be an alive human being who is concerned not with his own voice or with his own problems but with understanding and experiencing as far as possible the student and the student's voice.

Sometimes a teacher may become a god in his studio. He is no longer fully aware that it requires a certain imagination and a good deal of empathy to recognize in a student a human being who, though different from the teacher, is nevertheless sensitive and feels and reacts much in the same way the teacher does. The male and female prima donna--teachers with the "capital I" complex may find all of this a pretty difficult psychological task. Yet in it lies the essence of all pedagogical success.

The outcry of some students in the arts (particularly in the field of acting) against their teacher or former teacher comes often from their wish "to pay him back" for the psychological mistreatment that they feel they had to endure.

---

**Q.   What can interfere with progress in tone production?**
**A.   Physical, psychological and emotional problems.**

---

Physical, psychological and emotional problems can affect not only the vocal instrument but also the ability to concentrate. No student can get out of her effort more than she puts in. Through deep concentration, many minor vocal disorders can be overridden.

Sometimes we hear a beginner exclaim, "I'll get by with what I have." The step from zero to "getting by" safely is much bigger and harder than the step from "getting by" to "getting good." It is indeed doubtful whether that student will get by.

In the curious way in which most people tend to cherish whatever is theirs, the vocalist is sometimes in love with his own faults. Take the

tenor who talks and sings as if he had a potato
stuck in his throat. We hear it. We are amused
by it. Only the tenor does not hear it or does
not want to hear it. To him the unnatural sound
seems quite natural. The teacher can help the
student in this case by means of aversion technique.[4] Through the teacher's imitation of his
student's sound and, if necessary, through an
enlargement of the objectionable features, a-
versions can be induced. Once they are established deeply enough, the pupil, though at first
perhaps still not quite believing in them, will
eventually come to recognize the imperfections.
He will admit that, blunted by habit, he had accepted the constricted sound of his voice without conflict. A psychological reorientation toward good free tone must be the first step on
his road to progress.

The beginner who permits himself to be prematurely critical of his voice may be unsuccess-
ful in finding the desired progress. He is apt
to reject some of his sounds and abruptly interrupt others so that he does not follow up the
possibilities of development that can open up
for him.

The beginner must be advised that the success of his training depends upon his noticing
and communicating everything that takes place
vocally. He should try to sort out the impressions he receives while working on his voice. He
should be encouraged to make subjective comments
on his approach, his feelings and his impressions, but he must refrain from early self-eval-
uation. At the outset the beginner must also try
not to change the sound he produces, no matter
how much (or little) he likes it. If the beginner cannot produce his voice apart from what
appeals to his own taste and what does not, the
sound itself can get in his way. He resists what
he does not like. But unfortunately, what he
likes is not always good and what he does not
like is not always bad. Therefore, to like or

not to like, that is not the question. To let
go, to open up, and just to do it is the prime
task. It is only when the beginner succeeds in
just showing his voice and being impartial that
the barrier of reserve is bound to break. He
will then become aware of a vast number of vocal
possibilities that would otherwise have eluded
his grasp. The true value of these sounds---
their vigor, form, flow, substance---have to be
spotted for him and pointed out to him as he
makes and experiences them.

This, of course, is the job of the teacher,
who must give meaning, emphasis and urgency to
the sound qualities the student produces. In
this way, a new frame of reference is gradually
established out of which the student's judgment
is formed. The beginner learns from experience
to identify what he is doing when he is doing it
correctly and to know what is really desirable
in his own voice. That is seldom learned spontaneously. It is based upon the art of being
objective about oneself, which comes mostly from
education or even reeducation.

Sometimes the beginner is afraid of sounding
too wild, too mannish or effeminate. At other
times, he may tend to suppress a sound because
it does not seem "pleasant" to him. Then, again,
the attempt to exchange his innate voice for an
assumed voice or to match preconceived ideas as
to how he would love to sound (which may be a
far cry from what the nature of his voice wants
him to sound like) may have misguided him.

The situation is much the same in other
fields of art. In the study of acting, the beginner will sometimes be tempted to work in
terms of what it looks like instead of what it
is. In the study of dancing, the beginner who
learns to stretch his leg muscles should be interested only in the degree of efficiency he can
obtain. Eye appeal does not matter here. It happens in the course of vocal study that the student who at first rejects some of his sounds as

undesirable will later reclassify them and eventually accept them as desirable.

The idiosyncrasies of the beginner may interfere with progress. The student exclaims, "Oh, I could not stand to sound 'brassy'; one can't sound like that without being like that," and she bemoans the vulgarity that assails her ear at any time she hears such a sound. As an example she mentions a musical comedy star who symbolizes her own distastes and who happens to be her pet hate. While it may be true that the star indeed sounds very brassy, the concern of the student that a similar sound may lastingly dominate the character of her own voice may be totally unjustified. Even if she occasionally does sound brassy, that still may be no cause for concern, since it may play only a transitional role in the growth of her voice. The beginner lacks perspective. She can only hear the primary color in her own voice instead of the blend.[5] In her fear of sounding unladylike or vulgar, she tends to censor and to withhold sound. The idea, though, is not to hold back but rather to help sound to sail, and to make it sail under its own colors so that it may exercise its own colors. Otherwise, if one cuts down right from the start, one will never gain strength.

In order to reveal and use her vocal potential fully, the beginner must learn to overcome the fear of sounding ugly or of making herself unbecomingly conspicuous. She must learn to familiarize herself with the world of vocal sound. She must also learn to understand that values can exist in many different vocal types and breeds---in delicate as well as in rugged ones. Above all, she must become more tolerant.

Just as one student protects herself unnecessarily against brassy sounds, another will perhaps unnecessarily protect herself, though in quite a different way. Her pet hate is a wailing, off-key sound. In a well-meant effort to

stay exactly on pitch, she becomes a fanatic who
drives herself pitch-crazy. Even when she produces tones that are not troubled by any noticeable pitch impurities, she still does not leave
good enough alone but makes an extra effort to
control the pitch. As a result, she is forever
trying for the right pitch rather than for the
right tone quality, and she mars the production
through too much conscious control. Her voice,
robbed of sufficient leeway to function freely,
becomes stiff.

Another case is the student who blasts right
from the beginning. When his teacher tells him
to take it easy, the student exclaims, "I
thought this sounded too thin." Still another
case is the student who deliberately tries to a-
void the ring or "ping" in the voice and thus
reduces the penetrating and carrying power of
tone because, as he says, "I thought this sounded too hard." Again another case is the student
who, at the slightest sign of a pulsating effect
or vibrato (when the voice begins to float), reacts negatively and complains, "Why does it
shake? Isn't there enough support behind it?"
Though the same student accepts or admires the
vibrato of other singers and instrumentalists
(especially of violinists and cellists), and
though a lack of vibrato bothers him (especially
when a boy soprano sings a solo), as soon as he
hears it in his own voice it seems either dis-
jointed or exaggerated. Or the student may be
afraid of acquiring a wobble or tremolo, both of
which are vibrato imperfections, and so deliberately cuts down on the tone streaming. Or he
obstructs the flow of his voice and does not
allow the natural buoyancy of the voice to come
to the fore, thus tossing the baby out with the
bath water.

We can see, in addition to personal dislikes
and to the ego aspect, the desire to please and
an unbalanced sense of one's own potential turn
out to be factors that often hinder vocal progress.

A premature obligation to the sense of beauty also impairs the progress of the voice. Beauty does not come from an indication thereof. Vocal beauty may result from making it real, knowing what sound one can make, encouraging the individuality of this sound and perfecting the four essentials: freedom, form, flow and substance.

A typical example of a pupil who holds back progress is the immature vocalist who exclaims during his lesson, "I could have done this before but I did not think it sounded 'pretty.'" In an early attempt to sound "pretty," we rob ourselves of an earthiness that is essential. We must remember that we have limited the use of our body as a result of the conventions of civilization. We have repressed body functions. We have to relearn in order to do things that should come naturally. The squatting position, for example, one of the most natural positions of the body, is not used in civilized behavior because of furniture and clothing. Loud and unrestrained laughter as well as a good healthy yawn cannot be indulged in, lest people consider us rude. As the dancer must sweat to attain that primitive force that enables him to produce and sustain dance movements with strength and flexibility, so must the singer and speaker work in order to produce that wealth of free sound that is needed to fill the hall. From the coloratura to the bass, we can hear certain primitive, animal characteristics in great voices. In fact, the sheer animal excitement in the voice is often hard to resist. We say, "She sang like a bird." Many compared the voice of Chaliapine ---in the quality of its roar---to that of a lion. Hagen in Goetterdaemmerung is most effective when the sound of his voice is properly barbaric. However, when the primitive force and animal power in the voice are not appreciated and the dealing with these raw materials are not considered in the training process, the use of

the vocal instrument is often more significant
for things left out than for things accomplished. (This is true except for the chosen few who
are born with a birdlike quality, a roar, a
growl, silver in the voice, and who usually take
these blessings for granted.) To aim early for
"prettiness" means to choose superficiality at
the expense of vitality. A premature aim toward
refinement leads to curtailment.

A premature desire for absolute excellence
is prone to cloud progress. Unfortunately, many
students have a natural tendency to judge themselves harshly or to be fussy. They suffer from
a lack of work enjoyment and are busy being unhappy with the voice. Resentment rather than
effort exhausts them. Other students become an-
noyed with themselves for not doing better. This
chokes them up. Their own partial failures crush
them. Still others suffer from the disease of
the twentieth century: unseemly haste. Their
steady complaint is, "I feel so slow" or, "I
thought if I don't push, it won't grow quickly."
All of these students must learn to overcome
their negative, self-defeating attitudes and to
be more patient with their own problems and in-
eptitudes. They must acquire a more long-range
viewpoint and view study time in terms of months
and years rather than days and weeks. They must
realize that they have chosen a medium that is
indeed very demanding and puts them to a severe
test. Above all, they must learn to have more
respect for the voice and for the stature of
vocal art, for art requires long, diligent and
devoted training in order to lift itself from
the level of a sorry craft to that of a distinguished, superior one.

Indeed, what matters most is the spirit with
which the student meets the challenge. The important factors are first, his faith in training
his ability to live in peace with his own potential (however big or small), and second, his
trying to be a good sport. By this we mean to

accept without unreasonable fear or fuss the various development struggles, dead ends and reversals that come up in the learning process and without which no real progress in physical and psychological functioning can be made.[6]

The beginner who patiently explores the possibilities and variations in her tone production will go beyond the surface level, leave familiar vocal patterns behind and, in her quest for the hidden powers within her voice or for the qualities that lie somewhat beyond the boundaries of her conscious technique, will venture into the unknown. Surprise, embarrassment or even delight may sometimes throw her, perhaps upsetting her progress temporarily. The student exclaims, "It does not seem to belong to me." The type and amount of sound that comes out startles or overwhelms her. She finds it hard to endure the leverage exerted upon her by the new vocal extension. She blanks. Her faculties are numbed by newness.

A period of self-consciousness may follow. Even the praise of her teacher may affect the student adversely and, as after eating rich food, mental indigestion will follow. An element of frivolity then seems to enter, providing an escape from strong commitment and temporary relief from the stress of studious attention and deep concentration. The student is so much involved that she tends to break up. This is nerves. Or she may lack the inner courage to follow through and exploit the newly discovered possibilities.

Diversion of attention can help at such a time. The teacher can aid the student to absorb the impact of such experiences by introducing exercises with additional, related problems. These will keep the body and brain of the student occupied. Eventually the ear of the student will get used to new standards, and the body will become geared to the new sections of the different mechanisms that have come into play.

The various experiences assume form. A portion
of work has been completed. An additional vocal
weapon is won.

---

**Q.  How can one measure progress in tone pro-
     duction?**
**A.  The student can judge by his own bodily ex-
     perience, by his own hearing, feeling and
     sensing. He will find confirmation of pro-
     gress in the lessening of his vocal prob-
     lems.**

---

If the student is in good health but feels vocal
strain continuously, if his throat aches after
each lesson, if he gets hoarse frequently after
practicing, then the result is far from healthy
and what he is doing is not right. If the freedom, form, flow and substance of the voice do
not improve, and range, size, dynamics and sustaining length do not grow, the work in tone
production is not progressing.

Progress in tone production is not made and
cannot be judged by a regulated order of occur-
rences. There is no sure way in which we can anticipate fully the events that bring about tone
development, and we are unable to predict with
any certainty or precision how far a voice is
educable or can go. We must therefore take into
account a certain number of unpredictable elements which confront all who study and teach
voice.

Progress does not come overnight. Nothing
comes suddenly into existence in the voice.
Everything is gradually developed in a particular, individual way. The proof of improvement
may become evident overnight, but it is always
the result of newly acquired coordination, balance and, finally, growth. A student often has
the impression that certain correct functions do
come within reach overnight. He exclaims, "Why

couldn't I do that before?" These functions have
not become available miraculously or in the
twinkling of an eye. They have become ripe for
usage. They were not ready before because the
unripe organism was able to function only in an
unripe way. In the beginning we can feel only
our potential, and all we can hope for is to do
the right thing in the right direction. Sometimes the beginner can only stumble in the right
direction, which is at least more beneficial
than walking straight in the wrong one.

Improvement does not come about smoothly. No
voice student mounts the ladder to achievement
in an even progression of steps. The "normal"
course of vocal development is quite irregular,
with ups and downs. In this sense, vocal learning, like most other learning, resembles a re-
volution; it passes through many contradictory
stages. Sometimes the voice may pass through a
bad spell, which drags and tries our patience,
and no matter what we do, progress seems to e-
lude us. But the effect of consistent plugging
is cumulative. Eventually, something new is
bound to appear.

When an improvement is discovered, the student alone can cement it. When something new
happens, it must become part of him, not something to be repeated by rote. Repetition by rote
is useless. It cannot be applied to the finished
product; it cannot be used for artistic expression; it cannot serve as a means to convey inner
emotions.

Improvement cannot be forced beyond the limitations of nature. If we force, if we try to go
beyond our strength, nature will surely catch up
with us and throw us back.

When working correctly, the individual possibilities of development and the variations in
tone production must be searched for and explor-
ed. In this process, the teacher can try to establish within the student a point of comparison. By means of comparison, the student can

learn to discern the essential qualities of his voice. This is, of course, of vital importance to the realization of progress.

When the student, for example, sustains a tone and when in her aim to improve the tone, changes in production occur, the teacher---after evaluating these changes for himself---can simply say, "First part (or middle or last part) of the tone was the best part" and then ask the student to repeat the tone. Or, instead of saying it, the teacher may want to convey his message by means of sign language. Signals, received by the student while she sings, serve as guideposts and give her a sense of teacher participation. The latter may bolster her will and strengthen her morale.

The student can then go along by saying to herself, "If I can do it in the first part, I can do it also in the middle or last part," or "If I can do it in the last part, I can also do it in the first or middle part." Even though no technical directions are given, the perceptive student will nevertheless come to know what to aim for because she can hear and/or feel the difference.[7] She will learn to recognize what opposes what in the voice. She will begin to distinguish between the free and the unfree, the ring and the nonring, the flexible and the inflexible, the steady and the unsteady, the round and the not-well-rounded tone.

A measuring mark is won. Once it is won, an awareness of what it could be and a longing for it results. From then on the student can try to work it, ooze it, coax it, will it, manipulate and stretch for it. When she reaches it, she can capitalize on it until it is there in ever stronger presence. Repetition and practice will ultimately enable the student to stay with the best part of the tone and to maintain the degree of tonal excellence by habit.

The fact that the student is able to proceed without the use of technical rules will simplify

the course of study. The crucial, technical
question of how she did what she did will not
mystify her. As a matter of fact, she can bypass
or ignore it. She goes for tone and works on the
tone. She thereby learns to control the effect.
In the process, the "How" will include itself
automatically.

Before the beginner has learned to distinguish between what is right and wrong in his
tone work, he cannot progress in his homework.
It is not easy for the novice to separate the
wheat from the chaff. Having no full, innate
knowledge of what is good or bad in his own
voice, he must learn discrimination. That consists of developing a sense perception of differences so that he will come to recognize on
his own what contributes to his vocal well-being
and what does not.

The prime concept here is the one that has
the greatest functional relevance to the learner, namely tone freedom. Distinctions are to be
made between various degrees of tone freedom. At
first these distinctions may go unnoticed, or
they may be perceived but not retained. This is
usually not so much because the beginner lacks
the sense equipment for distinguishing, but because in the past he was quite indifferent to
vocal differences, so he simply is not used to
the process of differentiating but must now get
used to it. Only with time and through vocal
work and experience can the distinguishing vocal
marks and fine points become ever more relevant
and meaningful and will he be able to give verbal definitions of them. Gradually he recognizes
tone freedom in his voice with fuller certainty,
and eventually, it is hoped, freedom will persist. All of which goes to show that, to develop
sensitivity to good vocal functioning versus
malfunctioning is a task that in most cases has
to be achieved bit by bit.

Premature self-study is a risky procedure

that can lead to a peculiar bypass of the effectiveness in practicing or may even result in malpractice. One mistake frequently made in premature self-study is to become overly fascinated with some new element that has appeared in the course of development and to overwork that new element. This tends to unsettle the equilibrium of the vocal organism at work, and it upsets the quality of the previous voice work. In consequence, lesson time must be spent to balancing various factors that led to the undue emphasis.

Granted, we must catch new things while they are "hot" and, unfortunately, a new technical advance tends to disrupt the old pattern, sometimes causing confusion and setbacks. In the midst of both, let us remember, when a new element comes in, the other good and actively functioning elements should not be neglected. Otherwise, the new element will overpower the production until the effect is distorted.

Keeping the voice student away from doing the wrong vocal thing and weeding out what might misdirect him are among the chief objectives toward which the voice teacher must work. If this work is omitted, and people (particularly when inexperienced) try to improve vocally in a "do-it-yourself" fashion, they are apt to reinforce their bad habits.

Only after the voice student has established reasonable control over the right tone can he trust his direction and will he know what it means to work correctly. It is then his responsibility to try to continue by himself the things his teacher started for him.

In all physical as well as psychological development, the retention value must be considered. Disruptions of continuity should be avoided as much as possible. A time lag between lessons can undo progress. It is easy to get out of shape quickly, but it is difficult and time-consuming to get back into shape.

Particularly in the first stages of voice study, a continual battle against sinking back into old habits has to be waged. The beneficial effects of a lesson are prone to ebb away quickly. The "treatment" has to be renewed, and the sooner the better. In later stages of study a voice lesson should have an ever longer-lasting effect.

Without consistent work on the instrument, the technique cannot be incorporated completely; it cannot carry over fully from lesson to other use or application; it cannot settle into a habit. Good vocal technique is not a value that, once achieved, is automatically maintained ever after. We are dealing with a living organism, and living organisms do not tolerate stagnation. Work is necessary, not only to gain but also to maintain. There is always a challenge to technique. In all art forms the quest continues. The adventure never ends.

The voice student who does not learn how to work on her own and who cannot depend on her own judgment is in trouble. She has not developed a scale of values with which to test her vocal impressions and with which to evaluate her future vocal experiences. Therefore, in the absence of accumulated awareness, self-confidence and conviction, she bases all her hopes on the opinions of others and is pulled in a thousand different directions. Smitten with self-doubts, frightened by criticism and vulnerable to other people's suggestions, she is easily taken in by catch phrases and tends to become a gullible victim for quacks and vocal sharpies.

We cannot deny it, our vocal minds are very conventional. Thus, angels sing soprano (at least in the movies) while God is a basso. Our reactions to vocal problems are often typical human reactions. For example, one hears the comment: "He already has a good voice; why does he study voice?" The vocal market is full of quick answers, slogans and oversimplifications, such

as "Smoking is good for the voice because when
one smokes one coughs up phlegm." Or, "To
strengthen the voice, shout into the sea." Or,
"When one practices low notes, one will lose the
high ones." Or, "To project, always speak high."
The opinions we hear depend entirely upon whom
we listen to. In the end we have to blame only
ourselves for taking opinions of this sort seriously. Particularly when we do not resist suggestions of a violent nature can we hurt the
voice. Shouting is a case in point. We can easily shout ourselves hoarse and sick. The vocal
damage suffered by many a cheerleader proves
this point.

A person who has suffered vocal damage but
was able to repair it will probably be unusually
qualified to teach vocal technique. The discoveries he made in the course of his own re-
covery were priceless. Since he went through the
mill, he seems to be able to understand and help
others in a way nobody else could.

Success in voice training should be judged
not only by the result but also by the size of
the task. Therefore, the criteria for judging a
voice teacher differ. For example, if a teacher
works with a student from the hopeless category
(who may need voice work as a sort of therapy)
and he is able to advance the student, that may
be more to his credit than all of his other
teaching achievements.

The criteria for judging a voice student also differ. Each voice student should be judged
in terms of his equipment and by the technical
efficiency reached on his own particular level
of ripeness.

Nobody can judge a person's progress and
tell whether she is taught correctly or incorrectly, unless he has observed her objectively
over a period of time. A voice may sound good
now but it may have sounded better earlier. A
voice may sound bad now but may have sounded
worse before. Snap judgments should be ignored.

---

# THE CHRISTMAS TREE THAT COLLAPSED

### (A Parable of Ambition)

There was once a young fir tree whose heart's desire was to become a Christmas tree. Thus, one fine day he got into his Sunday best and went to a studio that had advertised in the Sunday supplement. There he was greeted with open arms by the factotum, whose cosmopolitan and secretive manner fascinated him. He was ushered around the studio, shown the picture of the factotum himself adorned in all his Christmas ornaments, and invited to gaze worshipfully at the gallery of other Christmas trees whose fame and glamour covered the walls. After witnessing so much greatness, he asked hesitantly, "How about me?"

"I can see at a glance," said the factotum, "that your material is exceptional. After a year or so with me and my method, you will be as beautiful as these."

This wonderful promise flattered the fir tree beyond his wildest dreams, and the picture of fame rushing toward him left him breathless. After setting an appointment for the next day, the fir tree respectfully took his leave. He was floating on air. He told all his friends about his experience. All were impressed, except for one skeptical fellow who doubted so rosy a future.

And so the process got under way. The factotum took the fir tree in hand and, after a few pat phrases on how to stand and hold his branches, began to apply the ornaments. Tinsel, multicolored balls, stars, lights and artificial snow were assembled. As they were applied in profusion, the fir tree was almost blinded by his own glory as he stood in the sunlight.

Meanwhile, time passed very quickly. The fir

tree was pleased to find that the design of his
own ornamentation was exactly the same as the
designs of the most beautiful and famous trees
pictured on the studio walls. But one day, while
standing resplendent before the factotum, he
complained of fatigue throughout his branches.
This did not worry him because he thought it was
just a matter of his own momentary disposition.
Yet, as the factotum continued the decorating,
the burdensome feeling increased.

One day, when the factotum was entertaining
some friends who he said were "important people," the newly adorned fir tree was called upon
to display himself. The guests put down their
glasses long enough to applaud politely. After-
wards two of the guests came to him and asked
him whether he might like to appear at their
cocktail parties so that he could meet some even
more important people. Rapt with the wonder of
it all, the fir tree said to himself, "Gee, now
I am really a celebrity."

As the party progressed and the flattery
reached a higher pitch, he was again asked to
perform. It was in this second appearance that
his strength, sapped by the weight of his decorations, finally gave out. With every eye upon
him, he collapsed to the floor. Worse, the decorations collapsed too and were ruined. After a
nightmare of apologies, the fir tree hurried
home alone.

Dark days of depression followed. As this
unhappy period continued, the fir tree started
to do some thinking. The two years the factotum
had said would make him famous had passed. He
had accomplished little. Gone were his dreams of
glory. The praises that had been heaped upon him
became a mockery. All of the factotum's promises
seemed wild and meaningless. The latter's mys-
terious evasion of questions now suggested ignorance. The arty aura he had displayed that
once had impressed the fir tree so very much now

became superficial and false. Yes, even the "in-fluential people" whom the fir tree had tried to please so much seemed no longer quite as sophis-ticated and glamorous as before. As a matter of fact, some of the party guests actually turned out to be types merely out to satisfy their cu-riosity, while others---behold---appeared to frequent these offerings for the sake of free cocktails and free entertainment; and, at second thought, still others, with their chatter and gush, seemed perhaps a bit snobbish or blasé or both.

Just at this time, when life was at the low-est ebb, the fir tree encountered the one friend who had doubted the validity of the factotum's promises. Had he been able to, the fir tree would have avoided running into his friend. How fortunate that he could not. Instead of the "I-told-you-so" attitude, the friend was most sympathetic. He assured the fir tree that all was not lost, and he even came up with an idea as to how to get him out of the mess. Speaking from wounded pride, the fir tree thanked the friend for his kindness and for the new glimmer of hope given him.

The next day the friend took him to a cer-tain nurseryman of his acquaintance. Now this man had raised hundreds of fine fir trees. He had never decorated Christmas trees, but he did know all about them, especially how to develop the strength and beauty in their branches.

After examining the fir tree, the nurseryman sighed: "This is a typical case. I see more and more of this sort every day. In your ambition you have disregarded order in Art. You tried to skip. That is impossible to do."

"Order?" questioned the fir tree in amaze-ment.

"Yes, there is order in all Art," replied the nurseryman. "It is impossible to apply heavy ornaments if your branches are not strongly enough developed to carry them."

"We have to decide separately in each case whether the time is ripe for applying ornaments. Some trees are stronger than others. These can cope with earlier decorating. Nothing should permit us to overload. There are many parallels to this in Art. Take the vocalist for instance. What intelligent singer would overload himself by applying expression, style and finesse before his voice is strong enough to carry them? The unready voice would bend under the load, just as your branches did, and eventually would end up, just as you did, at the hands of your factotum, a decorated skeleton, bloodless, all embellishment and surface gloss but without earthiness and natural beauty."

"But, please tell me," asked the fir tree, "how about all those beautiful pictures of Christmas trees on the studio walls?"

"Those, my dear, were wise enough to take time to ripen before they rushed to be decorated. They were, by that time, strong enough to stand upright under the load. In addition, there were the 'blessed few,' exceptionally favored by nature, who were ready but did not know why. All these could be decorated without any danger to themselves.

"Still, when you judged the factotum by those pictures, you not only credited him with the decorations, you also credited him with the condition of the trees that supported the decorations. In this you were mistaken. Many people seem to be impressed by the wrong things when they enter a studio. Also," continued the nurseryman, shaking his head, "it is a typical mistake to judge the factotum by his best Christmas trees only."

"But, why?" asked the fir tree in astonishment.

"Because it is the average tree that counts. You were looking only at the exceptions. No picture of an average tree will hang on a studio wall."

"Oh," exclaimed the fir tree in surprise, "such thoughts never occurred to me. I guess I was just swept away by the glamour, and the atmosphere of fame almost blinded me."

"I know," said the nurseryman, "you created your own happy emotional dreamland. Perhaps, too, there was a bit of vanity involved or you even took pleasure in boasting when you were able to tell your friends that you were working in the same studio in which celebrities study."

The fir tree blushed. Just then a thought occurred to him, and he said hesitantly, "You know, my factotum told me that he too did some tree nursing."

"My friend," replied the nurseryman gravely, "it isn't what you say, it's what you do. Nurseryman and decorator are two different craftsmen. They require different abilities and interest. Similarly, a teacher of vocal production practices a different craft from that of a conductor, coach or accompanist. People go to a voice teacher for the technique of vocal production, to any of the others for the study of musicianship, interpretation and repertoire. An expert nurseryman will be so fully occupied with your health and quality that he cannot concern himself with other professional activities without losing some of his superior skills and perceptions. The expert decorator, on the other hand, who aspires to productive, artistic work, will be so busy and involved with his ornaments that it would be unseeming for him to apply himself profoundly to professional problems of another nature.

"Whenever a decorator tries to perform the duties of a nurseryman, or whenever a nurseryman tries his hand at decorating, then a conflict of interest arises. A high standard of specialization no longer prevails; instead, a two-in-one business is going on, and the danger exists that the one is being performed at the expense of the other. The latest proof of such a two-in-one business is your own case."

After a short pause the little fir tree said: "There is one more thing I would like to know. Why do I have to worry about developing? Don't we all mature and develop naturally in the forest?"

The nurseryman smiled at this and answered: "That is just what I wanted you to ask. How many trees in perfect condition have you ever seen in the forest? Is it not true that, crowded as they are, they never develop their lower branches and that only the tallest ones can escape being stunted? The only tree that has the opportunity of growing freely, uncrowded by its neighbors, is that one which, by good fortune, is isolated in a clearing."

The fir tree had to agree.

The nurseryman continued: "Here in the nursery, however, we space every tree so that it has plenty of room. We treat the soil so that it is well nourished. We train the branches gently so that they may grow symmetrically and strong. But without appropriate training, even those who are most richly endowed by nature may fail to bring their gifts to full fruition.

"So, you see, there is a great difference between simply attaining maturity and developing one's potentialities toward a goal. Nature alone will bring the first to us. The second, in the great majority of cases, must come from wise direction and constructive development."

Moral: Nature follows a regular order and never leaps toward that which she will eventually accomplish.

Goethe

---

**Q.   What causes the conflict among voice teach-
ers?**
**A.   Above all, a difference in terminology. In
addition there are personal differences in
hearing, feeling, sensing, taste and approach. Last but not least, there are idiosyncrasies.**

---

We cannot deny that all of us perceive our fellow humans through our own limitations and
bias. This is not a question of moral failure or
slackness, though it can indeed be greatly increased by a lack of moral sensitivity, in an
age of interstudio rivalry and cutthroat competition. It is an inescapable result of the
fact that each voice teacher has no choice but
to listen to the vocal world through his own
ears. Hence, each voice teacher is speaking a
vocal language that describes more or less the
kind of vocal world he hears and feels.

It is another well-known fact that voice
training can be described in technical as well
as in artistic language. The use of either of
the two may offer a correct description of the
same thing but from a different point of view.
In common voice teaching practice, the two are
often loosely used and intermixed.

Let us look, for example, at the voice
teacher at work in his studio. He will search
for expressions to describe his students' sounds
and sensations; or he may use words that explain
the technique of voice production in terms of
experiences that the student can learn to verify
by himself; or the teacher may want to bring the
attention of the student to some aspects of
voice production that so far had been unverba-
lized or only unconsciously implied by the student. As a result, a familiar yet unnoticed part
of voice production is suddenly perceived by the
student on a more conscious, significant level.
Vocal learning often means simply the uncovering

of something that has always been there but has
been hidden from the ear and the feel by the
blinkers of habit. Verbalization can thus formu-
late a bit of new vocal knowledge and put it in
a more revealing light.

In seeking a mutual understanding or verbal
rapport, a teacher and student develop a language that employs both fantasy and fact. Such a
language has reality and significance to the
teacher and student who use it. However, such a
hodgepodge of imaginative and technical terms is
not much concerned with strict definitions. Its
main aim is communication, in whatever way suits
teacher and student best.

Once this aim is achieved and a higher level
of communication established, the teacher may
want to give the student a term of his own coin-
age, a stimulus word that is meant to trigger
the desired vocal action. The voice teacher thus
transmits orders in a sort of compressed, personal language or code.

Other teachers will, upon hearing such expressions, question their scientific validity.
Science itself does not approve when its conceptions are flavored with talk of sensations
within the vocal tract. Musical terminologies
that in themselves are vague increase the number
of languages clamoring around our modern Tower
of Babel.

In these---the hodgepodge language of sensations, musical terminologies and scientific
claims and counterclaims---lies the main bone of
contention among so many voice teachers.

The battle of vocal terminologies that now
rages can perhaps be fully understood only in
the light of the historical perspective of the
development of singing as an art form. There is
thus an important historical story of vocal terminologies. The latter, after all, were derived
from the traditional store of beliefs and experiences that comprised the collective heritage of
vocal performers and vocal teachers.

One of the confusing by-products in the history of voice teaching has been the multiplication of names to represent the various vocal schools that establish separate positions within the field. In the vocal profession many a term is differently used by different users. This does not necessarily alter the usefulness of terms, but it makes it hard to break through and find a common ground of understanding among the different teachers and students who use these terms. Affected by semantic confusion, many of the terms now cry out for further elaboration. Often one is forced to painstakingly spell out specifics so as to avoid being misunderstood (and to escape the muddle created by freak theories that fill the vocal market and obscure rather than illuminate anything).

Instructions like, "bite into it," "up and over," "sing down when going up the scale" are sometimes used in voice teaching. Those are terms that some voice teachers and physiologists view with grave misgivings. "You are ignoring physiology," or "You are making ambiguous, scientific statements" is their frequent argument. However, teachers with a different point of view will reply: "So what? Art in its essence is effect. The end justifies the means. Everything is right that makes the voice come out right. Now look at yourself. You are unfamiliar with psychological reactions. Moreover you let your convictions limit your perceptions. That's why you refuse to understand the results that may be obtained from such suggestions. You may go on and single out this or that term and prove it false a thousand times, but it will still endure because it is true as an expression of feeling."

Indeed, as suggestions, as stimulants and perhaps even as muscular imagery, such phrases may help to arouse desired vocal action and may then be of value for adjusting individual needs of the moment. They cannot serve as a system of voice teaching lest we reduce the whole training process to a play with one or another device.

Such terms may even be ridiculed when they are analyzed from a purely physical angle. Anyone foolish enough to take figurative terms literally will consider many terms especially invented by voice teachers foolish.

A maestro claims: "Caruso did not develop his voice. He just did not know how to use it at first." This teacher defines negatively, in contrast to one who might say: "Caruso did develop his voice." It seems reasonable to assume that Caruso developed fully what was undeveloped in his voice. Be that as it may, the fact remains that one cannot create something out of nothing. There is no difference between developing a voice and learning how to use it. What is unused or undeveloped and what one can learn to use and develop are unknown quantities of equal dimension in the voice. Both to develop the voice and to learn how to use it mean to uncover, select, reorganize and combine already existing vocal abilities and to bring them from potential to the fore.

We should not quibble. One maestro claims: "The term "voice building" is ridiculous. We cannot build the voice. We can only build up the skill and proficiency, and hence a more satisfactory use of the voice." Another says: "Never, never can tone be focused. Tone can only be concentrated." Still another proclaims: "You can neither place the voice nor direct the sound of your voice. You can only produce different positions of tone through resonance adjustment."

We should not be pedantic. If the student complains about lack of support due to nervousness, by referring to the butterflies in his stomach, it is not necessary for his teacher to bring out a net and specimen box in order to catch the butterflies. Neither should the teacher scold because the student did not describe his difficulty in technical terms. It is not necessarily the strict scientific definition that will register with an individual. Similarly, in acting, a personal or active verb such as <u>cut</u>, <u>get warm</u>, <u>open</u> or <u>clear</u> gives a mental picture that can be made personal and therefore actable, whereas scientific or intellectual terms are rather cold, cut and dried and less open to response.

In all creative teaching, imagery has always played an important part. The use of imagery (as well as of the metaphor and analogy) is a proved teaching device. It consists of referring to one object in terms of another, of recognizing essential likenesses and of discovering how such likenesses illuminate the interrelation of things. Meaningful analogy serves to draw fruitful parallels in the presentation of study material. An image can produce a short-cut to a sensation and enable the beginner to gain a concept of vocal events that are not always in themselves intelligible. With the help of an image, too, we can find a more familiar way of dealing with the voice and of reducing the complex phenomena of vocal functioning to the plain and distinct, which slip into comprehension more easily. An image may sometimes not produce an immediate response but must grow on the sensory powers until it makes sense and is of help. An image may be most helpful when it refers to an object outside of the frame of human nervousness and self-consciousness. For example, when a voice teacher wants to encourage the vibratory or resonating power of a voice, she may proceed by telling the student: "Think of a bumble bee." After the student has identified the buzzer action of his voice with the buzzing of the bee, the teacher can go on: "Now the bee is increasing its buzz," and the student will try to increase the amplitude of his tonal vibrations.

In the final analysis, the definitions that are used and the way they are used in voice teaching do not matter, provided the experiences are adequately described or the desired sound effects well defined.

The meanings and values of vocal sound can be conveyed to us in many different ways. Take the phenomenon called by some "resonance," by others "vibration." Resonance is an accessory, vibratory factor in voice production. Will it lose its value by having a different name? Hardly. In voice teaching the emphasis should be on treatment rather than on terminology.

It must be admitted that sometimes in order to understand a voice teacher one has to discount his odd formulations and his strange way of saying things. Not every teacher is always able to state vocal goals in an ordered, precise and simple way. But to convey with clarity a vocal experience as it manifests itself in its physical and aural properties is often a tough job. Therefore, first and foremost, let us assure ourselves of what a voice teacher really means by his verbal expressions, for even though his theories explaining his practice may be wrong, his practice may still be right.

---

**Q.   Which of the different teaching approaches is best?**

**A.   The approach that searches for the most effective work balance among all parts concerned in voice production and then perfects that balance.**

---

Regardless of what approach we are willing to apply (a subject of argument), there is at least some agreement as to what the structures and functions are that produce the voice.

Theorists of voice as a rule acknowledge that the main structures and functions that produce the voice are:

1. All parts concerned with the breath: The Motor Power
2. All parts concerned with the vibrator: The Generator of Sound

3. All parts concerned with the resonance
   cavities: The Amplifier of Sound

To put it briefly and loosely: Breath, Vibrator, Resonator constitute a Vocal Trinity. The
action of the Breath upon the Vibrator produces
sound. Resonance of sound takes place in head
and chest.

In the act of tone production, the three
simultaneous elements are always interrelated
and condition each other in various ways and
degrees.

Yet, in the act of tone production these
three are not really distinct and separate. The
human organism functions rather as a totality
and does not form subdivisions that the conscious mind can be aware of.

The very fact that one can perceive these
subdivisions intellectually may be misleading.
It may lead to a concept of division rather than
wholeness of the vocal organism at work. As a
result, we may be tempted to compartmentalize
our vocal efforts in an unrealistic manner.

Because sound comes out as a unit, people
are frequently unaware of the fact that three
mechanisms are in operation. The simultaneous
work of these three main mechanisms in everyday
speech or singing is often overlooked or taken
for granted, but when one is indisposed or sick,
each afflicted mechanism makes us quite conscious of its existence. One's breath, vibrator
or resonator suddenly becomes a center of attention. The fact that an abnormal condition of any
of these will make itself felt in a vocal way
proves the vocal influence and importance of
each of the three.

All of us at one time or another have had
chest or head colds. We were congested and our
resonance suffered. Most of us have had laryngitis. Our voice lost vibrant power and we were
unable to make a clear sound. Instead, we produced a false or abnormal vocal depth[8] or we

were hoarse. Some of us know people who have asthma. Their difficulties with breath, accompanied by a wheezing sound, affect the voice noticeably.

The actor is sometimes called upon to portray people who have asthma, laryngitis or colds. He may be asked to play a character with a Donald Duck type of voice. Other characterizations may require a cavernous type of voice. An actor can accomplish these various vocal tricks by the many different ways in which he can make his vocal instrument work. A ventriloquist and a yodeler give further---if unusual---proof of the control that we can gain over the different actions of the voice.

The human vocal instrument is the only instrument that can vary the action of the breath, the vibrator and resonator according to plan and needs. This makes it the most versatile instrument there is. Since, in addition to sound, the human voice also produces text or language, it serves as a unique instrument through which people may gain valuable clues to their physical health, emotional state, character and personality and through which people may work for fuller expression of their personal needs as well as their creative, artistic and musical reach.

In the vast effort to accomplish this task, rather sharp differences exist in points of view and in voice teaching techniques. Of course, there is more than one correct approach to the fundamental vocal goal. However, not every vocal way will always lead to the goal.

Proponents of one school of vocal thought will claim that if the lips are moved in a certain way, everything else will fall into place naturally. Those of another will say that when the tongue is moved a certain way, everything else will follow automatically. Still others will claim that the secret lies in diaphragm control. Again, others place faith in fixed combinations such as jaw, palate and rib control.

None can deny that all these elements are active. Each tone is always the result of the action of all the parts that enter into its production; hence, all parts are of importance. The mistake is to concentrate with all students on the same, favorite features at the expense of others. By emphasizing only fixed, single parts, one forgets about the complete organism. One does not have enough faith in the entire cooperative effort, but concerns oneself only with fixed details.

If we attempted to do justice to all details concerned in tone production and tried consciously to direct them, we would drive ourselves mad. We would feel like the centipede who, questioned by the toad as to which of his hundred feet he would move next, became so self-conscious that he could no longer move.

The so-called studio singer is an unfortunate example of a technical person who drives himself crazy. In his attempt to put ever so many vocal details together, the details get in his way and plague him. As a result, he remains perpetually glued to the impossible task he has set himself and never progresses out of the studio-singer category. In time he loses the impulse or the instinctive capacity to sing and finally gives up singing as a bad job.

We have seen so far that there is no successful approach to voice teaching through any or all fixed, detail work. Consequently, we have to approach it from the vocal organism as a whole---the entity.

Our first task is to conceive of all the functions concerned. This is possible only through the one effect into which all vocal strivings unite, the produced tone.

Our second task is to analyze the whole organism. This can be done by discovering and identifying the positives and negatives of the produced tone.

Our third task is to improve the whole
organism. This can be achieved by encouraging
and gradually expanding the positives and dis-
couraging and gradually diminishing the negatives.

To sum up, there are vocal approaches that
prescribe to all, that if one stands a certain
way or places these and those elements in this
or that way, the right tone will result. Whichever way and however we lock parts into fixed
positions, we shall not help the variable elements that produce voice to find their balanced
contribution to the whole. On the contrary, the
struggle for the fixation of separate parts will
actually overdevelop some while others will be
left underdeveloped. This applies to fixed
placements of mouth, lips, tongue, palate, larynx, chest, diaphragm, abdomen, ribs, spine,
pelvis, knees or buttocks (the latter being employed by some fixed-posture methods in a vain
endeavor to build the inside through the back-
side).

Human tone is an entity. Produced by a living organism, it has life. Like life, it is individual, complex and unique. It varies in its
needs. The living organism, while producing tone
and satisfying the constantly varying demands of
tone, is of unique complexity and will be hindered more than helped in its work balance if
fixed, mechanical body patterns or prefabricated
body gimmicks are imposed.

Vocal sound that strikes the ear is the product of an entire instrument. The living function cannot be mechanically assembled nor can it
be taken apart; neither is there available a
supply of spare parts. But a voice has to be
judged in its parts through analysis of sound.
Upon analysis of the produced sound, the possibilities of expansion on the one hand, and the
possibilities of correcting deficiencies on the
other, can be estimated. This will allow an expert teacher to conceive an image of the direction in which a voice can develop, of future de-

mands upon it that will have to be met and of what she expects the student to eventually produce.

The ability to perceive glimpses of the vocal path, the ability to look into the future of the vocal potential and the capacity for advanced knowledge of the ultimate effects are all features that a voice teacher---one who is perceptive and lucky enough to possess them--- should apply in a highly flexible way. Nature must be permitted to follow her course, and the many surprises she has in store for us, vocal attributes yet to be discovered as well as unborn constituents, should not be hindered in their growth by rigidity and dogmatic approaches.

In the aim to bring all vocal abilities from potential to the fore, we must plug along through the use of selected, custom-tailored exercises. The correctness of the approach will become apparent in the improvement of the product: the tone.

## Notes

[1] This is decisive in an audition, where the task is to get something going and to get it going fast. It is a well-known fact that many actors have audition problems. The voice as a factor in auditions should not be underestimated. If an actor's voice can make instant communication, there is hope, but if his acting is off and his voice does not come through either, things are pretty hopeless.

[2] The voice is not an absolute whose properties are the same in radically different circumstances. A mistake frequently made is to forget about the acoustical conditions of a theatre, opera house or recital hall and to judge a voice by studio standards alone. The danger then

exists of cutting down a voice to make it sound "sweet" in the studio. In consequence, the voice reduced to a size good for small effects may emerge as inadequate in the larger size theatre. A quality that seems most frequently misunderstood or misjudged in this connection is ring. The layperson and perhaps even the inexperienced teacher may be bothered by the degree of ring or "ping" that a voice produces in the studio. The teacher may even classify it as shrill and may subsequently discourage it or try to get rid of it. As a result, a voice may lose much of its "silver," and then no longer be able to cut through an auditorium. Because space eats up voice, diminishing vocal returns are to be expected in an auditorium compared with a studio. Generally speaking, it takes a lot more than one thinks to sound rich in a theatre. In order for a performer to prepare correctly for the needs of a stage (particularly for the radical proportions or brutality of size of many contemporary houses), an excess of vocal virtues when working in the studio must be developed so he or she can rise fully to the challenge. For not only the size of the theatre but also the nerves take more out of us in the heat of performing.

[3]The serious student will be interested in them, as well as in the exercises that bring about the changes. He will have a taste for the technical groundwork. He will be willing to exercise as long as they help him, no matter how simple or monotonous they may seem. The less serious student gets bored more quickly. He wants to be entertained. The variety rather than the quality of the study material is the important thing to him. The question, "I have done this exercise for so long, can't I do another one?" is indicative of his attitude.

[4]The use of aversion technique may be an es-

pecially useful tool in accent correction. For instance, if a person has a regional or ethnic accent and wants to get rid of it, he may not succeed entirely unless his feelings against the specific accent are so strongly developed and the aversions so deeply established that whenever he slips back into the old habit his taste buds begin to react and revolt.

[5] The blend of the voice is much like that of a perfume. When some ingredients are judged by themselves, they may be hard to take, while others are so faint that by themselves they can hardly be perceived. Take them away from the blend or leave them out, and the whole effect will suffer badly. Yet, they all fit in, and in unison they thrive.

[6] Of course, the artistic temperament cannot always be taken at face value but may have to be understood in terms of the law of reversed conduct. For example, some artists throw fits of boredom to "unbore" themselves. Others display dissatisfaction to satisfy themselves. Still others show fear in order to encourage themselves.

[7] The majority of female students seem to feel the differences first and hear them later. In contrast, most male students tend to hear first and feel later. We can see that a woman's approach differs significantly from a man's.

[8] Admiration for vocal depth makes some people wish for a permanent cold while others, through the consumption of liquor, may seek to create a similar depth with a so-called whiskey voice. Granted, it sometimes helps vocal roughness when we sin. Unfortunately, an exploitation of such imperfections for voice training purposes is not feasible. Vocal sounds produced by such means cannot be relied upon.

# THE STUDY OF VOCAL TECHNIQUE: HINTS, WAYS AND TRAPS

Q. At what age should voice training begin?
A. It is not so much a question of age; it is more a matter of mind, will, spirit and maturity. Setting an arbitrary age may prove to be quite unfair to certain gifted individuals.

The study of voice production by children should be regarded as the exception rather than the rule. The training should be modified so as to protect a child from practice that may prove to be too demanding and therefore harmful. A child's voice should not be subjected to obligation. Rather the inclinations of a child's voice should be followed. This goes for production of volume and range, as well as for sustaining length. The stretching of any vocal function should best take place in self-regulation or, if consciously done, to a minimum and with utmost caution.

Unfortunately, many courses for the young are geared to a lower or amateur level. The attitude toward "the kids" is to be blamed for this. The young are not taken quite seriously nor treated with respect. Voice training for children is fundamentally the same as for grownups and should be given with the same care and expertness as for adults.

As a rule, it is reasonable to begin the study of vocal technique after voice change is complete. Before the change, the voice is not structurally set. In fact, even after the change the voice is often still embryonic. The general direction that it wants to take and the correct weight for it to assume are then still in the balance. At such an early stage usually one can perceive the voice merely within the frame of its predisposition. The vocal identity is still hazy.

Careful testing should first uncover the various individual vocal possibilities. Careful training should then bring these possibilities to a state of harmony. Only after this is done can the voice live through all the phases of its natural development.

Singing prior to the change of voice can influence the voice correctly or incorrectly. If a child has been fortunate enough to come under the guidance of a careful and patient choir director who understands the youngster and wants to preserve his voice, he quite possibly will be on the right track.

Unfortunately, however, many times he is directed by one who does not understand and has neither time nor patience. In school the youngster is perhaps excluded from choir practice. The teacher singles him out with the typical remark: "You can't sing," and the stepchild in the music department is sent to the scullery. Such an early rejection may leave a very deep psychological mark. It harms the youngster with vocal inferiority complexes. The child withdraws and closes up instead of being able to open up. Because of an anticipation of trouble, his future attempts to sing are more painful than joyful and often end in an alarmed retreat. On the other hand, if a youngster is accepted as a choir member, then the conductor often feels that he must get everything he can out of the child's immature vocal mechanism, regardless of consequences.

The singing time before the change of voice is short in comparison with the time thereafter. It is a pity to abuse the voice during this short period. The long period to follow then becomes a distinct echo of this unfortunate time. It is not able to pass through the various stages essential to its future development.

Singing in the wrong key is unfortunate but not uncommon in choir voices. The classification of a new choir member is often haphazard. The teacher tests the voice of the youngster by letting him sing a few scales or phrases. Then his voice class is decided upon immediately, and he is perhaps put with the contraltos. Or, worse, still, classification is dictated by the needs of the choir. If the conductor, for instance, is short of sopranos, a child may be stuck in the soprano section---for better or for worse.

Forcing is another typical factor that steers the natural tendencies of a young voice to wrong tracks. One can observe in religious concerts the boy choirs, carried away by emotions, driven on by their directors to painful, damaging vocal extremes.

Add to this the ambitious glee club director who, in his eagerness to keep his group intact, does not have the moral courage to dismiss those members whose voices are breaking and cracking because of voice change. This is where most of the damage occurs in the young male voice.

To any male who expects to use his voice seriously, it is beneficial to rest the singing voice at the time of its most striking transition in life. Just as the caterpillar rests in the cocoon during its physical change, so it is best for the singing voice to be dormant during its metamorphosis.

Of course, the voice change takes place during puberty in both the male and female. The range of the voice will grow larger during this period. Since the larynx of the male grows suddenly, a shifting of the voice range takes place. The male larynx will grow considerably bigger than the female larynx and therefore the range of the male singing voice, which approximately equalled that of the female before voice change, will sink about one octave. This brings about a more or less drastic change in the abilities of the male voice. The lower the voice, the more obvious and radical the change.

The change of the female voice, in contrast, is not revolutionary. It is usually a gradual expansion. Frequently, the transition cannot be observed clearly. Sometimes it remains altogether unrecognized. As a rule, the higher the voice, the less noticeable the change and the less the vocalist is bothered by it. We therefore find many coloraturas but hardly any contraltos who make the mark in their teens.

After the change of voice, a young man finds himself in a new world. Like a child with a new toy, he is very apt to overexploit the newly found sonorities, unless he is guided by a wise teacher. How many would-be basses, impressed with their manly depth, have tucked their chins into their necks and, unguided, have gone through life never aware of their full possibilities. They have remained stuck in the vocal cellar and dead upstairs.

On the distaff side, young contraltos, intoxicated with their newly introduced sonorities, sometimes emphasize the break in their lower voices for comic effect. They crack just for the fun of it. Other times, they seriously strive to imitate the yodeling sounds of some

older contraltos, with equal, if unconscious,
comic effect.

After the voice change, all the component
parts of the voice are active and can, through
guidance, be brought together harmoniously. The
mistake is to consider some components "child-
ish" or unnatural sources to be abandoned in our
maturity and to ride exclusively on the new,
massive sonorities. By doing so we are bound to
rob ourselves of some of the sources that are
necessary to complete the whole.

It is only after the work (or struggle) to
balance all the component parts of the voice has
progressed to the point where everything is beginning to work together that a sense of unity
results and a more leveled production comes to
light; only then will a voice be in a condition
to indicate its own true inclinations.

---

Q.  How do you classify a beginner's voice?
A.  Any line that is drawn to demarcate or clas-
    sify a voice is purely arbitrary. As a re-
    sult, labels are imposed upon a voice that
    are often not accurate or durable. Before we
    classify the beginner, it is advisable to
    wait and see, in order to give his voice a
    chance to classify itself. Hence, in most
    cases classification is best served by
    lay.

---

The process of finding the true class of a voice
is by no means a parlor game. It is one of the
major issues on which a voice teacher must pass
judgment. It is an essential aspect of any serious analytical effort and, as such, demands a
penetration of vocal designs that are neither
immediately nor totally self-revealing in most
beginners. In fact, the tendencies that do
reveal themselves, particularly in young voices,

are often so faint that they serve mainly as a clue but not as a solution to the complex problem of classification.

To be sure, accurate classification takes time as well as deep, detailed probing, for in spite of the fact that many voices carry the same group name (such as tenor), they differentiate into such diverse products that it is impossible to lay down the law regarding the normal sound and the normal technique for a tenor voice.

Unfortunately, we often find the young singer halfway through her first lesson asking, "What am I?" She is eager to know immediately. Classification will give her a sense of belonging and a notion of professionalism, which flatters her.

When the teacher is honest and wise enough to reply: "I don't know yet what you are; let nature decide," the prospective student will probably be disappointed. Her family may not understand, either. They expect her to return from her first lesson at the very least proclaiming herself to be, perhaps, a dramatic soprano. When she can only answer, "My teacher does not know yet," the surprise may be so great that her father may well say, "Why don't you go to a teacher who knows his business?"

Yet, if the teacher had said that she was a dramatic soprano, think how such a statement from the department of vocal forecasting might have affected her impressionable mind.

As soon as she is labeled or classified, she may want to pick up the prototype (or the stereotype). The girl tries to sound as---she thinks---a dramatic soprano ought to sound. So, the young student often hurries enthusiastically to the music shop and returns home with records of her favorite dramatic soprano. Then she sets off immediately upon a course of imitation and thereby slips into a voice pattern that is organically foreign to her. Like the famous mimic on stage, she can, through artificial twisting and coloring, come to a vocal caricature. These obtruded habits become like scar tissue, and adhesions in the vocal organism result. They never lessen but become thicker and more ingrained, always keeping the voice from its natural balance.

Perfection cannot be imitated. Imperfection can. Vocal imitations usually result from a desire to duplicate. Two persons with different makeups cannot produce the same sound with the same approach. Vocal duplication is therefore the wrong goal. All "second Carusos," for example, have little in common with the original. Unless we believe in reincarnation, there will never be another Caruso.

To follow a vocal example that others may wish to follow is valid only if one has the means to do so. In order to apply Caruso's---or anyone else's---technique, one must also possess his equipment. This does not mean that a vocal model is without value. On the contrary, a model can serve as a stimulant in whose presence we shape ourselves more readily, carrying out the work that builds technique.

The saying, "A little knowledge is a dangerous thing" is true of our young student. We can see that early classification is not the best thing. A wise teacher will keep a young student's mind completely engrossed in the search for and establishment of the best tonal possibilities, which themselves will determine the eventual range, weight, size, character and type of the voice. All of these factors combined will, in turn, determine in what repertoire the learner should be engaged.

Pupils may be tempted to skip the search, just as in reading a detective story, we peek at the last chapter for the solution. The comparison ceases here, however. Voice building is rather like building a skyscraper, where security depends upon the foundation, and each one of the many floors depends upon the solidity of the others.

Of course, whereas the plan of the architect can be followed to the letter, and one may assume the calculated result will be obtained, such is not the case with a voice. It is only by persistently searching and exploring with an open mind that the best vocal results can be obtained.

If we thus give nature a free hand, she may reward us with surprising developments, which sometimes even exceed all the hopes of teacher and pupil. However, if we make snap judgments in classification, then the danger exists that a fixed direction will be imposed upon the voice, and its natural possibilities of development cannot assert themselves.

It is true, though, that even young voices now and then possess certain characteristics that label them unmistakingly. We say: "She is a born coloratura," or "He has a typical 'Irish Tenor' voice." To resist the temptation to classify is difficult here and, in extreme cases, perhaps even impossible. Such voices fit into one voice class and sound misplaced in any other. However, beginners whose voices possess sufficient distinctive characteristics that lend themselves safely to an immediate classification are by far in the minority. The majority do not fall naturally into any category conforming to traditional labels. They must wait, work and grow into it.

Unfortunately, however, even if the true class of a voice seems to be established, that still may not be the end of the matter. In the process of study, or even later, in the course of a career, a singer may have to revise the decision.

Reclassification may become unavoidable with the growth of a voice, for as a voice grows, it forges new patterns and in the process it may simply outgrow or overthrow original assumptions. A voice may suddenly want to go higher or lower. It may want to work at a lighter and more

lyric or heavier and more heroic level. Then the
classification prophecies, no matter how emphat-
ically proclaimed, have gone awry. The voice
teacher's crystal ball was obviously clouded.
Moreover, age and bodily changes, which occur in
the process of growing older, may take their
toll and cause a voice change.

Just as some artists may be forced to give
in to a voice change that nature dictates, others may try to bring on a voice change by means
of study. Laurence Olivier, when well into his
fifties, accomplished the stunning feat of adding a bass range to his voice.

Also it must be stressed here that we do not
always find a clear dividing line between different voice classes. The boundaries are vague.
A high baritone voice will usually come across
with a certain tenorial suggestion. The sound of
a Wagnerian tenor, on the other hand, will usually reveal some baritone qualities. Throughout
the history of opera, many singers have switched
from one voice class to another. Some have even
switched and switched again. A recent case in
point is Ramon Vinay, who started out as a baritone, switched to become a tenor (his Otello under Toscanini and at the Metropolitan Opera was
highly acclaimed) and later returned to baritone
roles.

All of this goes to show that the classification of the human voice is a subtle thing and
many times subject to change. With this in mind,
the answer to the question, "What am I?" cannot
always be final and can rarely be given with
total certainty.

Q. Now, where do we start?
A. As in all physical development, we start with what we have, the strongest potentials. These must be established, nourished and developed. From there we can expand, gradually solidifying our gains on the installment plan.

Strengths must be searched for individually. No matter how good or bad we are, how great or small our gifts, each of us has some best potential.

The strongest starting point will be that sound whose pitch and volume offer the greatest freedom and the most promising qualities of which a voice is capable at the moment.

When we speak of discovering strength, we do not necessarily speak of producing strong (that is, loud) tones, but of testing natural potentialities, of becoming aware of the best of them and of gaining confidence in them.

Our training plan is this: Utilize strength where tone strength exists, and thus establish a strong point. Perfect the strong point until it offers a model for the rest of the voice. Then, infiltrate into the weaker tones, gradually, until they match the model.

Voice range consists of a series of halftone steps up and down. In closer intervals we go from one step to the next. In larger intervals we jump over some of the steps. If one of a series is insecure, we are in danger. In any tread on that weak step, there is danger. Before we can successfully connect tones, all the steps must be securely established, because the success and security of the connection are based upon all the tone-steps involved, their freedom and "qualities."

**Q.   Are breathing and diaphragm exercises really
      helpful?**

**A.   Breathing and diaphragm exercises can be of
      general value but we should not overrate the
      importance of unvoiced exercises to voice
      production.**

Unvoiced breathing and diaphragm exercises can
exert a conditioning influence upon our physical
state. In much the same way, physical culture
exercises or calisthenics can give us a workout. Because of a general human need for exercise and because of the satisfaction obtained
from almost any constructive physical workout,
the latter may very well improve our sense of
well-being.

       In the process of voice study, unvoiced
breathing exercises are often used for conditioning purposes, mainly to stimulate and ac-
tivate the breathing system. One can produce
noises with the breath and vary them in shape
and color through the various shapes and sizes
given to the resonance activitics. Thus, whis-
pering different consonants and vowels can, in a
general way, exercise the action of the breath
as well as the shaping of the resonators. At the
same time, practice of the articulation agents
also takes place.

       It is an error to assume that once breathing
exercises are perfected, correct tone is bound
to follow. A "master breather" will not make a
"master singer." An individual who has learned
to produce very good, free breathing exercises
may still produce very poor, unfree vocal exercises. Until one realizes that, for the purpose
of tone production, the rate of breath emission
should be slow and the quantity small, one might
do better to omit unvoiced breathing exercises
entirely. All too often they lead a voice student to aim for force alone, when he should be
emphasizing ease, buoyance and flexibility.

In the mechanism through which excessive breathing is produced there exists an obvious danger to the attainment of the normal, regular vocal aim. A harmful circumstance is conditioned by the fact that we linger over the act of breathing, which is preparatory to the act of tone production. The emission of breath is thus prevented from merging easily into the new combination, which makes up the act of tone production. The completion of the act of tone production is hindered.

We must realize that the emission of breath is an integral part of the whole vocal function and must be treated as such. The breath and breathing as isolated functions may be perfect, but it is only when they are joined to the other functions of vocal production that we can judge their adaptability to those functions by the final criterion: tone.

Since breathing function is the most easily isolated part of the overall function, it offers an ideal target for exploitation for those who judge the virtue of the whole picture by its detail. Many methods approach breath as a feature unto itself, separating the breath function from the vocal function. But the very act of separating misrepresents the nature of the vocal act. It breaks into segments what is essentially one and, by so doing, works against the integrative processes of the vocal instrument.

We have observed classes in which the student is given a lighted candle and told to blow against the flame. One rate of emission is recommended to keep breath support steady. When the breathing muscles are thus activated, the student is told to apply this candle experiment to the tone function. This is analogous to a driving school that instructs its students to drive at a uniform speed, regardless of the fact that the demands of safe driving require a constant changing of speed, for traffic lights, curves and obstructions.

The task of the breath is to supply that
specific energy that the vibrator needs in order
to produce even-flowing and vibrant sound. The
need must be determined by the condition of each
individual instrument and will vary in accord-
ance with pitch, volume and duration.

The application of correct support requires
that we make constant physical adjustments to
constantly varying vocal conditions. To meet
needs as needs arise is the problem. It is not a
matter of one-sided detail work. What we must
look for is not located in any one particular
part of the body. We depend upon a variety of
elements, their interdependent functions and the
precision of work and division of work between
them. The correct mode of interdependency cannot
be obtained by any local, voluntary control over
isolated muscles. Action and interaction along
correct lines are produced and controlled by internal processes. Muscular sensations may be experienced from these internal processes, but
they are not under any voluntary control.

The temptation is to oversimplify the control and the development of the muscles as well
as their relationships. Many people build up the
area around the waist. All of us know the type
of singer who delights in showing off the won-
ders of the human body. His friends and fans are
cordially invited to punch him in the stomach.
He insists "It does not hurt," and he is very
pleased with himself. Surely he is tough. Unfortunately, this is not always something laud-
able in itself, nor is it necessarily a tribute
to the function that the vocal instrument must
perform. It is easier to build up great muscular
strength than it is to know how to use it. How
the toughness can be put to the needs of tone
production is the crux of the matter. In most
cases the toughness and the voice refuse to fit
into a balanced coordination. The he-man might
better have spent his time and energy preparing
himself to participate in the "Mr. America"

strong-man contest. In respect to singing, in
his aim for muscular development, the he-man
type usually builds up a force that will prevent
the necessary coordination and elasticity.
Similarly the dancing student who previously was
an athlete may have to trim his bulky mechanism
before he can learn to coordinate muscles
without force so that dance movement will come
freely.

Does the tennis player use dumbbell exercises to toughen his arm muscles? Hardly. He
practices the swing that projects the ball. This
gives a workout to the arm muscles concerned
with the particular functions of tennis.

Specific muscular training is required for
specific needs. Exercises to strengthen the
diaphragm will accomplish nothing but a strong
diaphragm. Exercises to strengthen the arm muscles of a tennis player will give him a strong
arm. Just as a strong arm has little to do with
the specific needs of a tennis player, who must
get the ball over the net, brute diaphragm
strength has little to do with the specific
needs of a singer or speaker, who must produce a
phrase. Just as it is better to take an average
arm and develop it in the movements necessary
for the game than to take an arm that has been
built up with dumbbell exercises and expect it
to perform all the specific tennis strokes, so
it is better to take a normal diaphragm and develop it through the act of tone production than
it is to build it up through breath holding,
book lifting or furniture moving.

A tennis player would think it very strange
if, after a skillful stroke, a person felt his
arm muscles and enthusiastically exclaimed,
"Hard as a rock---that's what I thought." But a
singer is often flattered by remarks referring
to his diaphragm, because of a misplaced
emphasis on muscle glory, or he makes a fetish
of the name. Since the diaphragm has attained
something of the status of a glamour term, the

attention lavished upon it is often quite enormous, and voice students are, of course, often told to watch the diaphragm and to control it. Unfortunately, this is not telling them much, since they are given very little advice as to what to do with it when they watch it and control it.

Some teachers like to punch a student in the stomach to find out whether he "supports" correctly. This is like a tennis coach who feels his student's arm during a swing to check his wrist action.

It is obvious, when we speak or sing and someone punches us in the stomach, chest, back or throat, that vocal changes are going to occur. (The same is true of forcing down the jaw and thyroid manipulations.) Naturally, the same stress will evoke different responses and yield varying vocal results. If the sound "pays off," then the end justifies the means, odd or radical as they may seem. Generally speaking, the use of radical and convulsive measures will steer us toward an approach of violence, and violence breeds violence. When this mode rules the voice, we are likely to produce results (and sometimes startling results) of an abnormal, ambiguous or transitory nature. The grim vocal school, particularly the grunt and push methods, are often the breeding grounds for vocal disorders such as hoarseness, laryngitis and unpredictability in response. Moreover, vocal methods that advocate the use of external controls and tricks may involve the risk of dependency or addiction.

It is more difficult to attain balanced co-ordination of our inner resources and to equalize the play of muscles from within than it is to strengthen muscles that can be touched. Concern with the latter will always appeal to those who believe only in what they can see.

Granted, there is a physical adaptation to an occupation. A cowboy, for instance, tends to become bowlegged. However, he need not perform

any special exercises in order to become bowlegged. Nor will he do anything special to his
body to support or further his bowleggedness.
The physical condition of his legs is merely the
natural result of his riding. A singer's body,
too, will usually reveal certain occupational
traits, particularly in the development of the
area around the waist. But, in this case too,
let us not confuse a natural result with an artificial or superimposed one. There is development and there is pseudo-development.

Let us remember, the voice as produced is
not characteristically the result of the influence of the diaphragm, abdominal muscles, ribs,
or other area but rather is dependent upon an
intricate combination of all these influences
working together. To make combinations work is
the task in voice production.

The right combination does not take on visible form, cannot be directly observed and cannot even be defined for practical use. It can be
recognized only in terms of its effect. Only the
result is experienced and the "how" is felt in
internal processes.

If we are careful to study the work of the
breathing muscles in terms of the vocal result,
we shall be less liable to commit the error of
directing our interest toward purely external
matters. The latter are never decisive factors
in voice production.

The vital capacity of the diaphragm as well
as the other muscles concerned with the breath
are parts of the body whose vocal worth cannot
be judged until it is proved in practice by the
quality and quantity of the produced tone.

**Q.  Should I take a deep breath?**
**A.  No. Effective breath action needs no con-
scious physical preparation. Conscious
breath preparation tends to lead a vocalist
to overpreparation.**

A large quantity of breath intake can overburden
our system. We should be free from the mechanical limitations resulting from consciously fill-
ing up with too much breath. Otherwise, supply
will exceed demand and will impede the correct
use of the vocal instrument. Rather than pro-
moting coordination, too much breath will delay
the proper connecting of the muscular network
that enters into action in tone production.

Our breathing system must be elastic, not
rigid. Just as a girdle or garter belt should
have a certain give in order not to bind, so
must our breathing system be flexible. It follows that breath intake must be moderate so as
not to create restrictive pressures or tensions.

Shoulder lifting, noisy breath intake, ath-
letic or militaristic approaches are not desirable. Neither are heaving bosoms. Our law of
economy must be: with natural breath we shall
produce as much tonal vibration as possible.

A natural breath, however, is about the same
as minimum breath. When merely entering as a
necessary minimum, the breath---the most aggres-
sive physical force in the vocal act---is modified into a more useful, controllable vocal
force. In its extended form, our law of economy
reads: with a minimum of physical force we aim
for a maximum of vibration value.

Some will doubt whether such economy can be
applied in vocalization. However, breath economy
is evident in nature all around us. A canary,
for instance, sustains tones of fine quality and
definite pitch for a surprising length of time.
Does he take a big breath? No. He utilizes the

normal breath within him. A human being does the same when uninhibited, for example, when he becomes unconscious of tone, as in a laughing spell. He laughs without a conscious intake of air; then he simply replaces the air spent and continues.

Nature shows us the process: without extra preparation, S P E N D: then, without extra preparation, R E P L A C E. Applied to voice training, the process is: without leaping to a breath and without doing something to the breath, S T A R T, S I N G. Sing as long as you comfortably can in one breath. After finishing, P A U S E to refill, that is allow breath replacement to take place. Then start off on the next tone and repeat the process.

This is most economical because each refill or intake will occur in self-regulation. We will take in no more than we need. The intake, which is the preparatory act, is then automatic. We do not have to worry about it. We are not trapped in confusion and controversy: how, where, with what or what not to breathe.[1] This liberates us from the necessity of paying attention to the management and placement of the breath. We can give all our attention to the act of tone production. (When a dry sponge is compressed, air is expelled. When released, the sponge sucks up as much air as is necessary to regain its shape.)

Insufficient breath in vocal production or a feeling of insufficiency is usually the result of simply not knowing how to make the most of normal breath intake. This may be due to a beginner's inability to slow down the action of the breathing system during tone production, or to a lack of proper coordination of the parts concerned, or even to a lack of confidence. This last condition sometimes preys on people's inferiority and occasionally develops into a deep-rooted insecurity about physical strength and breath capacity.

The fear of not having enough breath to get

through a vocal exercise or phrase makes people fight for breath. In order to prevent their breath from failing them, they resort to frantic ways of pumping in more breath. This accounts for all kinds of body contortions which singers go through for breath support.

Many interferences in singing occur in the form of carryovers from breath worries, miscalculations and excessive physical and nervous preparations prior to singing. Many of these interferences may be decreased by economizing the work and the attention of the learner, by asking him to cut out extras or to do as little as possible in matters where he can do very little well or where he need not do anything special. The means whereby this may be progressively achieved are: (1) taking in less breath; (2) lessening physical preparations and "overtures" just before tone start; and (3) adjusting posture so as to offset any tendency to contort, convulse and cramp.

Getting rid of breath problems, which directly or indirectly cause voice problems, and using just as much breath as each tone needs is for many a step-by-step process. The simplest feats are usually the most difficult to achieve.

The singer who works with surplus breath and who wants to correct herself by trying to gain normal, regular breath may at first find it difficult to trust in her natural "wellsprings." By force of habit, she wants to pump up. In addition, she may at first also feel naked without extra breath preparation. But she will soon find out that there is breath reserve to fall back on and that she can rely on this reserve force. Moreover, she will discover that, when all the natural breath supply is correctly utilized, maximum intake is unnecessary because proper utilization comes from normal functioning and not from overextension. It is not the quantity of breath intake but the quality of breath utilization that must be cultivated.

Once the technique of utilization has been

perfected, it will be possible to distribute
more and more breath with the same economy. It
will be possible to sing more on one breath than
before. The amount of breath will grow automatically in response to vocal demands. Longer and
longer phrases can gradually be produced without
the desperate gulp we so often hear.

Of course, we must not altogether frown at
the gulp or noisy intake. Both, perhaps, are not
always avoidable. This is particularly true in
those songs and arias where the composer has allowed very little time between two phrases. Then
the singer cannot wait for his breath to be re-
plenished naturally but is forced to hasten the
process. If we then occasionally gulp a bit in
singing, it may be normal and acceptable.
However, gulping a great deal from conscious
preparation for singing is unnecessary and
disturbing. Thus, the reason we gulp and the
degree to which we gulp must always be considered.

Let us stress here that a hastening of the
breathing process, as required in some songs and
arias, constitutes physical extension that can
easily lead a beginner to tighten. Therefore, it
should best be left for later stages of vocal
training. Moreover, a need to hasten the breathing process is the exception rather than the
rule. Techniques should be based first on rules
rather than exceptions.

Increasing the naturalness of the use of the
body must be the first aim in physical development. The stretching of the faculties can then
follow without undue effort.

The vocalist who bases his technique on a
natural intake will produce with less effort
than will the big breather. He will not waste
energy prior to the tone production and can
spend that much more in the act of tone production. He will not first accumulate and then
discharge a load of big breath. He will avoid
the double action of first inflating, then

singing. He will pump less. He will need less time to get a phrase rolling.

---

**Q.   What is the purpose of vocal support?**
**A.   The purpose is to produce an even, vibrant tone flow and to sustain vocal phrases, full-length, with ease.**

---

Support is accomplished through the balance of a number of parts concerned with our motor power and our vibrator. The balanced contribution of these parts varies and cannot be determined on analytical scales. Hence it is impossible to fix the amount of activity that might be designated as normal. The demands of each tone point the course for the parts to follow. When we do not restrict or overdo, when we permit the various parts to adjust the balance of the tone, a normal voice will grow in the act of singing as an avalanche grows in the act of rolling.

A singer is often praised as having good support because he can sing in one breath a phrase for which most singers require two. Even though quality suffers in the process, some observers remark that his support is nevertheless exceptional. Quantity is stressed over quality. We have had great voices that could produce only short phrases, but these were of great quality. However, it cannot be said that there ever existed a great voice that produced long phrases of poor quality. Therefore, the question is, "How good is the quality of my phrases?" and perhaps thereafter, "How much can I sing in one breath?"

Let us think again of an uninhibited laughing spell. In this completely natural and effortless phenomenon, it is interesting to note the vocal improvement that usually takes place. The voice peals forth more freely, more vibrantly, bubbly, flexibly and easily than it is or-

dinarily produced. This is a result of liberation. Body and mind have become unfettered.

Psychological inhibitions and conscious physical efforts deriving from instructions such as
"Now lift the lower floating ribs and expend the
waist line," or "Raise the chest and draw in the
abdomen," or "This muscle must go in, that one
out," or "Tense this muscle and relax that one"
are forgotten. Likewise forgotten is the puzzle
as to which groups of breathing muscles are supposed to act on one another or against one
another.

The sound of free laughter has great carrying power. Often when we leave a party and are
quite remote from the guests, we can hear hearty
laughter from far away. We speak of pealing,
silvery laughter and can all recall a laugh suddenly ringing out through the night. The produced tones have much vibrancy and buoyance. An inner muscular action is felt in a continuous,
buoyant, accordionlike propelling sensation.
Such action has amazing vitality. We can observe
an innerspring action contributing to the looseness and buoyancy of tone plus a compressing,
consolidating action contributing to the tone's
firmness and vibrancy.

Our task in voice production is to develop
as much firmness and looseness for each pitch as
is required for tone quality and steadiness. Our
innerspring and inner compression systems are
the two component parts that possess regulatory
powers, helping us to produce tone with a harmonious balance of stability and flexibility.

It is up to the teacher to diagnose the student's tone and then to see that tone productional demands dictate his inner compression and
innerspring development. A stiff or straight
tone, which must attain enough looseness and
buoyance for healthy use, will be helped by the
innerspring action. A wobbly or tremulous tone,
which must gain firmness and steadiness, will be
helped through better compression.

Imagine a soap bubble held aloft by a column of air. The bubble is balanced evenly and continuously on the column of air. Now compare this evenly and continuously balanced bubble to a steady tone flow. If we wish to send the bubble higher, or if we wish a tone to go to a higher pitch in an even vocal scale, we add breath strength. When we do not add enough breath strength, the bubble will sink lower than desired, and the tone may become flat. When we add too much breath strength, the bubble will go higher than is desired, and the tone may become sharp. In the correction of pitch, variable strength of breath is an important factor.

In addition to the breath's being sympathetic to the needs of the tone in pitch, the action of the breath must adapt to the needs of the tone in dynamics. In swelling and diminishing a tone, the workings and adjustments of the breathing muscles are usually strongly felt. The more softly we sing, the more careful and skillful we usually have to be in order to maintain an even and vibrant tone flow in diminution and to prevent the voice from sounding breathy, dull or unsteady. One mistake frequently made in diminishing a tone is to concentrate on the changes rather than on trying to hold on to the vibrancy and pulsating of the tone as we carry it through the different degrees of volume. To be sure, the process by which tone volume is reduced should not result in a lessening in tone quality.

To keep the tone flying under all varying conditions, at all times, is our supreme task and the one in which support will be prominent.

It is when this "flying" balance is well established that a good cantor in a synagogue begins his colorful vocalizing, allowing his voice to follow its own inclinations, improvising cadenzas, runs, coloraturas and trills.[2]

Many believe that fast vocal exercises will build up buoyancy and flexibility. However, speed is a tempo; flexibility is a quality. A tempo alone cannot develop a quality. Speed is not necessarily a proper preparation for competence in singing. It is the other way around: when we have conditioned the instrument to such an extent that a work balance has been established, facilitating an even flow of tone so that sound floats forth, flexibility in tone production also is gained. As a result, a controlled speed will be possible and technical proficiency or bravura may be attained. The same applies to everyday life: a person who, for example, walks stiffly will not improve her condition by running.

Some stage directors are under the illusion that tempo can create quality. When they see that the production of a scene resists efforts to bring life to it, they try to speed up the so-called dead spots. As a result, a good deal of rushing around and hysteria take place on stage (and some actors are prone to catch their director's panic) but no real bounce. Some elderly orchestra conductors tend to rush tempo to prove how young, virile and bouncy they still are. To quote Eddie Foy, the famous comedian, "If you can't dance well, dance fast."

Nevertheless, even some untrained voices tend to do well in fast vocal passages. This ability is particularly evident in light voices. Countertenors, coloraturas and soubrettes are examples. But let us not confuse cause with effect. These voices are not light because they sing fast. They are endowed with a high degree of muscular elasticity, which enables them to sing swift passages well.

Muscular elasticity, strength, skill and control, as well as all other related aspects that figure in vocal support, can be achieved only by practicing the whole work order together, for in the overall function no muscle or group ever operates independently. If we do break up the team and develop the members sep-

arately, we find---when we try to reincorporate
them---that their relationships to each other
are many times irreparably lost.

It is more logical to develop the members
together in relationship to one another because
in this way their affinity is never lost. The
group relationship grows and improves. If developed without regard to its adaptability to
the needs of the others, a muscle can easily
grow out of its original form. When the time
comes for it to rejoin the group, we find it has
been trained out of proportion and does not pull
with the rest of the team. The improvement of an
individual muscle through cooperative effort
must be the aim in voice development.

We should remember that no conscious muscular preparation is necessary before the act of
tone production begins. It is a mistake to fix
any one group of muscles before others are
brought into play. The separate use of any part
of the whole may work against the cooperative
effort of the various contributing parts, because of advanced tightening.[3]

In the act of support, it is true that the
breathing muscles assume a state of tension, but
they must arrive at this state because of the
need to sustain tone. We should not tense them
arbitrarily in order to produce tone.

Tension is indeed a delicate and subtle matter. When consciously and locally created, it
tends to lead to tightening, which is harmful.
When involuntarily created, as an integrated
part of the whole, it will support and help us.

The arm of a golf player has to be in an i-
deal state of tension during a swing. If he
tries consciously to create such tension---when
he tenses in order to swing---the swing may go
wrong because of the pressure and tightening.

The ideal state of tension---that produced
involuntarily---allows us to perform with an e-
conomy of effort. But a voluntary effort to
tense will usually result in no economy of effort.

To gain tension without tenseness, we must permit the muscles concerned in our support to act in as natural a manner as possible, allowing them to take care of themselves in the tone creation, rather than tensing them for the tone creation.

Muscular coordination, as required in singing, dancing and sports, usually has to be attained through hard work. Forcing should not be employed. An effort can be made for the purpose of correct functioning, but strain will result from forcing, which, in effect, is incorrect functioning. Even in a relatively easy sport such as swimming---which most animals perform instinctively---the human adult usually needs considerable time to "let go" and to coordinate the necessary movements. At the outset, most of us have a tendency to overdo, to involve too many muscles and to throw more force than necessary into the muscles. However, if we let up or relax before we reach the point at which we can keep ourselves afloat, then the letup will turn into a letdown and we will sink. Through hard work and experience with our bodies, we progressively learn to apply effort more efficiently. The more coordination and balance we develop, the less we overdo.

The temperamental and emotional makeup of a person influences her work attitude. There is the underworker and overworker. The overworker, in her extreme, will throw herself from a bridge to find out that it hurts. The underworker, in contrast, is hesitant and overcautious and tends to hold back. In between these two opposites we find mixtures of both types, complex and contradictory. People with an ideal balance do not exist. However, a talented person is usually endowed with a relatively good sense of balance. Conversely, a lack of a balanced attitude toward vocal functioning is generally apparent in voice students who are less talented. The main question to be considered is: How much off balance is an individual? It is a matter of learning the degree. The goal must be to arrive at as close a middle-of-the-road approach as possible. Progress depends upon the elimination of excesses (perhaps at first using the extremes and gradually normalizing them) and upon the development of balancing factors. In the process of technical study, the underworker must learn to gain more vocal courage, to apply herself in a bolder way and to make proper use of all the zest and vigor she can muster up. She may then discover that she does best when she dares most. The overworker whose capacity is far greater than her eagerness and tenseness allow her to go, must learn to budget and channel her drive in order to gain better control over her resources.

The very nature of low notes, for example, will compel the overworker to apply himself with relatively less tenseness and to push or oversupport less. The student may complain, "I hate that low note because I can put so little behind it," which is, of course, the purpose of the exercise. In contrast, the production of high notes, particularly when done in full voice, will make the underworker give out more heartily and put in more of an effort. He may admit with surprise, "I didn't know I had the physical stamina to stay with that kind of output." Generally speaking, the energy expenditure of the vocalist increases on higher notes and decreases on lower ones. Through the way in which we design exercises for use on different pitches, we find a means of exploring various degrees of energy expenditure. Our task is, of course, to find that degree with which we apply ourselves most efficiently and then to build from there.

Experience gives us judgment; we learn what to look for and what to avoid. Through repeated, graded exercises we acquire skill, ease and proficiency. Ease in sports, dancing and voice is usually the result of hard persistent work. Ease does not result from taking it easy. If we follow the motto "easy does it" at all times, as some vocal approaches suggest, we throw the seeds too loosely and skip the hard work through which one develops strength and growth. In consequence, our full potentialities are never realized. To be sure, we must learn to master ease, and must exercise the voice until it gains ease.

Strength and endurance are developed through use and practice. In the beginning we may tire easily; any unaccustomed physical work may cause fatigue. The training process should be so planned and executed as to enable us to build up to it. In time, we will catch our second wind and acquire a capacity to produce with endurance.

A certain measure of muscular discomfort or pain is sometimes unavoidable in the hardening process. Granted, pain hurts, whatever its source. However, even hiking or sightseeing can make us footsore. Such pain usually does not occur because we walk incorrectly but simply because we are not used to the activity. A student may admit, "I am very easy on myself," or "I am always afraid of hurting my voice." This student may have to readjust his mental attitude in order to accept the fact that he is not going to hurt his voice just by using it.[4]

However, generally speaking, and in its simplest form, the pleasure-pain mechanism in the body of the vocalist provides valuable clues to her vocal health and can serve as a guardian to preserve her voice. The physical sensation of pleasure derived from making a sound indicates a general vocal well-being. Conversely, physical hurts tend to be danger signals.

Of course, the location of pain is always significant in physical functioning. Occasionally, a voice student may worry about strain felt in the stomach area or may fear he has injured the muscles there. This fear is baseless because the stomach muscles are not vulnerable

in the act of voice production. If the discomfort in the stomach area is due to pushing, the
tone production may suffer and an adjustment of
support may become necessary. If, on the other
hand, this discomfort is merely the result of
normally exercising the voice (as is often the
case), then pain accompanies accomplishment, and
the muscular reaction is much the same that we
get from a workout at a gym. However, if the
throat hurts from speaking or singing, then the
vocal mechanism is giving us a warning that
should not be overlooked. The throat is a vulnerable area; it is to the singer what hands are
to the pianist and legs are to the dancer. Where
we give out or expend ourselves the most we also
get hurt the most.

    If a person is feeble-voiced or suffers from
constitutional weakness (a rare case in point),
any workout or practice session may at first be
a sort of shock treatment, which may cause temporary discomfort in the throat area. In most
cases, however, throat aches from speaking and
singing indicate that the individual has gone
beyond his immediate capacities---perhaps in
volume, weight or range. The voice has been
overtaxed. Experimenting with softer or louder,
lighter or heavier sounds on higher or lower
pitches may then bring about a more comfortable
level of vocal functioning. The latter, once it
is established through repetitious practice, can
serve as a starting point for future, gradual
expansion.

    Let us emphasize here a point that is often
overlooked. It is not only the breath function
that determines the strength and size of a tone;
it is the balance of all functions concerned.
When the tone volume changes, a balance must
remain and a ratio be maintained. Some vocalists
do not understand this. They lose tone quality
and carrying power when they try for the biggest
tone possible because they increase breath expenditure without maintaining balance. An in-

crease in breath must be utilized immediately; otherwise it becomes a dead weight upsetting the balance. Energy that cannot be properly utilized takes a wrong path in vocal functioning.

Right or wrong energy utilization in vocal functioning manifests itself in a feeling of satisfaction or frustration, depending upon the amount of physical effort spent and the amount of sound received in return.

The act of making sound is a personal experience, which leaves our urge gratified or ungratified. There is, of course, the aesthetic satisfaction (or dissatisfaction) derived from the experience of producing good (or not-so-good) sound. Also there is the physical satisfaction (or dissatisfaction) derived from the presence (or absence) of economy in production. When the physical effort is proportionate, we feel rewarded and, of course, when the effort is out of proportion so that we work too hard for too little, frustration results.

The same is true of the attack and ending of a tone. The way in which we attack or end a tone can serve as an indication of correct or incorrect voice production. The question is: Does the attack or ending of the tone require due or undue effort?

There are vocalists who start with too much of an impact, they shock into the tone attack and pounce on the notes. Such an excessive effort cannot be maintained throughout an exercise or phrase but tends to collapse shortly after the attack. In consequence, a constant punching and then fizzling-out effect results. Extremes of this sort are always bad. They lead to a jerkiness or choppiness. To convert "spurty" energy release into a consistent one, these vocalists must learn to go for a more leveled production, for a flowing kind of line, and must sustain with more of a legato feeling and "schmalz." On the other hand, there are voice students who always slide into a tone attack.

They lose precious time and energy before they find the kernel of the tone. As a result, they feel spent before they have even started. These students must learn to strike more quickly. They must try to attack tone in a more crisp, intense and concentrated fashion and maintain or even increase the tonal intensity throughout the exercise or phrase.

Sometimes the beginning of a tone is preceded by a sort of plucking noise, which is frequently called "glottal stroke." The breath seems to knock the vocal cords, as in a defective piano where the keys knock in their sockets. This extra activity in the voice tends to obscure or spoil the very first part of a tone effect. In an ideal vocal attack, the action of the breath upon the vibrator is no more audible than is the action of a hammer upon string in a good piano. The productional means should be concealed by a perfect tone effect.[5]

Often the ending of a tone is produced with a sort of explosion. (Some call it a grunt, others a sigh, groan, or sob.) This "grunt" is perhaps added by the vocalist as an effect for the sake of expression or just to let the audience know that it is a little difficult. If so, the use of the grunt must be dictated by the style of the composition and by individual taste. An overgenerous application of the grunt, for the purpose of embroidering, defeats its purpose; it cheapens the singing or reduces the singing to a vocal caricature. Many times, however, the vocalist cannot help but end with a grunt. In such a case the grunt arises from functional necessity. Like buoys in the water, the grunt can indicate danger as well as safety, depending upon the range in which it appears and the degree of force with which it is produced. In the upper range, the ending on a grunt is widespread, if not standard practice, especially in the male voice. This is particularly true when high notes are cut off in full voice. However, sometimes the middle or even lower notes cannot be emitted without a grunt. The latter is a danger symptom of the first order. It supplies evidence of undue force in functioning. The produced tones are either overheavy or oversupported or both. When they are oversupported, the pressure of the breath often condenses to the point where it creates an intolerable vocal condition. The student complains, "I can't get off the note," or "I can't ease it off." Adjustment of support and/or vocal weight may be required.

In addition to the grunt, there is another phenomenon we sometimes hear when a singer ends a note, a slight crack or "breaking to a stop." This is typical of some not-so-good Wagnerian tenors and of some baritones who are trying to switch to tenor. It is usually an indication that the voice is struggling with the tessitura. The phrases lie high for the voice. To stay that high continually tends to tire the organism or creates overloaded tension. The slight crack or breaking to a stop is the manner in which that overloaded tension is released.

It is often assumed that the cure for such a condition as well as for similar vocal complications lies merely in the handling of the breath. The implication is that all other functions will fall into line by themselves if one concentrates on the breath function alone. This is not quite so, though it is perhaps one of the most common illusions in the field of voice. It is true, the breath function will influence the other vocal functions but not to the extent that an automatic, total dependence exists. There is, furthermore, an influence for the better or for the worse. If the condition of our breathing system is not commensurate with that of the other component parts of the vocal mechanism, this influence will be for the worse.

Many singers and speakers naturally possess great stamina in the breathing system while other parts of their vocal instrument are weak. Un-

less through practice the other parts catch up
and can match that strength, no progress in tone
production can be made. If these singers and
speakers are then advised to do breathing or
diaphragm exercises, which will further
strengthen the respiratory system, they will
merely strengthen something that does not need
strengthening and thereby increase the imbalance
from which their tone production suffers.

We can see that the development of the
breathing mechanism for voice production is not
the same for all. It is an individual problem,
which must be solved after a careful diagnosis
of the entire vocal organism as revealed in the
tone.

We should always remember that in addition
to the action of the breath, the tone depends
upon the action of the vibrator and resonator. A
mistake frequently made is to forget about the
vibrator: the vocal cords. A great many voice
students torture themselves exclaiming: "I don't
know how to use my diaphragm" when actually
their troubles with insufficiency of breath,
breath escape, breathiness and tonal unstead-
iness come from not knowing how to use the vocal
cords. As pointed out, the action of these is
for all practical purposes involuntary and can
be trained only in the act of tone production.
They are physiological factors that can be dealt
with effectively only in a psychological way.
The teacher must therefore direct the student
toward an effect---a desirable tone---thereby
gaining access to and improving the cause---the
use of the vibrator. The audible product reflects the skill, good or bad, that brought it
into being. "By their fruits ye shall know
them." As the student explores and experiences
more and more the different aspects of vocal
production and support, the part of the vibratory cause may suddenly become real to him as
one integral aspect of the total understanding
of what he is doing.

For the production of sound, a resistant action is needed. Our vocal cords are the forces of resistance. This very resistance is of a variable nature. When a tone cracks, for instance, the unexpected (yet so typical accident of the trade) happens; suddenly our intention falls into a different muscle pattern, and a spectacular change in vocal cord activity becomes apparent. Because the involuntary side is responsible for this perplexing phenomenon and the voice discloses itself from the angle of suddenness, of something totally different and uncontrollable, a performer considers cracking to be grim and fears it. Fear is a communicable disease which feeds on itself. After experiencing trouble on some notes, he may be afraid of cracking other notes, too.

In order to avoid mishaps[6] and to support the tone correctly, we must learn to find the most effective working balance between our respiratory and vibratory organs in speech and singing. The most effective working balance is achieved when the tone remains vibrant and steady in flow, regardless of pitch, volume or duration.

When a voice is breathy, the tones lack vibrancy. It is plain that when two voices produce tones of the same volume, the more breathy voice has less tone intensity. On the other hand, when a voice is brittle, the tone suffers from over-intensity. A breathy voice has too big an air escape, a brittle voice has too little. One can learn to add intensity and decrease breath escape, by aiming for more vibrancy and tone concentration. One can learn to ease the intensity and increase breath outlet during singing, by aiming for more tone flow.

Voices that by nature possess an even flow of vibrant sound throughout the range are by far in the minority. Most are either uneven or stiff or disconnected. These qualities limit them. To establish a well-supported tone all through the range is usually a gradual development.

Vocal support can be developed and adjusted through basic tone exercises of: (1) varying duration---depending upon how short or long we sustain altogether in one breath; (2) varying dynamics---depending upon how softly or loudly we produce sounds in one breath; (3) varying range---depending upon the lower, middle or upper pitches on which we choose to produce sounds in one breath; and (4) varying rhythmic patterns ---depending upon where we put the accent and how long we hold each of the sounds produced in one breath.

As a dancer acquires a muscular memory of the organic positions and balance of functions that keep him "moving through space," so will a vocalist establish a muscle sense and muscular memory of the positions and organic work balance that "keep his tone flying." This, in collaboration with his ear, will help him to reproduce. Once his muscles have proved their tonal usefulness that way, a vocalist can try to induce and stimulate those muscles, thereby increasing muscular efficiency.

Muscular control as a conscious mechanism in tone production must be subordinated to sound control. Whatever the muscles do is correct if the sound is correct and the throat is not subjected to strain. Some students tend to drive themselves muscle-crazy. They try to put all the muscles together in order to make tone. Others have overdeveloped certain parts of the body and in consequence are too muscle-bound or muscle conscious. Both types of students tend to "complicate" themselves. They can learn to correct themselves by temporarily disregarding all muscular activities, by using or working the muscles without thinking about them, letting the voice come from psychological sources---will power, mental demand for sound, concentration on sound, self-abandonment, surrendering to the sound---letting tone and ear be their guides.

Because there are so many conflicting theories in regard to support, let us conclude this section with the following summary for the benefit of those vocalists who are tortured by a set of mechanical rules and suffer from breathing complexities. All we can gain from proper support is an even, vibrant, tone flow and sustaining length. The latter can be achieved through the practice of tone holding. The former can be attained through the search for the best possible steadiness, vibrancy and flexibility that rest within the vocal equipment, and a subsequent effort to improve these qualities through use and practice and through the elimination of the forces that oppose them.

In sustaining tone and in gradually improving its steady flow and vibrancy, we will automatically improve muscular skill and the coordination between our respiratory and vibratory forces. The more advanced our development, the more rapid, precise and constant will be our ability to produce a vibrant and even tone flow, and with ease to sustain exercises or phrases in their full length.

In dealing directly with tone, the mechanics establish themselves, in an unconscious response to the thought process, while the work of the supporting muscles is eased or reduced to its simplest state.

---

Q. Everybody yearns for resonance. Where is it found and what is its value?

A. The upper and lower vocal cavities are our resonating sources, which contribute quality and quantity to the voice.

---

Let us imagine that our different resonance spaces, along which the sound travels, act as

communicating pipes. We must take into account
the phenomenon of collective vibrating.

Sound is created by the action of our breath
upon our vibrator. The vibrations of the throat
can be felt. This is an entirely healthy and
correct phenomenon. We have observed speech
classes where the teacher touches a student's
throat and exclaims: "Oh, your throat vibrates
so noticeably---that is wrong. The vibrations
must be in the head and chest." Let us not confuse vibration with constriction of the throat.
Assuming a normal voice, when we are trying to
produce sounds without noticeable throat vibrations, we are trying for the impossible. The vocal act involves simultaneous coordination of
all vocal functions. Hence throat vibrations
plus head and chest vibrations are concomitants
of the tone production, and no voice can normally function without all three.

Sound travels from its origin---the larynx
---to its exit---the mouth and/or nose. It follows the curves of the different parts of the
upper chambers, putting into vibration the air
in the resonance spaces above the vocal chords.
As these spaces vary, so will their resonating
capacity vary. (Sounds produced in the bathroom
sound different from those produced in the living room.) It is assumed that the resonating capacity of a larger vocal cavity---as for instance, the naso-pharynx---which is a relatively
low resonance zone, contributes depth to a
voice. In contrast, the resonating capacity of
the smaller vocal cavities and passages---such
as the nasal passages---which are higher
resonance zones, add ring and brightness to a
voice.

In a pinched, twangy tenor, the bright elements can be so predominant that the tone takes
on a harsh and overconcentrated character. The
tone sounds a little like that of a faulty loud-
speaker with the base missing. It lacks depth.
The "droning bells" are missing.

Hooty and hollow voices, in contrast, lack concentration. Their tone, even when true in pitch, sounds as if it came from a record player that is running too slowly. The "silver bells" are missing.

Sound travels in two opposite directions, putting into vibration the air in the cavities above the vocal cords as well as in those below the vocal cords. The upward stream of tonal traffic and the downward stream of tonal traffic make for a simultaneous, two-way traffic.

The resonance spaces below the vocal cords are considered to be in a less favorable condition for amplification. Unlike the spaces above the cords, they are not between the laryngeal origin and exit (mouth and nose) of sound. The air vibrations in these spaces below the vocal cords are more or less closed off. Because of this, some teachers doubt whether these vibrations can influence amplification at all. Others, admitting the possibility of such an influence, claim it is overshadowed by the vibrations in the spaces above the vocal cords, which occur simultaneously. Still others insist that the voice should be centered in or on the chest. This approach, of course, applies only to a sensation. Centering the voice about the chest brings about a downward development of tone production into the deeper respiratory tract. This may be of benefit for exploring the sonorities of the voice.

It is this author's opinion that the spaces below the vocal cords (which include the tracheae and bronchi) do influence amplification. In consequence, a sound phenomenon results. We might compare this phenomenon with a drum, which adds a sort of boom. When it is not there, we miss it, and a voice is somewhat like a ship without ballast. Many vocalists, when temporarily indisposed, have experienced the sensation and complain, "My voice feels as if the bottom had dropped out," or "I can't get grounded today."

When we produce voiced G or D consonants
without releasing them, slight froglike sounds
will result. As an example, sing or speak the
word "Go" or "Doe." Then skip the vowels and
sustain just G or D. The sound of these unre-
leased consonants will be unaffected by mouth or
nose openings or closings. Even when we squeeze
our nostrils or close our lips tightly, no noticeable sound change will occur as we sustain
the G or D. These sounds have no exit except
through the body walls and can be heard through
the walls.

Pupils, in their search for amplification,
are sometimes advised to aim a tone toward one
focal point in the body walls. It is a common
belief that the chest walls and the bones of the
head and back function as amplifiers of tone.
While it is true that our body walls co-vibrate
with the air vibrations that occur in our resonance cavities, this co-vibration does not necessarily contribute to the amplification of the
tone. The G or D sounds, which travel through
the body walls, lose in power by comparison with
other vocal sounds, which stream out through the
mouth and/or nose. It follows that in a general
way the walls themselves dampen the tone. Also,
because of the irregularity of the bony structure within the body walls, a tone may be damp-
ened in varying degrees depending on where it
strikes, like a vacuum cleaner that changes its
noise when it goes over different parts of a
room. As a result, the quality and quantity of
the sound may be affected.

Hollow and muffled voices, which need sharp-
ening and more ring, must aim for as little
dampening as possible. In contrast, shrill and
strident voices, which need gentling, may gain
mellowness through increased dampening.

It is up to the teacher to make a diagnosis
of a student's tone production and, on the basis
of his observation, to develop those resonating
sources that the individual requires in order to
improve tone quality or quantity, or both.

To sum up: upper and lower resonating sources provide a variety of contrasts and a wide selection of possibilities from which to draw, in modifying, magnifying and adorning tone. The combination of these will vary as pitch, volume and color of tone vary---and must be allowed to do so.

---

**Q. How can resonance be improved?**
**A. Through the different form and size that we give to our resonance cavities. The form and size of our resonance cavities are influenced by moveable parts, mainly: mouth, tongue, soft palate and larynx. The combined positions of these parts provide a channelling system. The task is to channel the tides of the sound to best individual advantage in order to produce a free, rich, round tone.**

---

The problem is to use and move these parts in a way we normally don't use and move them, to get used to different positions and to develop the ability to hold those positions. Indeed, in voice, as in dance, all the parts concerned have to be held in the proper position. To do so, we have to be steeled to the task. In the beginning we are not and cannot expect to be. Every once in a while the positions give. Then we may stumble, slip or miss.

In the quest for freedom, all the moveable parts must operate in a constantly flexible and friendly work exchange. Nevertheless, in voice training, positions of mouth, tongue, soft palate or larynx for all are often superimposed or fixed.

To state a case: One school of vocal thought works on the theory that tone is strongest and pitch most easily controlled when the larynx is in its lowest position. With this as a premise, all pupils must produce all vowels through an

"OO" formation with the larynx in the lowest possible position.

There are voices that, through structure or habit, naturally speak and sing with an extremely low larynx position---the "Mortimer Snerd" types. To prescribe the lowest larynx position for them would be advice in the wrong direction. The larynx position is usually highest when one is swallowing and lowest when one is yawning. If the Mortimer Snerd voice were to yawn more, the hollowness of tone would increase. In order for this type of voice to take on a brighter shade and more ring, the course of its development would necessitate the raising of the larynx.

"White" voices as well as throaty voices, which operate with an extremely high larynx position, will have to lower it in the course of their development, in order to improve sound.

We can see that no fixed larynx position is advisable. Its relation to the overall function must always be considered. The larynx position must be dictated by the needs of the individual tone.

Of all moveable parts, the tongue is the most abused. Since we can move and observe it, it offers a golden opportunity to those who try to build the inside through the outside. According to one method, a flat tongue is prescribed. By another, an arched tongue is recommended. By still another, a curled-up tongue is demanded. Up or down or all around, what shall we do with the tongue? One particular position is defended because of its supposed beneficial effects on another part of the organism. Detail is moved to please detail. One "tongue teacher" may insist upon the tongue's being held in a concave position so that a larger space in the oral cavity will be provided. This advice, while giving more space in the oral cavity, can for some easily shut off resonance space elsewhere and may therefore prove to be of more harm than help for

the overall function. Through fixed tongue prescriptions, the relationship to the whole organism is forgotten and with it the needs of the
individual tone. The right tongue position cannot necessarily be seen but a wrong one can
surely be heard. When the tongue interferes,
vital space is narrowed and as a result the
produced tone is characteristically choked off,
constricted or distorted. To be sure, the tone
is the criterion for the treatment and position
of the tongue.

The tenor Richard Tauber's mouth and tongue
positions were indeed awkward. This externality
would have tempted a number of teachers to get
out their spoons, corks, and special instruments
in order to alter his unorthodox positions. Had
they done so, they might have easily thrown his
production out of gear. A dogmatic insistence
upon this or that position makes for rigidity,
which is prone to upset the overall function.

Many of us are too easily influenced by ex-
ternalities. We may become suspicious of certain
visible traits. We may even interpret them as
abnormal or as signals of a need for speedy correction. However, these physical manifestations
are often merely surface effects, which do not
interfere with the real thing. The "essential
underneath" may be very normal indeed.

Generally speaking, the more biased and narrow a teaching approach, the stricter is its
conception of the normal and the readier it is
to condemn any peculiarities and deviations. In
dancing, for example, we find cases of students
whose muscles, while well under control, move
independently. Thus, in a high arabesque a thigh
muscle may quiver. Bothered by this, some dancing teachers may try to eliminate this personal
trait and thereby overdevelop the misunderstood
part with unfortunate effects.

Granted, not only what the sound reveals but
also what face, body and gestures reveal can
serve as general clues to a person's way of

functioning. Good teachers are supposed to be intuitive clue readers. However, from the technical point of view, the various external characteristics of the vocalist may or may not exercise a conditioning influence on the tone result. In order to avoid unnecessary correction, we must not quickly condemn unusual body positions, quivering,[7] veins popping out, getting red in the face[8] and other peculiarities as subversive vocal elements or bad symptoms. We must add the appearance (what we can see) as a supplement to the existing aural facts (what we can hear) when we judge the total vocal performance. A good tone may be produced with visible peculiarities, which need not be bothered with. Bad tones, in contrast, may be produced with paralyzing external factors, and these have to be corrected.

Just as some people tend to overcorrect all visible peculiarities of a vocalist, so others will perhaps overrate the vocal value of structural peculiarities that they notice in the body of a vocalist. For instance, at a vocal recital a person in the audience may observe the performing artist through his opera glasses and then exclaim admiringly, "Look at the mouth she has." But for all that mouth, bones and torso ---and for reasons often necessarily obscure ---she does not let out anything good. Hence, the significance of individual visual peculiarities in voice production must be determined only by the final criterion---the tone.

Witch hunting for body tensions has become quite fashionable in the study of voice as well as in acting. In view of the confusion that prevails, it may help to draw a dividing line between interfering and noninterfering tensions. Interfering tensions are those that stand in the way of our technical goal. In the study of voice, they oppose tone freedom and fullness. They must be eliminated by means of remedial, technical exercises. Noninterfering tensions can

be dismissed as unimportant. We may as well
learn to live with them. Many singers and actors
plague themselves from morning to night, trying
to detect tensions. Relaxation becomes an obsession; they are getting tenser and tenser trying to relax. Their motto should be: pay less
attention to your tensions and you will be less
tense---and less self-conscious.

Let us emphasize that manipulations that are
visible in good vocalists are made in order to
give the moveable elements the best possible
position. As was pointed out, it is an error to
assume that, by one's imitating the facial play
or other outer manipulations of any person, the
inner or overall function can ever be duplicat-
ed.

A famous basso of a European opera house did
most of his singing through the right side of
his mouth. As is often the case, he was invited
to teach voice at the State Academy. Pupils
flocked to his studio. Emerging as from a frank-
furter machine, each student, regardless of inner structure, sang out of the right side of his
mouth. But since not one inner structure out of
a hundred called for this outer manipulation,
these voices were one-sided in more ways than
one.

There are also outer manipulations employed
for the sake of appearance. Let us point out
here that there is a vast difference between improving the product and improving the way it
looks. Unfortunately, work on the instrument and
work on eye appeal are sometimes confused in the
field of voice.

A pleasant expression, especially since
television has come into existence, is certainly
an asset. However, this should not be achieved
at the expense of the voice. One thinks of the
musical comedy star who, while singing, suddenly
remembers that she must give with the "tooth-
paste smile." Putting looks at a premium, she
assumes an expression that is at complete vari-

ance with the needs of her voice. As a result, she disrupts the singing function to the point where the tone suffers as much as the audience.

A typical falsification for the sake of appearance is the dubbing of singing, done in some movies and television shows. The dramatic climax of the composition approaches. The singer is singing his heart out. The top tone, which is supposed to give us goose pimples, is finally coming. We are in suspense. We expect the singer to be in a state of utmost alertness as his nervous system prepares his body to bring about the responses for the "kill." We hope to catch the artist in as many characteristic and revealing body positions as he can manage, in order to deliver the goods for the production of the climax. But instead of a mobilization of the body's energies and an added dynamism in the body, which alter facial expressions and cause postures and motions to shift and stretch, we see such a casual bearing and banal facial expression that the dramatic impact is lost.

The conflict between sight and sound becomes apparent. For the sake of the sight, an amputation of the physical extensions takes place. As a result, the much-heralded top tone seems to be produced with a strange aspect of unreality. We miss the real work, joy and satisfaction of the artist. Because the state of his body was not shown in the act of making the top tone but was deliberately prettified for the screen, we feel cheated.

A casual bearing and a lackadaisical use of the instrument make for a lack of intensity, which is obvious in some crooners on television. Their kind of nonchalance and half-doing becomes a monument to boredom. No wonder that, in our day of relaxation crazes, "taking a nap" while performing is often mistaken for the calmness of know-how.

Even relaxation, when misapplied or overdone, can lead to a mannerism and turn into a defect. Banal facial expressions and a lack of proper keying-up of the vocal instrument can be observed in some students who have undergone so-called relaxation training. "A relaxed voice from a relaxed body" is perhaps the motto of this school. Unfortunately, it is not as good as it seems. It is too easy a formula to be truly effective. All too often the student mistakes a lack of energy for relaxation or mistakes effort for tenseness. We must always remember that the controls that keep the tone supported and reson-ant must do their job when we sing. "Relaxation within a well-supported and well-resonated tone" should therefore be the motto. In other words: "Improve your technique and you will relax nat-urally." Preconceived ideas, resulting in gen-eral advice to keep the whole body or a specific part of the body relaxed, are prone to reduce the productive state of those parts or to pre-vent the parts from finding their balanced con-tribution to the whole. Underwork results. Ef-fort and will go down. The total capacity of the voice is devitalized.

Let us remember, the prime task in voice training is to bring the vocal instrument to the right state of adjustment. This goal implies a need to establish the body in relation to the needs of the tone. Ease in voice also depends upon the existing condition of strength. Unless strength bolsters the ease, the lag will be great. Ease without strength is just a bore. Unfortunately, the type and degree of strength and ease that a tone must have to fulfill itself cannot be defined for practical use. It follows that general relaxation and energizing exercises are extraneous; they fail to develop the needed skill for the act.

Some believe that the size of the mouth opening should determine the size of the tone. When singing loudly, they open the mouth; when singing softly, they close it. Yet, mouth open-ing and volume of tone do not necessarily have anything to do with each other. By deliberately changing the mouth position during a change of tone volume, one can easily lose the correct tonal balance.

In order to produce a tone with an open throat, the mouth need not be opened widely in all cases. The same is true in the formation of vowels. Particularly on the vowel "ah," some schools of vocal thought are of the opinion that a conscious effort to open the back of the throat should always be made. However, in many instances the formation of "ah" obeys the mere thought process. All we have to do then is to think "ah" and do it. Any additional attempt to consciously manipulate the mechanics is unnecessary and undesirable. It can easily lead to overopening, overstretching or spreading. In fact, by closing the mouth more, some vocalists even gain better control and, with it, a more correct open tone. The saying, "The open jaw makes for a correctly open tone" is an erroneous generalization or too simple to be wholly true.

On the other hand, it is equally wrong to generalize by prescribing a small mouth opening for all.[9] The mouth opening must be allowed to vary and adjust according to plan and pitch. The degree and shape of the mouth opening must be dictated by the needs of the tone.

We can see that positive generalizations regarding detail manipulations are unfortunate. We must now add that negative generalizations are equally unfortunate.

One school of vocal thought will claim that the raising of the soft palate cuts off the upper pharynx resonators. With this in mind, no student is permitted to raise the palate. Again the claim is based upon examinations of details only. One detail is not moved in order not to displease another detail. The relationship to the whole is forgotten again. Such palate action, with its influence on the size of our resonating cavities, may well benefit the overall function and improve tone in one case while it may be of disadvantage to the overall function and interfere with tone in another. Twangy voices, which function with an extremely low palate position and at the same time with the back of the tongue in a high position, may counteract narrowness and improve tone with the help of palate raising. No fixed palate rules for all are advisable, then. The tone is the criterion for the treatment and positioning of the palate.

To sum up: larynx, tongue, palate and mouth are certain distinguishable mechanisms whose positions exert a decisive influence upon certain distinguishable resonance zones. Hence, varying the larynx, tongue, palate, or mouth positions can bring about tone changes.

There are changes for the better and changes for the worse. Because of our individual makeup, these changes affect the overall function of each of us differently. Therefore, some may better and others worsen the tone. To ensure against changes for the worse while still not shutting the door on any possible advantage, we must not generalize. There is no best larynx, tongue, palate, or mouth position. The relationship to the whole organism, as revealed in tone alone, is the deciding factor. Only through tone can we tell whether we are directing the use of these parts to advantage or disadvantage.

These parts can serve only for the purpose of tuning and adjusting each tone. The when, where and how much are individual problems that have to be solved in a practical way, depending upon a careful diagnosis. We may test. We may explore. We do hear the results of our manipulations revealed in the tone. That flexible combination of all the moveable parts that produce a tone with the most freedom and "qualities" is the right one.

The same principle applies to posture. The right posture for vocal production can be out-

lined as that flexible but composed state of
body that lets the vocal instrument function
correctly so that the best tone result is a-
chieved with the least physical force. As a
foundation, we need alertness and readiness for
the act of tone production, but we should not
pose ourselves. Self-consciousness comes from
posing. Studied and stilted movements are easily
detected. Since they do not spring from any inner source, they are obviously artificial or
phony.

The idea is to stand in any way that gives
free and full release of vocal sound. After the
body attitude best suited for the needs of sound
has been found and established through use, it
will then be possible to produce the voice with
more and more variations in posture without losing the proper instrument adjustment. Changes or
corrections for the sake of appearance can then
safely be made.

It is worth noting that, in order to make a
tone change, we need not be conscious of a body
change that takes place. Body changes are not
always perceivable to the eye or clear to the
mind. Tone changes are, however, perceivable to
the ear. Hence, when making vocal changes or adjustments, it is usually more reasonable to follow the needs of the tone. It is true, we cannot
create a tone change merely by wish or will power. These can give us direction, but by themselves they cannot bring about fulfillment. A
physical agent is required for that purpose.
Every aspect of tone production involves muscular activity. Therefore, tone changes cannot
take place without body changes. However, to
produce the proper tone, we need not necessarily
know the ways in which the adjustments operate
and what the body does to achieve them.

Tone can be adjusted and expanded through
tonal terms and description. When, in correcting
tone, one teacher says: "Your tone sounds too
yawned" and another says, "Your larynx position

is too low," both may be right. Both are using different means to achieve the same end. For psychological reasons, the teacher who deals with tone will probably be more successful. The mentioning of larynxes, pharynxes, and the like is often not much appreciated in artistic circles. Moreover, when there is a vocal fault or shortcoming, usually more than one detail needs adjustment, for the misuse is usually not limited to one specific part. Hence, we must also prevent those other, associated wrong uses that bring about the fault. However, making a student conscious of a number of wrong uses in the production of one faulty tone will overinvolve him technically and consequently harass and confuse him. In addition, the moveability of the parts that produce voice is tremendous. Besides, many of these parts are invisible. An attempt to improve a tone by manipulating some parts of the vocal mechanism is sometimes offset by counteractions of other parts. For instance, the influence that the position of the jaw has on a sound may easily be offset by counteractions of the tongue. Thus, jaw and tongue may cancel each other's technical effectiveness. Hence, in expanding and correcting, it is usually beneficial to give the tone first rank and the body secondary rank.

In the voyage through our pipe and chamber system, sound has one major obstacle: blockage. This may be the result of organic problems, such as a deviated septum,[10] hay fever, sinus trouble, enlarged tonsils, or elongated velum. Such abnormalities should be looked for, and a physician consulted, if marked deficiencies in resonance exist and persist.

A cold may temporarily cause shutoffs, depending, of course, on where it settles.[11] Usually narrowness and narrowing, the latter due to muscular tightening, are the greatest offenders. Structural and psychological factors are to blame for these conditions. Sometimes the vocalist is unaware of them. At other times, being aware of them, he tries to help himself by "counterpushing." As a result, the voice, fed by forbidden sources, gets worse.

To work away obstacles so that sound can always stream unhindered is a step-by-step process. The smaller the organic changes we make at one time, the more subtle the transition and the better the result will be.

Interferences with tone freedom, such as twangyness, nasalness, "the potato in the throat," and similar narrow formations, can gradually be eliminated through the realization of more resonance space by means of reshaping the resonance cavities. In this process, the ability to open up, to mold and stretch, may become apparent in the mouth and throat areas. As a result, a student may discover, "The tone slipped into a groove I never knew I had."

A student whose tones suffer from overopening or overstretching and whose voice sounds spread may also improve production by means of adjusting and reshaping the resonance cavities. In this case, however, the work to be done on the tone-form is subject to modification and control.

With smog and other environmental conditions, our pipes and passageways are often not clean. Tones appear to be cloudy or sounds are eaten with static. Granted, this is an annoying condition, but even when we turn on the radio and static interferes, we don't shut it off; we still listen to the music. Much the same goes for the voice; we must continue to work on our craft all the time, even when we have to pick our way through the grime, the mucus and the static. The task is to find ways of dealing with the obstacle, provided, of course, that the degree of our trouble does not make the work impossible.

The quality of our technique is often revealed by how we handle adversity. Under adverse vocal conditions even an experienced singer, when warming up, may do best to wake up his voice with a gentle nudge so as to work gradually into tone clarity rather than tearing it in order to come through.

The process of establishing tone clarity can be approached in two different ways. One can shape the resonators in an effort to find those sound directions that bypass or avoid phlegm. This is the negative way. On the other hand, one can try to increase the intensity, vibrancy and brilliancy of tone. Drawn to a taut and concentrated formula, the voice will crowd out the phlegm. This is the positive way. The mucus, fog or fuzziness of the voice will then disappear in proportion to the more ringing sound that appears. Inasmuch as the ring acts as a destroyer of foreign influences in vocal sound, we may regard it as an important vocal element of purification.

There are spaces that are influential in the resonating as well as in the articulating of vowels. If we use these spaces for articulation (i.e., clarification) before we use them for amplification, the carrying power and quality of the tone will suffer. Before we clarify, we must first fully establish what we want to clarify. Full establishment includes amplification. If we disregard this order, we may be apt to articulate away from the tone.

Good diction is certainly important, yet if we articulate with poor tone, the whole operation is wrong from the beginning. To avoid this, we should establish the tone before we attempt to clarify the vowel. The tone is the vehicle, the articulation.

We find among singers and voice teachers a variety of opinions as to resonance. Let us examine briefly three typical cases. The first teacher is an ardent believer in "mask" resonance and frowns upon the use of other resonance zones. He points to his forehead and says, "The secret is all here." He encourages manipulation of the moveable parts in order to gain that mask resonance.

The second teacher accepts all types of resonance. He states that it will come of itself, when everything else in the production is correct. However, he claims that nothing should be done to get it. He maintains that any manipulation to adjust resonance is wrong and will hurt the entire production.

The third teacher has no favorite type of resonance. He accepts any and all that benefit tone. Any manipulation that will bring resonances into action is encouraged.

These three teachers might be compared to three hunters who have comparable ideas about duck hunting. The first hunter shoots with a rifle which, we know, fires a single bullet. (This is the teacher with one favorite type of resonance.) In order to attract the wild fowl within easy gunshot, he sets out a number of decoys. The wild birds, seeing the decoys, settle in the marsh around them and offer a perfect target. However, if the hunter fires only a single bullet, he will either bring down only one duck or miss entirely.

The second hunter uses a shotgun that fires pellets. This can bring down many more ducks because the shot covers a much greater area. This fellow, however, scorns the use of decoys to bring his target within range. As a result, he may have no success at all. (He corresponds to the teacher who has an open mind about resonance but claims it must come automatically and rejects adjustment.)

The third hunter employs every possible advantage. Decoys bring the game within proper range and in position. With a shotgun fired from his vantage point, this hunter naturally has huge success.

Everyone possesses a number of targets or resonance areas, all of individual proportions.

Each person, because of his or her particular makeup, possesses different resonance combinations. The voice of one may naturally possess more nose resonance, of another more chest resonance, and so on. We should follow the path of nature and utilize strength where strength exists, first using---as the foundation for future building---the best resonating powers with which nature has endowed us, that is, the resonance that can be produced with the greatest freedom and fullness.

In order to bring out and test available resonating powers, humming may be a purposeful exercise.[12] A free, full, sustained hum (charged with ring, buzz, crackle, rumble or purr---whatever the case may be) can make us conscious of vibration and resonance values. The hum may very well be a source from which good vocal resonance may spring. It may then provide a starting point from which we can try gradually to expand.

In order to reach or tap as many productive resonance areas as possible, we must arrange (that is, shape) the targets so that they are all in range and can be utilized for the benefit of the tone. However, as pointed out, if we assume that resonance comes automatically or if we are satisfied with as little as does come automatically, we will either miss or hit these areas indiscriminately.

Clapping the hands in applause may serve as a simple example. In clapping our hands, one person may indiscriminately beat one hand against the other. He ends up with sore hands, all in an effort to make some noise. Another person will discover that, by arranging the targets, that is shaping the palms of the hands, hollowing them a trifle, he can produce with rather little effort a plentitude of sound. He will come to a better result than the first and will not get sore hands.

Disagreement about the acceptance or rejection of nose resonance in tone production has been going on for many decades. This is mainly due to a confusion of definition. Some experts feel that the nasopharynx resonance belongs to the so-called nose resonance, because of its connection with the nasal passages; others believe that it belongs to the pharyngeal areas. Additional confusing factors are the various vibratory sensations that may be experienced in nose areas and that are sometimes mistaken for symptoms of sounding too nasal. In their fear of sounding too nasal, some voice students do not always take full advantage of these resonating possibilities. A loss of vocal power results.

Our law of economy must be: Avoid waste. Sound on its journey outward must take advantage of all productive areas.

Our principle must be: Everything is correct that enriches tone without impeding its form and freedom.

The more resonance areas we utilize and the more resonance we add, the more vibratory sensations and reflexes we will experience. Sometimes the vibratory sensations are felt all over, and the voice seems to come from everywhere and nowhere. Then, the produced tone is blended so that no particular part of the resonance areas seems to stand out. At other times the tone seems to be centered or focused on some specific point. To notice and remember where it is gives us a sense of position, or place memory. The latter is also called <u>voice placement</u>.

What we experience is, of course, mainly sympathetic vibration. The resonance does not necessarily originate where we feel it. Thus, the process of producing resonance and the process of experiencing it may be different from each other and yet simultaneous.

This very difference, however, has brought about another vocal controversy: Which comes first, the chicken or the egg? Because the manifestations of resonance are so often felt in the head and chest areas, the terms <u>head resonance</u>

and chest resonance crop up frequently. These very terms are branded by some voice experts as misnomers. Let us point out here that even in medical circles the terms "head cold" and "chest cold" are used. To condemn such terms because they do not necessarily specify the origin but perhaps only the symptoms of a condition seems futile and merely proves the inclusiveness of words.

In the act of tone production, however, the seats of sensations can be of indicative value. They become sensatory guideposts by which teacher and student understand each other. They also collaborate with the ear and muscular memory in acting as road signs by which the student, once he has found the right path, will be able to find it again.

Also, when a student auditions or performs under adverse acoustical conditions where that happy "bounce off the wall" feeling does not exist or where background noise (air conditioning, for example) bothers him, he may find it difficult to judge the carrying power of his voice. Then, vibratory sensations can serve as test devices and inner controls. Once established, these inner controls basically remain the same while outer acoustical conditions vary with each auditorium.

Vocal carrying power, then, is something the vocalist can feel but cannot hear directly. The capacity to perceive the voice through other channels than hearing demands a certain shifting from one sense to another. (Similarly, a deaf mute dancer can feel the rhythm through the vibrations of the floor.)

The vocalist who cannot depend upon sensations of resonance for confirmation of correct voice production tends to worry about not being heard. He may then try to make himself heard and, as a result, often ends up giving too much.

There are teachers who deny the value of vibratory sensations that we experience when speaking or singing. They usually belong to the group of "science minded" teachers who feel that only what can be demonstrated in a laboratory can be true. The fact is that whatever enters into our sensory experience appears real, and sensory reality needs no scientific proof; it is enough that we feel ourselves affected. Such voice teachers may be compared to miners who, when they find a promising vein, do not make a map that will enable them to return to that spot.

Other voice teachers claim that it is difficult or perhaps even impossible to describe body sensations clearly. However, vocal vibratory sensations are relatively simple body conditions. As such they are subject to description. Similarly, the term "thirst" states a condition in the lining of the throat and the back part of the mouth. The term "hunger" describes a sensation of the stomach. Voice students are usually quite willing to put into words their own impressions of vocal sensations, provided they are not discouraged in the matter. Here are some student descriptions: "The vibrations are massaging the inside of my face," "It feels as if the bones are rattling in my head," "It's banging in my temples," "It bounces against the roof of my mouth where the peanut butter gets stuck," "It hits like a fan right behind my teeth," "The inside of my lips are quivering," "It beats against the breastbone," "I seem to have a xylophone on my chest."

In the voice finding process we should accept sensations and all vibratory powers, wherever they may come from and wherever their impact is felt, and should build on them, provided they are associated with good sound. The presence or absence of freedom and "qualities" decides if it is good sound or not. It must be the student, though, who discovers the sensation, discusses it with her teacher and stores it in her sense memory; the sensations must not be dictated to her by someone else's notion of what comprises her feeling or sensing.

The student must be induced, with proper aid and guidance, to pin down the vibratory processes that go on in her body, by herself. She must thus experience some of those flashes of insight that lighten the development of the resonance path. In contrast, the traditional methods of confronting the voice student not with the discovery but with a finished solution or dogma, such as: "Place it here or there," means to deprive her of excitement and to reduce the adventure of the vocal learner to a dusty heap of resonance theories.

The attempt to transfer to somebody else the sensations of one's own vocal processes is the wrong goal. Many of the controversies that exist in the teaching of voice placement, breath control and posture are due to the fact that many singer--teachers try to pass on their own way of singing and their own vocal sensations as the "right way." The ideal of vocal education requires a more universal approach. Hearing, feeling, sensing and the capacity for empathy will enable the expert teacher to identify himself with his student, to link together vocal phenomena, to make sense out of the ever-changing mosaic of vocal sensations, to understand the seat of his student's sensations and thus to interpret vocal sensations correctly.

Sensations that we have experienced in the production of good tones can be reexperienced and reproduced. They will serve as guides to effective action and contribute to the correct production of a tone. Additional confidence in the control of the tone will result. Particularly in the later stages of study, the vital points or maximum vibration spots upon which peak production and tonal fulfillment depend will become ever more clearly and sharply defined.

Following up vibratory sensations, exploring them and expanding or modifying them can influence sound. Any such influence for the better should be encouraged and any influence that diminishes the freedom and "qualities" of a tone should be discouraged.

It was previously said that the resonance combination varies as the pitch varies. Consequently, the vibratory sensation varies as the pitch varies. Many vocalists, however, think that in order to match and produce tones of even resonance throughout the range, the vibratory sensations must remain fixed. They mistakenly hold on to one vibratory sensation when producing several intervals. If they try to impose the sensation of one pitch upon another pitch, a new kind of need is not recognized. Then, part of the resonance is prevented from merging into the new combination of resonances that the production of the other pitch requires. As a result, the sound never quite keeps going where it should, and the produced tone never sounds as free and full as it should. When we produce small intervals, we may experience similar vibratory sensations in the same place, but they will then occur with different degrees of strength.

Sensation control must be subordinated to sound control in voice development. Wherever the voice is placed, it will be correct if the sound is correct and the throat is not subject to strain. Unfortunately, even when no strain or throatiness is evident, some voice students still worry about the throat. In their well-meant effort to protect it, they try to place the voice so as to save the throat. Granted, safety first, but there is no need to protect what functions well without protection. Unnecessary protection leads to overprotection. Because it is performed with no regard to necessity, the uncalled-for manipulation to save the

throat interferes with the action of the vibrator. The throat is prevented from vibrating
fully. As a result, no full-throated sound can
be made. Other students tend to drive themselves
"sensation-crazy." In order to make tone, they
try to put all sensations together, placing "it"
up, down, in between, front, and back. Still
others tend to narrow the direction of the tone
by localizing only toward one fixed point; in
consequence, they cannot find complete reson-
ation. All three types of students can correct
themselves by temporarily disregarding all vibratory sensations and voice placements, by con-
centrating on sound, allowing the tone and ear
to be their guide.

Often we find in a review of a vocal recital
the complaint: the voice is not resonant. The
assumption is that if the artist could only have
added some resonance, everything would have been
fine. For a critic to make such a statement is
just about as explicit as a coroner's declaring
that death resulted because the heart stopped
beating. One must remember that in order to produce a tone with resonance and timbre, other
correct functions must be included in the production.

It is a mistake to assume that when a tone
is not resonant, the cause is only a lack of
resonance. It can easily be a symptom of trouble
elsewhere, such as incorrect support. Not aware
that a resonant tone need not be made loud, the
inexperienced singer, when trying to imitate a
resonant tone, is often tempted to push. As a
result, loudness may increase, but the gain in
quantity is offset by a loss in quality. Pushing
constitutes a violation of economic principles
and mars the freedom and flexibility of the
voice.

Attempting to compensate for a lack of resonance by oversupporting is barking up the wrong
tree. Resonance cannot help a tone that does not
function properly because of other shortcomings.
Resonance concerns only amplification and timbre

of tone. It can magnify, beautify and adorn only a tone that exists.

Voices that naturally possess freedom, roundness, and carrying power throughout the range are by far in the minority. Most are limited by being either spread or hollow or too pointed or narrow. The establishment of a free, carrying and well-rounded tone all through the scales is usually gradual development.

Vocal resonance can be developed and adjusted through the use of basic tone exercises of varying duration, dynamics, range and rhythm.

In our development, our aim should be the greatest resonance with the greatest ease. In our aim to sustain tone with freedom, and in our aim to attain the most effective combination of resonance for the benefit of richness and roundness of tone, we will gradually learn to balance and adjust our resonating sources.

The more advanced our development, the more rapid, precise and consistent will be our ability to exact this tonal bonus from our organism, with a minimum of exertion to reap a maximum of tonal values.

---

**Q.  Is the same vocalizing vowel best for all?**
**A.  No rule or generalization as to the best vocalizing vowel can be made. It is up to the teacher to see that practice vowels, dictated by the needs of a voice, are selected, for each case and each stage of vocal development.**

---

Usually when a teacher prescribes the same fixed practice vowel for his students, it is because of a pet theory or because of his experience with his own voice or the voice of his most successful student. Let us repeat: it is impossible for any two persons with different apparatus to produce the same sound with the same approach. Any imitation of vowel sound should be avoided

in voice training, though it may be pursued with
success in diction and language study.

Some teachers, for example, will claim that
the "ay" (as in "gate") is the best practice vowel. Others prefer "oo" (as in "moon"). What
will happen when the "oo" teacher works with a
student who naturally possesses too much of an
"oo" sound, often characteristic of overdark,
hooty or hollow voices? What will the "ay"
teacher do when a student naturally possesses
too much of an "ay" sound, the kind we often
find in twangy, pinched voices? Insisting on the
"oo" with the hollow voice will probably make it
more hollow. Insisting on the "ay" with the
twangy, pinched type will probably make the tone
still narrower.

Just as some voice teachers have vowel fa-
vorites, others have vowel aversions. One school
of vocal thought will advise composers not to
use words with "ee" vowel on top tones, claiming
that the sound tends to become pinched. This
generalization would have made the tenor Leo
Slezak very unhappy. Slezak, one of the greatest
Otellos, altered many of the words on top tones
to syllables with "ee" vowels because he felt
the greatest comfort and tone wealth on these
sounds.

Through the different shapes and shades of
individual vowel production, the tone will reveal itself as part of the product. Vowels, correctly or incorrectly produced, are formations
by which we can diagnose the positives and negatives of a tone. Varying the shapes and shades
of a vowel gives us the means by which to vary
the quality of a tone. This relationship also
works the other way around. Varying the shades
and shapes of a tone will give the means with
which to vary the quality of a vowel. We can
thus reach a tone through a vowel and a vowel
through a tone.

There are innumerable ways in which we can
produce an "ah," "ay," "ee," "oh," and "oo" vowels and all combinations of these. Therefore,

the range of choice before us is enormous. We
can recognize all varieties of vowel production,
from that of a ventriloquist, who functions with
almost closed mouth, to that of a singer who
drops his jaw all the way.

Each vowel not only contains numerous possibilities or modes of production, but is precisely rooted and can be developed in many
ways. For the purpose of voice development, it
is first necessary to find out which of a student's available vowel formations offers a channel of least resistance to sound and thus can be
produced with the most freedom and "qualities."

---

**Q.   What is the best vocalizing vowel?**
**A.   The best vocalizing vowel is that which pro-
vides the freest and richest tone for each
individual.**

---

The selection of the best vocalizing vowel is a
decisive factor in voice building. In our search
for the healthiest tone, we must not decide in
the beginning. We are not yet interested in any
fixed letter of the alphabet. We should first
give the voice a chance to make its own vowel
decision.

In order to give the vowel the freedom to
design itself, we must put the emphasis on the
tone rather than on the vowel. We must think of
the sound rather than the vowel. We must set the
mouth for tone rather than vowel. Then, when it
comes to the production of sound, we should look
for the most promising tone colors and forms
that we can find, on different pitch levels and
with different degrees of volume. (The kaleido-
scope produces various colors and forms but no
fixed specific patterns or scenes.) In the case
of most beginning singers, tests with various
tone shades and shapes (like a kaleidoscopic
color and form shifting) must first be made
until the best are hit upon. We thus determine

the most promising sound effects by means of comparison. To make sure in the voice-finding process, we should patiently search for that sound whose pitch, volume, form and color offer the least obstruction and the greatest vibration value to tone. An unconsciously pronounced vowel will then result. This unconsciously pronounced vowel which produces the best possible tone will give each person his or her own basic vowel.

The vowels of an infant are unconsciously pronounced. Usually we do not bother to analyze them. We expect them to be nondescript or neutral, and we know they have no dictional meaning. However, if we analyze them, we will be able to hear a certain resemblance to the customary vowels of our language.

When, in our aim to establish the best possible tone, we yield to a chosen vowel, whatever it may be, and when we later examine the vowel in terms of its relationship to our customary vowels, we will likewise be able to detect a certain resemblance to some specific letter of the alphabet.

The sound that is produced by this basic vowel must at first be regarded as raw material. Because we do not worry about language, about tonal refinement and other related modifications, the unrestricted use of the basic vowel sound can assume power and can gain ever greater momentum, which, in time, may carry the whole voice along with it. We experiment with the raw material by trying to perfect the fullness and ease of the basic vowel sound. We continue with our work on the basic vowel until the sound is sufficiently well-established to risk a departure from it.

Consciously pronounced vowels should be avoided at first, since most of us have produced them incorrectly for so long that we have become fairly "efficient" in them. Moreover, consciously pronounced vowels are not primitive sounds, as unconsciously pronounced vowels are. The more

primitive the sound, the less inhibited and ob-
structed it tends to be. This is particularly
important at the start of voice training. We
want to make sure that our customary vowel channels, usually full of bad habits and interferences, are not used as a foundation for future
vowel development.

Rather than trying out different, unfree,
habitual vowel channels in search for the best
tone, we should go for free vowel sounds through
the best tone. The basic vowel is different in
each case. It is not an absolute, but it will
dominate vowel production.

The basic vowel is not just a beginner's
preferred vowel which later will be amalgamated
with much else, but it is often a voice characteristic associated with tone production
throughout a performer's career. Richard
Tauber's tenor voice, for example, had the "ay"
(as in "cake") as the basic. The phrase Dein ist
mein ganzes Herz (from the operetta Land of
Smiles by Franz Lehar) was, so to speak, sustained on "ay" sounds.[13] Caruso's voice, in
contrast, was carried on a comparatively darker
basic vowel sound. Ezio Pinza had an "oh" sound
running through his voice. Lauritz Melchior an
"oe" (as in the German umlaut). Frida Leider had
a mixture between "ay" and "ee."

Inasmuch as the basic vowel produces the
best tone, it provides us with a substantial
basis for efficient vocal functioning and serves
as a firm foundation for future vowel development. By means of the basic vowel we thus arrive
at a structure or building block upon which all
vocal and vowel development can be based.

The establishment of the basic vowel should
be the outcome of a reasoned procedure, which we
can consciously work for and learn to control.

Q. How can we exploit the best vocalizing vowel?
A. Repetitious practice of the basic vowel
sound will settle the voice into one particular and more stable vowel position. The
advantage gained from this position is the
ability to operate the whole voice from one
center. This provides us with a simplified
approach to voice control and voice work.
By our working through the center, the produced tone can acquire a columnar solidity
and monolithic character. From the central
foundation we can learn to ring out, round
out and flow out freely.

The basic vowel serves as a common vowel denominator from which we evolve all other vowels.

In the average voice of an untrained singer
one is prone to hear quite a difference between
one produced vowel sound and another. This difference may affect both tone quality and quantity. For example, while a singer might produce
the "ah" vowel with comparative freedom and
fullness, he might have some difficulty with the
"ee" (or vice versa). With the help of the basic, common vowel denominator, these differences
can be neutralized. Changes between the vowel
sounds can be lessened until sound freedom and
the "qualities" of all vowels seemingly remain
the same. Thus he will gain unity of vowel
sound. Strength through unity will follow.

Unification is accomplished by his first at-
tuning closely related vowels to the basic one,
then gradually taking up the less related ones,
until all possess equal tone freedom and "qualities." A oneness will then be established.

Variety (that is, different, separate and
distinct vowels) can then be produced, because
all vowels will come through as a part of the
tonal and vowel unit.

Producing separate vowels for the purpose of pronunciation at an early stage of voice training is taking the baby away from the breast too soon. Vocally, we take the vowel away from the tone. The tone is the mother of the vowel. If we separate the vowels too soon, we isolate them before they are strong enough to exist alone. Vowels are like children in a family. They must remain together until they are able to get along on their own. When immature, they are similar in appearance. Only through development do they take on individual characteristics. These and a separate personality, when developed later, will be stronger and more secure if the children grew up in a family atmosphere of love and understanding instead of having been isolated, like orphans, at an early age.

The big difference between tone and diction becomes evident. For example, in the fourth act of Aida, the bass Ramfis sings his accusing "Ra 'da'mes," all three syllables on one note. He is followed by trombones, which play the same note three times, echolike. A well-trained bass voice will produce three tones that resemble the tones of the trombone, plus articulation. A badly trained bass voice will lose in tone freedom and quality (compared with the trombone tones) in proportion to its deviation from the tone of the wind instrument. An untrained bass voice will tend to produce three different tones that vary in value. Between the "ra" and the "da" there will be a change. Even though the vowels are the same, the difference in consonants will make for a difference in the "ah" vowels. The third syllable, "mes," will have a different quality altogether because of its consonant and vowel change. The more a person with an untrained voice tries to enunciate the three syllables, the more the tone quality will suffer and deviate from the purity of the trombone sound.

He who wants only good diction will aim for distinct, pure and separate vowels. This can be achieved by emphasizing and perhaps even exaggerating differences among the various vowel sounds. As a result, consistent changes in sound quality will occur. The natural, wide changes between vowel sounds are then increased to a point where tone suffers because it is split into isolated fragments. This is the type of production we frequently hear in vocalists who enunciate well but sound bad.

He who wants only good tone will aim for evenness and fullness of sound. This can be achieved by seeking likenesses within different vowel sounds, by minimizing the changes between them, by emphasizing tone freedom and "qualities" in vowel production. If the development ends here, the sound of all vowels will then remain pretty much the same, at the expense of diction. This is the type of production we frequently hear in vocalists who sound well but can't be understood.

He who wants a good tone plus good diction will aim for unified, rich sounds plus different, separate and distinct vowels. He must first unite all vowel sounds so as to benefit from mutual assistance. Then he can safely go farther. Different, separate and distinct vowels can be aimed for because by this time they will come through as an integral part of the entire tone produced rather than as broken-up segments. The allegiance of all vowels to the tone will be established. The whole tone will shine through the tint of each vowel.

The proper procedure for vowel development should be: Neutralize and find the basic. Add dimensions to expand it. Unify all other vowels with it. From unity work for variety and pronounce with safety.

Q:   Can consonants help in vowel development?
A:   Consonants can serve as stepping-stones to a
     vowel, "Pied Pipers" which lure a vowel that
     follows them into position.

In searching for our basic vowel, we also seek
out those specific consonants that make the entrance into the basic vowel easier.

Let us assume that in one case the "hum" or
"m" is the best consonant for such a purpose,
and the basic vowel has been established as
something resembling "ah" (as in "Shah"). In
this particular case it gives us the syllable
"mah" as our basic syllable. We establish it and
solidify it through repetitious practice. Because we gain strength through use and practice,
we soon are able to expand the exercise without
any noticeable additional effort. The voice
seems to go on its own a little longer and
stronger.

Because the tone lives longer when it vibrates and pulsates, breath sufficiency seems to
increase as we find the proper basic sound (or
breath waste is avoided if we proceed on what is
right in the sound to be made). Then, we add
another syllable, "mah," and thus have "mah-
mah," to be practiced on single tones on one
breath, and later on with intervals also. This
time the second "m" consonant serves as a syllable joiner. It is important that, throughout
the exercise, from attack to cutoff, the tone
continues as an uninterrupted stream. If it is
correctly done, the second syllable "mah" sounds
like an identical twin to the first.

Our work will then go on in three directions. Their order is of no consequence; to let
it develop naturally is what counts. In each of
the three directions we will seek to gain ground
whenever possible, and, we should use that one
of the three, in which the voice works best as
we try it out in practice sessions.

1. After starting on one syllable and after
   learning to intensify, prolong and control this single experience, and after
   profiting from such control and discipline, we gradually add more and more
   syllables, to be produced in one breath.
   Eventually, we should be able to produce
   as many syllables in one breath as an
   average vocal phrase requires. The purpose of these graded exercises is to develop sustaining length in text singing.

2. After starting on the most comfortable
   pitch, we take syllables and words gradually up and down the scale. By not
   clinging rigidly to the basic vowel formation, we allow minute changes to take
   place for difference in pitch. The purpose of the graded exercises is, of
   course, to develop range in text singing. Eventually we should be able to take
   these syllables and words all over the
   range within which text singing is to
   take place.

3. After starting on the basic syllables, we
   vary the syllables without varying the
   basic tone freedom and "qualities." After
   "mah-mah," for instance, we try the related word "Mo-ther." The tone stream
   must remain the same. The following
   should be observed: First we should produce the "mah" correctly, then attune the
   "mo" of "Mother" to "mah," and when "mo"
   is correct, attune "ther" to "mo." It
   then becomes a chain in which we try to
   equalize each successive link. Eventually, all syllables and words in a
   phrase should be produced with the freedom and "qualities" of the basic. The
   purpose of these graded exercises is to
   equate the varying sounds used in singing
   so as to perfect the blending of vocal
   music and text.

As a tightrope walker depends upon balance, so do we depend upon our basic tone balance. As every position and movement a rope walker assumes is dependent upon and must include that balance, so all our singing depends upon the security and balance of our basic vowel. If any variation deprives our tone production of the basic vowel or its beneficial effects, our tones will fall out of position as certainly as the rope walker falls when he loses his balance.

Any combination of vowel and pitch is produced to its fullest through the framework of the basic tone.

Vowel exercises done without the benefit of the basic tone as an anchor, the routine ah-ay-ee-oh-oo, and similar conventional forms of vowel practice are merely surface activities. Because they are not combined with the striving toward optimal realization of tone, they just move the voice mechanically from one vowel prop to another. Of course, vocal routine exercises may sound good if the voice that produces them is already good. But they will, as a rule, not help to improve sound.

When a voice is good and free, routine exercises may serve as a means of limbering up. When a voice is not free, such exercises will merely limber up and move what should not be limbered up and moved. One can forever move the voice around and around, from vowel to vowel, from pitch to pitch, piling one tone on top of another, without ever exerting a conditioning influence upon the tone result. What good can it do to produce a number of vowels in a row if not one of them is established in its freedom and quality? The same is true of range. What good can it do to run up and down the scale and produce a number of pitches, if not one of them is established in its correct foundation?

Petty, routine exercises, vocal "drills" and similar bores and empty techniques will particularly appeal to those singers who suffer from "silence fright," who thirst for vocal activity. Quantity at the expense of quality.

Let us repeat the principle: Perfect strength where strength exists, and in that way develop a model strength. Then infiltrate into the weaker parts, gradually. This applies to the development of vowels as well as of range. After utilizing and perfecting strength where strength exists in the basic vowel, we incorporate this strength into all other vowels until they match the model vowel.

As the properties of the basic develop in ripeness and sureness, so will all tones and vowels develop. In other words, the more the freedom and quality of the basic are developed, the farther we can reach into all other vowels without losing our tonal balance.

Let us assume that in one case the basic vowel is established as something resembling the "oh", and we wish to expand its dimensions into other vowels. We can accomplish this through the use of a word such as "no-el,"[14] which will introduce the basic "oh" into the breadth of the "el." Starting with a "noh," which in this case contains our basic vowel "oh," we introduce it to the "el" syllable, which contains a broader vowel. By maintaining the properties of the basic as we glide into the position of the "el," we develop an "eh" vowel, which has the necessary breadth and still all the virtues of the basic.

Expansion then takes place because the roundness of the basic goes into a broad vowel, adding depth to it.

Now consider the "oo" vowel. This, in contrast to the "eh" in "no-el," is a deep or oval vowel. We can introduce the elements of the basic "o" to the "oo" by practicing the word "know," which contains both the "o" and the "oo." Expansion then takes place because the roundness of the basic goes into a long, deep or oval vowel, adding width to the same.

In implanting into the other vowels the larger dimensions of the basic, we add dimensions to the whole voice. Thus we expand its broadness and depth.

In exploring the variations and possibilities in vowel production, sustaining on vowel diphthongs may be a valuable exercise. Take, for example, practice words like "chow," "coy," "shy." When produced in an exaggerated manner, so-called split-sounds may result. Slavic voices, particularly some Russian basses, are famous for this trademark. When singing "shy," they tend to change abruptly from "ah" to "ee" and put almost as much accent and duration on the "ee" as on the "ah." Despite the fact that such a production constitutes an extreme, and the overstressing of the vowel contrast in the diphthong may actually resemble a vocal caricature, it is nevertheless interesting to observe the tonal differences. The "shah" sound of the singer may be freer or fuller than the "ee," or just the opposite may be true. For the purpose of voice training, any such difference is of significance. We can determine the better of two tonal values from the diphthong by means of comparison and selection. The tone must dictate which of the two different vowel sounds offers the more promising possibilities for development.

Also, the sustaining on diphthongs enables us to move or curl the voice from one vowel sound to another, on one pitch. In our vocal travel from "shah" to "ee," we find a variety of intervening vowels, so-called "vowel-inbetweenies." The slower we move at any one time, the greater will be the variety. (It is a matter of unfolding the sound like an artichoke rather than of opening a suitcase with a bang.)

In minutely moving the voice from one vowel to another on one pitch, we will be able to exploit the flux between the various possibilities and discover more and more rainbowlike colors and forms. Zeroing in on these, letting the sound go into them and sustaining it may add new luminous properties to the tone. Moreover, by doing the same, minutely moving the voice from one vowel to another on one pitch, we will arrive at a point at which the freest and fullest available sounds meet. This is the strongpoint. We try to start the voice at its strongpoint and maintain its position as we repeat the exercise again and again. This strongpoint or model serves as a framework. Through the established framework we later seek to gain a hold upon not-so-good vowels, by means of extension or modification.

The order in which we select the not-so-good vowels for "treatment" is easy to determine, because vowels, in singing, are interchangeable. Let us explain the term "interchangeable vowel." When a tenor, for example, sings the word "see" on a high note, we will most probably hear a certain percentage of "ay" that fills the "ee" and broadens it. Or we may hear an admixture of "ue" (as in the French word "tu") that darkens the "ee" and deepens it. This turning of single vowels into multiple vowels or letting the "neighborhood vowels" drop in, is often done unconsciously. However, the same thing, namely, the adding of another vowel ingredient to the existing mold, or calling the neighbor vowel in for help, can also be done as a conscious, technical feat. The latter serves two purposes. It gives the singer an increase of inner space in which he may function more freely and fully, and it gives the tone the shimmer that comes from two rays of sound that overlap and feed each other.

As another example, let us take the "ah" vowel. When modified or darkened, it takes on an element of "oh," and when broadened or brightened, a shade of "e" (as in "bell"). There is thus within each vowel sound a certain play or possibility of variation, which gives us room in which to maneuver. The very play or variation of the model can be used to determine the vowel "next of kin" to the model and to incorporate model conditions into these not-so-good "next of kin" vowels. If correctly done, the sound will grow through the process of building new connections between vowel stimuli originally less closely related to each other. Once the extensions and modifications of the model vowel are firmly established, a vowel chain of considerable diversity has been won. Then adjustment for the production of other vowels will be easier, regardless of whether we sing in English, French, Italian, German, or any other language.

In the advanced stages of singing, all vowels should be ideally related or linked. In the beginning stages, only congenial ones should be used. The noncongenial will gradually learn to go with the rest and thus come into the fold. If a certain vowel resists efforts to produce it with vigor and "qualities," it may have to be ignored at first and left until later.

It is a mistake to jump to a problem and practice on it. How often do we hear a well-meaning singing teacher tell a student, "Your EE sounds bad, now. Let's work on it!" Unfortunately, such work consists mainly of beating one's head against a wall. A less painful and more fruitful way of attacking the problem is through the use of the basic vowel. Practicing the basic vowel will ripen and automatically develop all other vowels, by association. It is the reverse of the story of the rotten apple in the basket of good ones. Good attitudes and effective techniques are contagious. Good vowels can influence all the others for the better. Later the enemy can be coaxed into the family. We transform it into a friend by neutralizing differences, unifying it with the other vowels and then, at last, by purifying. Let us give an example. When a person has a problem with the "ee" and her best vowel is "ah," then the "ee" can be coaxed through the "ah" with a combination word, such as "mine." In the beginning, the "ee" will lose much of its independence, because it is the aim to keep it more or less in the "ah" form. One foot must stay on home base. In other words, she should allow very little change in the "ee" to take place at that time, because it must first absorb the inner opening, freedom and wealth of the "ah," which it has lacked. Gradually, it will become independent and will have as much tone freedom and as many "qualities" as the basic.

The influence on a vowel by a preceding vowel occurs through assimilation. Through the assimilation of two vowel sounds, they will become more and more intimate. The intimacy can become so strong that they will melt together into a oneness. Our objective is gradually to inject the benefit of the basic vowel function into all vowels.

If in another case, the problem child is the "ah" (as in "car"), and the model vowel is the "ee" (as in "see"), then the "ah" can be coaxed with the help of "ee." Take, for instance, the Italian word gioia (pronounced "joy-yah"). (For clarity, the explanation of the needed exercise is given in phonetic English.) The "oh" is rather unpronounced in this exercise. The "y" (that is, "ee") is sustained as the vowel denominator. "Ah" is more or less equalized into the "y" (that is, "ee") position. In the beginning, "ah" will thus lose its independence because one foot must stay on home base. From there it must first absorb the inner opening, freedom and wealth that it lacked. We must also learn how to lose our psychological fear of the black sheep. Gradually, the "ah" will ripen to the point where it becomes independent, but it will not lose the qualities of the basic. In this way the hostile vowel is gradually converted with the help of a friendly one until, without losing basic freedom and "qualities," it is ready for direct attack and pure solitary usage.

Additional exercises of a similar nature may be found in the practice words "Lear" or "dear." Lea or Lee is sustained as the vowel denominator. The "r" consonant is transformed into a slight English sort of "ah." Thus, "Lee-ah." We add a short "y" as a syllable binder or connective tissue, thus "Lee-y-ah" (or "dee-y-ah").

Another exercise for the vocalist whose problem vowel is "ee" and whose model is "ah" might be "dah-li-a" (pronounced "dah-lee-ah"). We establish the basic "dah," sustaining it until we have reached peak quality or efficiency. Then we glide into the "lee," which is unaccentuated and rather short. Then we produce the final "ah," which is again the basic.

A similar exercise, for the vocalist whose problem vowel is "ah" and model is "ee," might be "vis-à-vis" (pronounced "vee-zah-vee"). We establish the basic "vee," sustaining it until we have reached peak quality or efficiency. Then we glide into the "zah," which is unaccentuated and rather short. Finally we produce the last syllable, "vee," which is again the basic.

The "taming of a vowel" can be likened somewhat to the taming of a newly captured elephant. The introduction of an untamed or not-so-good vowel is like the introduction of a wild beast that has just been put with a tame herd. In India this is standard practice. The wild animal is left among the tame ones, where he is "put in line" and taught. Two tame elephants stand on either side of the newly introduced animal and see to it that he does as they do. The already established vowel or vowels can get underdeveloped ones into line by proper exercise and procedure, and a unity of conformation will take place in the overall picture.

Let us consider, for example, as the basic, the syllable "bay" from the word "bay-o-net." We sustain the syllable "bay" as long as necessary to establish the tone in maximum freedom and wealth. The good attack is the entrance to the good tone. Once we start correctly, a whole chain of actions is set off by itself. We must learn to attack in the center of the pitch and in the kernel of the tone. Then we connect with the neutral, unaccented "oh," without changing the basic tone stream. We can add a slight "y" consonant between the "bay" and the "oh," thus "bay-yo." The additional "y" serves as a liquid joiner and expander. The syllable "net" is then molded into the same tone stream. Throughout the exercise, the freedom and wealth of the basic must be maintained. Each syllable must stream uninterrupted into the next. Continuity of tone stream should never be lost. All adjustments have to be made so that the tone stream blossoms, its properties never decreasing from attack to cutoff. We gradually develop one unbroken tone stream into which all consonants and vowels will eventually fit without fighting.

In the exercise "bay-o-net" we have only one attack, that at the beginning. The second syllable, "oh," as well as the third, "net," run through liquid consonants, which do not stop the tone stream. If the second syllable as well as the third were to be treated as a secondary attack, the continuity or liquid streaming would be broken.

We must learn to weave syllables together so that the seams do not show. For this purpose it is often expedient to modify, weaken and/or shorten some consonants while prolonging and emphasizing others and, especially in the case of the American unrolled "r," to eliminate it completely at times. This may be difficult for an actor who has gone through a lot of consonant drill. His strong and precise use of consonants in speaking, when applied to singing, may act as a cutoff to the singing sound. Hence, many an actor may have to learn to avoid a stress of consonants in singing.

A nonliquid consonant such as the "t" in the exercise "gay-e-ty" has to be flicked on to the tone stream in such a way that, seemingly, no interruption occurs. If we overemphasize it, we will stop the tone.

Let us stress here that it is possible to render an "ah" vowel with a rather closed mouth as a perfectly free and rich tone, if the inner conditions of the individual mechanism desire or lend themselves to such a form. On the other hand, we can produce an "ee" vowel (as in "see") freely and fully with a rather wide-open mouth. A ripe organism, however, can usually perform more than one possibility for each vowel. It can produce the same "ah" vowel on the same pitch with a more or less open mouth, with equal freedom and "qualities."

A mistake frequently made in tone development is to persist in forming the stereotyped vowels frequently used in speech and in phonetic study, with mechanical mouth adjustments--for example, to think that on an "ah" vowel we must open the mouth widely and on "ee" we must smile; for an "oh" we must form a funnel shape and on "ay" we must broaden the mouth. Of course, here speech habits also must be considered. They, too, may have established similar, set patterns, which may work against free tone production. In extreme cases, the vowels are overpronounced in speech and/or singing to such a point that they are forced into preconceived molds. The vowel sounds become stale and lifeless in their rigid, pedantic positions. Unfortunate examples of this condition are found in some speech and elocution teachers. Their way of speaking has more to do with mechanics than expression. In fact, in the scholarly effort and in the mechanical process, their speech has become more or less "dehumanized."

Mouth adjustments for vowels must at all times be such that they never damage tone. The liberty to open the mouth in any reasonable way that is beneficial to tone must be stressed. After a correct tone attack has been established, the less we experiment, the better the inner vowel development will be. In practicing the exercise "bay-o-net," after establishing the basic syllable "bay," the mouth position for the "o-net" changes little. Thus, the inner development is helped by the outer immobility.

There is a tendency on the part of a beginner to overdo the differences in the mouth positions for vowels. Let us point out that it is possible to produce any vowels very clearly without perceptible movement or change of expression. The ventriloquist proves this point. Speakers and singers on television confirm it. When the television picture is on but the sound is off, we are usually unable to make out what an actor or singer is saying or singing. If mouth positions were fixed or standardized, lip reading would be an easy feat.

Exercises with unvoiced "s" consonants, as found in "Syl-vi-a," "sa-ga," "Sa-va-nnah," "Sa-mu-el," "San-an-to-ni-o," "Si-am" and "sa-li-va," are of importance for students who are prone to work with too much breath. The unvoiced "s" permits a release of excess breath prior to our establishing the correct tone attack. Without this release, the surplus breath would flood the organism---like a steam engine that does not let off surplus pressure.

A rolled "r" consonant, as found in the word "Ro-me-o," is usually a new sensation for a young American. A Russian is, so to speak, born with it. When correctly developed, a rolled "r" has a pulling power that the vowel following it can rarely resist.

Just as a Russian or an Italian is born with a rolled "r," so the English-speaking person is born with a heavily voiced final "s" and "d." (At a gathering, when we pass into another room, away from the group, although we have not been able to make out the conversation, we often hear a strong buzzing and mumble emanating from the group left behind.) As the Russian uses the "r" consonant with its pulling power, so can many of us use our voiced "s" or buzzing consonant as a conductor of sound to enrich the vowel that follows. We can attack on the buzzing "s" and from there slide into the vowel that follows, retaining the position with which we produced the buzz, but prolonging the clean, free vowel sound.

In the choice of consonants and vowels, in the way we set up the connection between them, and in the way we blend one with another, we find a means of vocal development.

Our language contains many different connections and combinations in its syllables and words. We will therefore find in the choice of existing words many that will help such vocal development. The English language, in contrast to Italian, does not have a very good reputation among vocalists. There are, however, a number of English words that possess long, pure, drawn-out vowels, which in themselves are melodious, in which the connecting of syllables is mellifluous, in which there are few if any stoppages and which are bouncy in their rhythmic patterns. If applied at the proper stage of development, such words will be of value. (See the Appendix to this book for examples.) Syllables and words should be selected for each case. They should be grouped and regrouped for each case and each stage of development. The more precisely each exercise is tailored to fit individual needs, the greater the possibility of attaining maximum benefit, efficiency and originality.

In the early stage of voice training, this special way of putting syllables and words together should serve merely as a vehicle for vocal tone or as a means to improve tone freedom and "qualities." The student must learn to feed into the words the right tonal qualifications, to let the basic tone appear and reappear in various syllable combinations. As was pointed out, later use of these syllables and words can serve to establish and develop the unchanged, unified tone stream, leading to an equalization of all vowels.

After the unchanged, unified tone stream is secured and the vowels have been equalized, articulation[15] has to be considered also, and these exercises will help to lead tone and articulation together into a happy marriage, for the benefit of the produced syllable and word, which should have freedom, quality and intelligibility. This last is relative, in singing. We must be aware of the compromises that have to be made.

Intelligibility in singing cannot always be a hundred percent pure and accurate. Thus, especially in singing high notes, an "inspired cheating" in the enunciation of vowels and consonants is a characteristic and recurrent feature. If not carried to extremes, we may consider it a necessary evil to which we resort in the hope of freeing the sound from the chains of language, when exposed vocal demands make both a good tone and good diction hazardous.

We can now venture a step further in our development and turn to more challenging tasks. We can try to produce more syllables in one breath than the average vocal phrase requires. We should gradually try to go higher and lower than the range in which singing takes place. As with a runner who trains for 200 yards in order to be able to race 100 yards successfully, a vigorous training leading to a stretching of one's faculties is essential when, and only when, the organism has been patiently and thoroughly prepared for it.[16]

Such exercises will pave the way for the discovery and establishment of model tones, syllables, words and phrases that have vocal freedom and "qualities" and therefore lead directly

into the heart of singing; for singing, as a
rule, consists of the production of phrases.
Only exceptionally does it call for something
else.

Unfortunately, many present-day singers
practice the exceptions but not the rules. They
practice in a medium they will hardly ever use
instead of the one in which they are going to
work. They do not concentrate on the technique
necessary in the exercise of their craft but
turn out busy and dizzy sequences of notes that
may follow each other in rigorous musical suc-
cessions--always with the suggestion that something is about to happen vocally; but not much
does. These singers never stay long enough on a
note to get the feel and the hold of it. Their
mode of practice is strictly hit and run. Their
constant try for roaring scales and flying ar-
peggios seems to disclose a desire to compete
with the pianist next door. In fact, many vocal
routine exercises are derived from piano exercises. "Mechanical practicing" was carried into
the field of voice when pianists worked with
singers and eventually taught voice. In the process, they then began to apply finger exercises
to the voice.

When voice students do not carry out the
sustaining of tones, syllables and words, they
neglect the graded exercises that develop phrase
singing and use an approach that runs counter to
the tone-by-tone, word-by-word, phrase-by-phrase
working and reworking that make for thorough
craftsmanship and the kind of tone-sure, worry-
free delivery that enables a vocal piece to be
finely knit.

For his purpose, a composer usually uses
phrases consisting of constant changes in pitch,
volume, duration and articulation. To produce
these with freedom and "qualities" is a task
that requires at least a reasonable productional
ripeness. Therefore, if we want to do justice to
songs and arias, our attitude should be that

there are no easy ones, there are only more or less difficult ones. Successful song and aria singing is a result. In addition to the fundamental equipment, success depends upon the preceding vocal development.

Before we concern ourselves with the result, we must first concern ourselves with the groundwork that is to lead to results. Students who involve themselves more in results than in groundwork skip basics and spend their time and energy counting the chickens before they are hatched. They may never attain results.

To sing songs and arias, as is frequently demanded of vocal beginners, can become a burden to the unripe organism, causing it to break down all too often. In many cases the effort can also have damaging psychological effects. Songs and arias maneuvered under unripe conditions, by hook or crook, will often turn out to be total losses for a lifetime. Inhibitions, fear and carry-over anxiety will have become so deeply rooted in the mind of a student that he will not be able to free himself from them, even when his voice is finally ready. Though new songs and arias of similar type and range can be handled with ease, the old ones, crippled by old associations, go on limping forever.

The vocalist who has learned throughout his range to attack, sustain, end and connect tones, syllables and words, with freedom and "qualities," has mastered the productional requirements and solved the essential technical problems of text singing.

---

Q. How can vocal weight be determined?
A. The weight of a voice can be determined only through careful diagnosis of the produced tone. Vocal weight cannot be determined mechanically. It is not read off any dial.

---

The weight of a novice boxer can be determined mechanically. He steps on the scale, and his weight is simply read. His weight class can always be approximated, whether he is in good fighting shape or not.

There are several paths open for the young voice to follow. One, of course, will always be the best one. It is the responsibility of the teacher to see that the coordinated gifts of the student dictate his basic weight formula.

The makeup of an "Irish tenor," for example, usually provides him with a mixture of overwhelming lightness and very little robustness. On the radio his voice will often sound like a contralto. His natural lyricism enables him to produce a floating phrase and to spin out many of his tones to nothingness. Sometimes a fringe of falsetto at the end makes his tones tail off ever so smoothly and sweetly. Some listeners will consider his the finest "technique." Others will criticize him for sounding thin and "emasculated" or for being merely a confectioner of vocal "bon bons." Yet, in an overly lyric voice this is often the only way in which the inborn apparatus can function.

For that type of singer, it would surely be fatal to follow the path of a Wagnerian tenor. That would cause him to overextend, to perform tasks for which he lacks the native equipment, and to produce tones contrary to his basic weight structure. What he should do is to develop his mixture with and not against his nature. His goal should be to become a legitimate lyric tenor, who may sing lightly but not without fullness.

On the other hand, the fundamental equipment of a tenor voice may provide a mixture of overwhelming robustness and little lightness. Such a voice will often sound like a baritone. Many listeners will admire its power and manliness and think it to be the result of training. Others, in contrast, may claim that this tenor sings with "all strength and no elegance" and is tiresome to listen to. Still others may even say that this type of singer is merely a bellower who is prone to "bust a gut" at any minute. Yet, the native apparatus of the overheavy voice can often function in no other way. For such a voice, to attempt a steady diet of Mozart, Rossini and Donizetti lyricism would, of course, be unfortunate. It would mean a curtailment of the natural swing. The possessor of such a voice should aim to become a good dramatic tenor, who may sing with a strong and heavy voice but not with undue force.

Many times a singer is misguided or he himself chooses the wrong weight path. Since dramatic voices are comparatively rare, the singer, motivated by opportunism, is sometimes tempted to risk unwarranted excursions into heroic molds. He usually regrets such decisions later. In his ambition towards a goal weightier than his abilities permit, he takes roads over which he is not equipped to travel and forces something alien into his voice. His voice is pushed, thickened or twisted against its nature, into the opposite weight type. A falsification of type results. Eventually, the singer may perish in his own vocal effort. In order to rise above the effort and to dispel overloaded tension, his voice must return to its original weight pattern and recover its true character and function as a lighter, more lyric instrument.[17]

On the other hand, if a young person has a naturally heavy voice, he or she will not save the voice but sabotage a part of it by allowing it only light or lyrical vocalism, as is frequently done. Such treatment would actually force a young student to produce a voice lighter than is comfortable and keep vital parts of the vocal machinery out. The ugly duckling was misunderstood and abused by everybody because he was judged by duck standards. Had he fallen into the hands of a witless teacher, who would have continued to impose duck standards on him, he would probably not have grown into a beautiful swan.

Q.  Is it worthwhile to try to change vocal
    weight?
A.  Yes. Any evidence to justify the hope that
    more lightness or robustness may improve
    tone should be explored. Moreover, if a
    healthy balance does not exist naturally in
    the voice, then changes for the heavier or
    lighter are essential. Even innate ten-
    dencies, when extreme, may prove to be disa-
    bilities.

Let us think of the "Irish tenor" voice as an
extreme on the vegetarian side. Such an overlight voice lacks the meat of robustness. Its
vocalism, similar to that of some high, pallid
sopranos, can often become monotonous. Even in
comparatively undemanding songs like "Because,"
such voices often lack the necessary body to
perform the two climaxes ("me" and "God made
thee mine"). They cannot fill up their tones
sufficiently. When they try, they thin out,
spread or crack.

In order to achieve the necessary body, the
overlight voice must gradually be expanded.
"Meat" has to be added to the tone carefully,
however, so that the natural lyricism will not
be endangered.

We add, to strengthen, yet we should not
burden. We should nurse the overlight voice until it is ready to perform with body.

On the other hand, let us think of a tenor
voice with a mixture of overwhelming robustness
and little lightness, as an extreme on the
"meaty" side. Its "blood-and-guts" production
can become monotonous. Light "fruit and vegeta-
bles" are lacking in the tone. Such a voice cannot reduce volume and bring the needed half-
voice into play. If an attempt is made, the
voice may refuse to comply and is apt to crack.

Lyricism, as for example in the last act of Aida, must be replaced by brute force or isolated falsetto. In particularly high phrases, one-sided heaviness will easily lead to strain and fatigue. For instance, in the last act of Goetterdaemmerung, Siegfried, in his narration, has to repeat in the tenor key the high phrases that the wood bird has sung previously in the soprano key. In order to perform this or similar tasks, an overheavy tenor voice tends to squeeze and tighten.

The weight influences the range.

Such a voice, since it is carrying an abnormal load, cannot climb high enough and will therefore find the upper range limited. In order to achieve the necessary balance, a gradual ratio change will have to take place. "Vegetable and fruit" must be added to the tone, so carefully that its natural vitality and power will not fade away or become atrophied.

We add, in order to refine; yet we should not weaken.

To put it another way, let us compare an overlight voice to an Austin runabout automobile which was built with only high gears; to make this car complete, low gears must be added. The overheavy voice is like a Mack truck with only one gear---the low one; the motor, of course, requires the addition of high gears. To each must be added gears of its specific type. The high gears of a Mack truck are built for a Mack truck and would be of no use in an Austin machine. Austin gears are for an Austin alone and are of no use elsewhere.

In the matter of weight, therefore, each voice needs all gears, but "to each his own." A lyric tenor must be able to sing forte, but his own forte. A dramatic tenor likewise must be capable of piano tones, but his own piano tones. Each should possess the complete dynamic range of his own mixture and of the weight of that mixture.

To achieve this, each voice must go its own way. True to its fundamental composition, the heavy or robust voice, whose sound is best when it is big, will find itself most easily when it can give out heartily. It will commence development most comfortably from a somewhat strong starting point. Of course, there are exceptions, if a workable half-voice is already present. A light voice, in contrast, which responds more to the softer sound of the instrument at its best, will "find" itself most easily at a smaller starting point, and from there can pave its way to greater power and abandon.

Some schools of vocal thought impose the same starting point for all. One school, known as the "head-tone" school of singing, insists that all students should start from a soft voice. Another insists that all pupils commence with the half-voice. Still another will prescribe starting with a full voice. This is sometimes referred to as the "shout school" of singing. To apply a fixed rule for all is a mistake. Strength should be searched for individually. Strength should be augmented where strength already exists. The strong point for starting will be that amount of volume with which the vocalist produces his freest and most promising sounds. From that strong point we will gradually branch out.

Some singers, when changing dynamics, exceed the limits of their basic weight potential. Take a Wagnerian tenor (a more or less vanishing breed) who undernourishes his soft or piano tones so that they become veiled and foggy. His voice then sounds like that of a different person. (The vain try of a bull to find his place in a china shop ends insubstantially.) Or a voice may sound strained from holding back.[18]

A lyric tenor may start the "E Lucevan Le Stelle" from Tosca with a natural, floating quality. When it comes to the dramatic parts of the aria, he will blast. His voice, incapable of such weighty force and passion, increases in volume to unfortunate levels and gets distorted in the process.

Oversharp contrasts and excesses usually result from conscious efforts, at first for characterization, shading and special effects. Later, these effects are unconsciously overdone until the effort to embroider works against the correct use of the entire instrument. The substance of the voice gets lost in a sea of variations. However, generally speaking, the substance of the voice should never disappear, regardless of what we are feeling or expressing.

Similarly, an inexperienced actor will sometimes try to become intimate in a quiet scene. As a result, he swallows syllables, and his voice vanishes.[19] At other times, when he does a part in a comedy he deliberately lightens or raises his voice so far that he finds it difficult to sustain the talking level. As a result, his voice breaks, or he becomes hoarse. Then again, in a dramatic scene he is perhaps afraid he might not impress sufficiently unless he gives the voice an extra drive. In his effort for power, he makes noise, but at a cost: he shouts, which makes it hard to distinguish the words; or he pushes, which causes the sound to become paralyzed.

All dynamics, shading, characterization and expression must work with and not against the voice and should never exceed one's weight capabilities.

A violation of this principle is often evident, in speaking or singing, because of a fear of sounding dull. A similar violation is caused by vocalists who seek to stress the meaning of the words they are singing and go overboard. This is particularly true of some singing actors and actresses. When called upon to learn a new role, they approach the score first from the point of view of the text, and consider the music later. This order is due to their creative

or recreative instincts and is not just a matter
of choice. They are text-minded or text-bound;
that is how their psyche works. Others, following the opposite path, may conceive of a vocal composition in terms of the music. In this
case the music is the stimulus or primary force
having a direct access to their emotions. Regardless of the order, it is obvious that both
music and text have to be produced by the vocal
instrument, and we should never forget that we
are working with a human sound mechanism whose
responsiveness follows laws and is subject to
limitations that should be observed at all
times.

When a marked deviation from that weight
pattern that is healthy and desirable takes
place, a gradual readjustment becomes necessary,
in order to restore a voice to normality.

A doctor, when consulted by an overweight or
underweight patient, will prescribe whatever the
case may require: diet, exercise, thyroid treatment, and so on. A wise doctor plans treatment
according to the individual needs of the patient
and endeavors to bring about a weight change
gradually.[20] He will not allow the treatment to
endanger the patient's general health in the
process. Once a proper weight is attained, the
doctor will orient the patient as to what he
must do to maintain that weight. The whole process is gradual, with careful checks and readjustments when necessary.

A voice teacher, similarly, must introduce
functional exercises, which will bring about a
healthy change in vocal weight. These exercises
may have to be revised according to the various
developments that become evident along the way.

---

Q. How can vocal weight be balanced?
A. Different amounts of weight can be given to any one pitch. Thus there is an opportunity to select and combine those most beneficial to the overall function. Through practice, one can establish or add to the amount of weight; through temporary inactivity, one can soften it. A choice in balancing and counterbalancing exists, and it must be determined by personal needs.

---

Of the component parts of a voice, the falsetto (its lightest ingredient) is the extreme at one end. The element that appears after the change of voice, which we have called its newly found sonority and which is its heaviest ingredient, is the extreme at the other end. In between we have many, varying degrees of weight mixtures. To put the matter in everyday language, an adult can imitate the voice of a woman or man. Between these extremes, it is possible to produce a number of tone variations.

In voice development, we should not overlook "male" or "female" sound productions, which exist in each individual. Male and female sound productions are opposite characteristics. The natural attraction exerted on each other by opposite characteristics can be exploited as a means of unification. This enables the voice to bring combined forces into play and guards against the exclusive, excessive use of one or the other.

In the effort to put the male and female forces into productive use, the voice is prone to encounter resistance, for, in addition to the attraction, there unfortunately also exists an essential conflict between male and female forces in the voice. Both may operate in strong opposition to each other, one separating itself sharply from the other. This tendency can be observed quite clearly in the split sounds and violent contrasts for which a contralto voice is famous, particularly in tones of the lower middle range. Almost every voice contains some variations and combinations of such conflicts. However, on the distaff side, and particularly in a contralto, the gap separating the two is often so wide and the divergence so sharp that the struggle tends to be more obvious and acute.

The very fact that even many acclaimed singers are unable to eliminate vocal difficulties caused by these gaps, or so-called register breaks, testifies to the scope of the problem. Some listeners may consider the presence of these difficulties as an individual lack of accomplishment, while, in fact, it is primarily a sign of the human vocal condition. The basic predicament is inherent in the vocal structure. Peculiar to its own distinctive structure, each voice is affected by these built-in difficulties and operates in the face of them as best it can.

Unwilling to take account of these vocal peculiarities, and unwilling also to make a concession to these consistencies, some singers and teachers deny the existence of a register problem and thereby sidestep one of the toughest of vocal issues. Or, it may be that they cannot find the problem because they are not looking for it. However, the fact that even great singers suffer from this problem should be reason enough to consider it and to work upon it. Moreover, the identification of a problem provides the first step in solving it.

Registers are included in the code of rules of vocal functioning. Registers in the voice disclose the inability of the human instrument to produce with the same approach the many different sounds needed for singing. Head and chest registers, low, middle, and high registers, for instance, are typical concepts of vocal registration. And the vocal world has grown old disputing them. All of these concepts, regardless

of controversy, divide the vocal sound system
into subcategories according to various aspects
or attributes. Thus, vocal registers are marked
by sections, which label and limit them. Gaps
and breaks in the voice are signs of these limitations.

A possible solution to the register problem
requires us to overcome these limitations, to
bridge the gaps and establish harmony between
the opposite poles. It is a matter of searching
for linking vocal traits, most of which can be
established and developed only by means of a
step-by-step progress.

To illustrate the process (frequently called
"register equalization"), it may help to consider the different vocal ingredients that are
present after the voice change and compare them
to a stocked pantry shelf. Every normal voice
possesses a supply of essentials, all of which
have something to contribute to the overall picture, provided we recognize and respect the differences established by nature, provided we understand their peculiarities and learn to make
the most of them.

The more one-sided we are in the selection
of our ingredients, the more limited will we be
in the overall function.

One fortunate pantry shelf may be stocked
with complete, prepared meals. This exceptional
pantry, like the well-balanced voice of a "born
singer," is already adequate. In the majority of
cases, however, there are no such well-stocked
pantries. Therefore, a complete inventory must
be made. In some cases, the inventory may reveal
that certain elements require purifying,
strengthening or modifying before they can be
considered usable ingredients.

The next step is to decide which components
should and can mix with one another and are thus
compatible components, capable of and needful of
complementation. The exploration should clarify
all possibilities so that recipes for a variety

of dishes may be evolved. When this has been accomplished, it will then be possible to plan a variety of healthful, well-balanced meals.

Vocally, the status of the ingredients and their willingness to blend will influence the character of each tone. Just as each dish depends not only upon its ingredients, but also upon their blend and treatment, so does the voice. When we vary a dish we change either the ingredients, their mixture or their treatment. When we vary the tones of a voice, in range, color and dynamics, a proportional change in ingredients, mixture and treatment occurs. In an untrained or uneven voice, these changes are often abrupt or "clumsy," as in the case of the contralto who can produce certain range changes only by means of yodeling. Obviously, such a voice is the victim of the change. In contrast, in a so-called even voice, these changes are so gradual and graceful that they are often hardly noticeable. We are under the acoustical illusion that we hear a vocal oneness. This voice then has become the master of the change.

However, the oneness or evenness of a voice is relative. For example, a singer who is acclaimed by the critics as having an even scale will still reveal differences in loudness and intensity on different pitches. If a singer were to sing his top tones with the same loudness with which he produces the bottom tones, he would be criticized for the weakness of his high tones, because to be considered even in scale, a voice must vary throughout its range.

A knowledge of these variations is invaluable, in the fields of vocal production and reproduction as well as in vocal art. Let us assume that a composer writes a duet for two sopranos. Every so often she may want one soprano to sound louder or stronger than the other, so as to provide contrast and emphasis. She needs only to compose higher notes for the voice that is supposed to outshine the other.

The effects of rising and falling tides of vocal intensity are quite striking. Take, for example, the old-fashioned radio or recording studio. There the engineer had to adjust the controls on high notes in order to avoid having a singer "blast the mike," a manipulation that he certainly did not need to perform on middle or lower pitches.

Riding the ebb and tide of tonal intensity can provide a consistently effective use of vocal contrasts, which serve both artistic and technical purposes. The ability to change over from ebb to tide and vice versa prevents us from being stuck in only one vocal track, which is tiring. It also gives us a choice for tone quality control. If one degree of intensity does not produce good sound, we can change to another.[21] Thus we may find greater tone value through greater tone choice.

For the sake of voice culture, a student must learn to produce the changes and contrasts in the voice with as much ease, accuracy and assurance as is possible. The mistake is to try to prevent them. Such prevention, unfortunately, is common among a number of female singers, for commercial reasons. It is well-known that American taste makes a sharp division between Lieder, opera and operetta singing on one side, and popular, musical comedy, and nightclub singing on the other. For the latter, by and large, the public prefers a low, masculine or chest voice. The former, in contrast, is based on the use of the so-called regular voice, which employs both chest and head voice. In order to satisfy the taste of the musical comedy, pop and nightclub audiences, the exclusive use of the female voice for belting purposes has become more fashionable. When girls sound much like boys, the effect may appeal to our sense of perversion or may have shock value, but the question is, at what price? There are, of course, robust voices that can take this type of vocal work without paying a penalty.

Lately the entertainment field, with its typecasting, has also been seeking to get hold of lighter, higher and more lyric voices. However in working on the musical numbers of a show, a composer, director or producer may command: "Only chest voice, please," meaning: "Distort yourself for our purposes." This puts demands on a voice that singers can rarely fulfill without strain. This strain is often greatly increased by the cliché: "Let's put the whole song in a higher key to make it sound brighter." As a result, the songstress may eventually suffer organic damage.

Let us remember, however, that changes and differences are an integral part of vocal functioning. They must be permitted to occur; otherwise the various contributing vocal sources are restricted in feeding the voice. When we see a river flowing majestically toward the ocean, we may picture a mighty oneness. We should realize that what makes that river flow so evenly are the many streams, rivulets, brooks and other sources that are feeding it. A variety of developed and coordinated functions will result in vocal unity in the overall picture. The more ingredients added, developed and coordinated, the more resplendent the result.

It is a mistake to skip over the work of unifying and to seize immediately upon certain technical tricks. To even out a voice, the young student is advised, for instance, to "localize toward one point" throughout the range or to "cover" artificially. Let us attempt here to clarify the term "cover." When an untrained baritone, for example, sings an upward scale on the vowel "ah," he usually arrives at vocal crossroads. When he reaches the upper notes, he comes to a point where suddenly he finds two ways of voice production that appear to be rather far apart. The fact that the pathways diverge is characteristic of that range section. Now there is a choice to be made---unfortunately, one between two extremes. Whichever way he chooses will not seem to be quite right. (1) On the higher notes, he may try to use a production similar to that used on the lower notes. Still, the character of the upper notes will change. His voice will sound broader and brighter. (In singer parlance, this is usually called "open.") Eventually, the higher he sings, the more the open sound will resemble the shout of a barker. (2) He may try to change the production or, as the case may be, he may give in to a change of production that the voice seems to desire. Then, the upper notes will usually sound darker and more "gathered in." (In singer parlance this is usually called "covered.") In its extreme, a covered tone will eventually sound closed and "muffled." It is assumed that the terms "open" and "covered," which are used in the field of voice, derive from a comparison with "open" and "covered" (gedeckt) organ pipes, and the contrasting sounds that these produce.

As in most any case in vocal technique, where two possibilities of production exist, speculation as to which is better develops into a controversy. Vocal extremists stand ready to capitalize on the controversy, trying to convince the profession that only the one or the other approach is the right one. Thus, according to one vocal approach, which advocates open tone production, closed or covered singing does not develop an "open throat." In the view of another, open singing is bound to tax the muscular system of the throat whereas covered tone production is an important equalizer of the voice range and also makes the ascending into higher pitches easier.

To try to make both sides win must be the aim in voice training. It is the recognition of this double destination that is essential. In some range sections, the produced tone may appear as a bridge between the two modes of production. In both of these, the tone must be strongly rooted, and of the two the tone cannot afford to give up either.

In other range sections, the sound follows the accidents of the vocal terrain like a rivulet and makes detours around obstacles and obstructions. In view of these, the continuity of the vocal line is affected. The stream of sound becomes narrower or wider. As a result, some of the produced sounds may emerge as either too closed or too open.

For many singers the establishment of a level between the two extremes or the production of a happy medium requires a step-by-step process. In this process, the student must learn to gain full technical control over the combined vocal functions. This is achieved when freedom and "qualities" of tone are not reduced but fully maintained regardless of pitch and transitions.

In the effort "to get over the hump" and to conquer the technical problems that trouble tones at the transition point, one school of vocal thought, in its quest for quick results, will prescribe: "All baritones must place the voice 'back' from F flat on upwards." Another will advise: "Raise the palate"; still another: "Up and over." Such sweeping generalizations can do more harm than good. Granted, some of these devices may occasionally be part of a tuning or adjusting process, but we must not confuse a part with the whole. These devices are neither cure-alls nor short-cuts. They cannot serve as a substitute for the work necessary to develop and coordinate the voice. When that work progresses, those problem sounds that struggle at the transition point will become fewer in number. Eventually, when the voice has been unified through development, no need for fixing or arbitrary switching will exist. The automatic switch will be on. The functions will regulate themselves. There is equilibrium in the process of change.

The Irish tenor is, of course, the typical example of a vocalist who is riding the light elements of his voice. If he were to develop its heavier ingredients and integrate them with the rest of his voice, he might find new substance and solidity in the tone. In addition, this treatment should help him to overcome a fault sometimes found in such light voices; namely, that of being pulled up by a lack of sufficient weight and, as a result, singing sharp.

The overrobust tenor, in contrast, exemplifies a singer who is riding the heavy elements of his voice. If he could learn not to rely exclusively on the weighty production but could develop the lighter ingredients and integrate them with the rest of his voice, he might find new relief. Cushioning influences may be recognized. They loosen the tone and add mellowness to its quality. They also serve as a safety device that prevents the tone from breaking or, at least, diminishes the risk of its breaking or cracking.

In the development of tone quality, the incorporation of the lighter and/or heavier ingredients influences the sound. In addition, the admixture of the lighter elements should help an overrobust tenor to overcome a fault often found in very heavy voices; namely, that of being pulled down from the proper pitch by too much weight and, as a result, singing flat. In the correction of pitch, the development and coordination of light or heavy ingredients will play an important part by enabling a singer to hit the center of a tone rather than over or under it.

In addition, the limitations of range may be extended. In the development of range, the incorporation of the lighter ingredients will ease the load that an overheavy voice carries, toward the top. The incorporation of the heavier ingredients will add bottom to an overlight voice. As a result, an overlight voice can pave its way more easily toward the usually not-so-good low notes. The overheavy voice will find it easier to branch out toward the not-so-good or not-yet-possible high notes.

Before we expand range, we must make sure that our organism is prepared to cope with the stretching. If the voice is brittle or over-heavy, such expansion would be as difficult as an attempt to stretch a stick of brittle, dried taffy. As we must moisten taffy slightly to make it pliable and stretchable, so should we add the lighter ingredients before attempting to extend the upper vocal range of a heavy voice. If we stretch before adding the lighter ingredients, we will be stretching only a part of a voice. To stretch only a part over the whole required range, necessitates undue effort. We should never stretch further at one time than the mechanism can take without tightening.

In addition to ingredients, there is a se-cond factor that will help to balance the weight of a voice, and that is shades. In going from a bright and open sound to a darker one on the same pitch, we will observe differences in the weight of the tone. Conversely, when we go from a dark to a bright sound on one pitch, an equal change of weight will become apparent. As tone color changes, tone weight changes also. Hence, varying tone color offers a means by which to vary tone weight. In choosing vocal shades, we therefore find a means of vocal development.

Darkening a shade will reduce the brass of a tone. The brittle voice, one with too much brass, must therefore learn to add darkness in shade in order to improve its sound. In con-trast, more open and brighter sounds, especially when produced in full voice, will add to brass. Hence, the voice with too little edge, which lacks kernel, must learn to add brightness in shade in order to improve its sound.

We should remember, however, that even a slight change in vocal production may have large vocal consequences. Therefore, any vocal change should take place gradually and carefully, and when necessary with readjustments. To make this change a matter of impatient, artificial, trick work is a mistake. Some of us know the comedian who uses a "voice lesson" as skit material. His first voice teacher tells him, "Your voice needs more brightness" and tries to incorporate some parrot twang in a hurry. The next teacher says, "Your voice needs more darkness" and impatiently makes him yawn into a hoot owl. Thus the functions of singing, instead of being reasonably expanded, step by step, are thrown from one extreme to the other. The proverb "Less would be more" is all too true in this instance. All physical development depends upon wise step-by-step progress. The omission of any steps will endanger the entire result.

The same applies to all vocal adjustments. The bigger the adjustment at any one time, the smaller the result. In other words, when we jump at it, we throw something else out of gear.

In a well-trained voice, darkness and brightness should never be present in the extreme. One of the two may occasionally have the upper hand, yet a sufficiency of each should be present in every tone, to avoid isolation. If too much brightness exists, the depth and roundness of tone will be impaired; if too much darkness, the ring and brilliancy will be lost.

To arrive at the correct overall balance in shade, the student must gradually learn to produce all so-called dark vowels like "oo" (as in "who") with a certain brightness and all so-called bright vowels like "ee" (as in "see") with an element of darkness. When these extremes are brought together beneath one roof, it is not necessary to resort to deliberate covering. Covering, when consciously produced, in its extreme, can lead to tonal shutoff.

The in-between vowels "ue" (as in the German umlaut or the French word "tu") and the "oe" (as in the German umlaut), both of which combine darkness with brightness, can be considered two-in-one vowels. By the very nature of their shape and color, these vowels may serve as bridges in bringing brightness and darkness together.

In addition to ingredients and shades, a third factor can help in the weight-balancing process: dynamics. In going from a soft to a loud sound on one pitch we will observe a change from a lighter to a heavier tone. And, of course, when we go from a loud to a soft sound on the same pitch, an equal change in weight will become noticeable. As tone volume changes so does tone weight. Consequently, varying tone volume offers the means by which to vary tone weight. In the choice of vocal dynamics we therefore find means of vocal development.

To swell the tone will make it heavier; to diminish tone will make it lighter. The connecting function, the swelled tone, with its varying dynamics, has been recognized in its importance as long as singing has existed as an art. Our goal is to swell and diminish tone without a break.

While an overheavy tenor, in order to add lightness in texture, must learn to develop and gradually incorporate the softer dynamics, an overlight tenor, in order to add robustness in texture, must learn to develop and gradually incorporate the stronger dynamics.

In between extremely light and heavy voices, we find voices of many different proportions. For each singer, whatever his or her type, from coloratura to bass, it is of the utmost importance to consider this question: Do I have sufficient lightness and robustness so that they will counterbalance each other and make for a healthy coexistence?

Sometimes a proper counterbalance exists in

part of the range. This part, where opposites meet and merge, may serve as a starting point from which to establish proper balance in weight throughout the range.

Voices that are naturally well-balanced in weight throughout are by far in the minority. Most are either too light or too heavy and are thus limited. To establish a well-balanced texture throughout the range usually involves a gradual development.

In vocal development our aim must be to purify, integrate and link the light, the heavy and the in between elements so that they complement the whole as much as our natural gifts allow. A tonal fusion will then result. The sound evolves as a product of the interplay of the lighter and heavier elements. Then, lightness and robustness can pass from one to the other, letting themselves be carried, nourished and fulfilled by each other. This will condition the voice so that a well-balanced texture will be present at all times. By comparison, in an intricate woolen fabric, parts of the design may be of a close, thick weave and others of a loose, porous type; the basic material, however, is all wool.

The more advanced our development, the more rapid, precise and consistent will be our ability to produce a well-balanced texture and to acquire a firmly spun tone, so that, whether we use it in a thick or thin vocal weave, it will wear equally well.

**Q.  Is it wrong to use falsetto?**

**A.  As a last resort, it is wrong. As an end in itself, if not overdone, its use can be a matter of taste. As a means toward an end, the function can be of great value. It may help us to add to a voice as a whole both contrasting and complementary components.**

As to its use as a last resort, let us take, for example, the tenor who was forced to replace a required softness by singing certain top tones in an isolated falsetto. This, for him, was the only choice. A drastic example in this connection can be found in a recording of the opera Tristan and Isolde. In the duet close to the end of the first act, the tenor has to sustain a high A in forte on "Lie" (beslust). The previous phrases are high, and the whole duet is certainly not easy. In this recording the tenor, incapable of attacking and sustaining the full tone, was forced to switch to an isolated falsetto tone as a last resort before capitulating.

As an end, the falsetto is sometimes used for an effect. As such it has its admirers as well as its enemies. The tenor Richard Tauber, for instance, used it and thrilled so many listeners that few critics dared to find fault with it. Cantors, too, frequently use the falsetto.

As a means towards an end, falsetto is one of the component parts of the voice. If we abandon it, we waste it. Hence, we deprive ourselves of an ingredient that, if treated correctly, may contribute materially to the whole voice, enhancing its value and health.

Compared with the rest of the vocal instrument, the falsetto is the most unused or virginal part and thus it is usually not affected by the same bad habits that may invade the regular voice. Switching to the falsetto, therefore, may give a student a feeling of more vocal freedom.

Because of its light texture, the practice of falsetto tones can give a student a feeling of vocal looseness and floating ease. Because of its higher range, the falsetto can give a student a feeling that top notes can be produced, after all, without strangling. Because of its different vocal cord action, switching to the falsetto and then returning to the regular voice may have a conditioning influence on the instrument. Making the vocal cords vibrate in a different way and using this different mode of vibration as a sort of vocal cord treatment or massage may help people who suffer from vocal disorders or from voice strain. In addition to therapeutic value, this treatment may serve as a cleanser for the voice. Its use is appropriate when the sound of the regular voice is bothered by phlegm, cloudiness or fuzziness. Finally, since opposites attract each other, one type of tone production can serve as a vehicle for its opposite. Juggling the opposites or switching to a falsetto and then returning to the regular voice---sometimes called a protest technique---may supply added voltage to the original charge and benefit the sound of the regular voice. Precisely this action-reaction phenomenon, which may be used to fuel the sound of the whole voice, may serve as a potent means to improve tone quantity, quality or both.

It is clear, then, that falsetto is a study in vocal contrast. Since we can work on the falsetto as well as on the regular voice, we can work on both ends of the voice and see what each of the two can do for the voice. The task would be to exploit the contrast between the two functions.

Some vocalists have an aversion to the falsetto, a matter that brings us to the emotional factor in reactions to vocal sound. The use of falsetto in such cases may have to be avoided in order to prevent mental tortures and vocal "allergies."

To some male singers, "falsetto" is a word of disrepute. Perhaps the type of sound they produce in falsetto is a bit of a threat to their masculinity. It does bear a resemblance to choir boys, eunuchs, or castrati.

To quote Lilli Lehmann, How to Sing: "Most male singers---tenors especially---consider it beneath them, generally, indeed, unnatural or ridiculous, to use the falsetto, which is a part of all male voices, as the head tones are a part of all female voices. They do not understand how to make use of its assistance, because they of- ten have no idea of its existence or know it only in its unmixed purity, which is its thin- nest quality. Of its proper application, that is, its necessary admixture with chest reso- nance, they have not the remotest conception. Their singing is generally in keeping with their ignorance.

"The mixture is present, by nature, in all kinds of voices, but singers must possess the skill and knowledge to employ it, else the natu- ral advantage goes for nothing.

"The most perfect singer that I remember in my Berlin experience was Theodor Wachtel, in this respect . . . . Phrasing, force, fullness of tone, and beauty were perfect."

In addition to Wachtel, one of the greatest lyric tenors of his time, Lilli Lehmann also mentions as an example Betz, one of the greatest dramatic baritones of his time.

In the face of such vocal magnificence and in the light of historic fact, and inasmuch as falsetto has in many cases been a help, could we not believe that those who generally condemn falsetto are biased?

Undeveloped, the function may sometimes sound impotent, depending upon the fundamental composition of the voice and the stage of its development. The more meager the falsetto, and the more it is isolated, the less it will com- plement a voice as a whole. The more the freedom

and "qualities" of the falsetto are developed
and the more it is integrated with the regular
voice, the greater its value. When two, originally independent vocal functions interact with
each other, the result is a fusion of them in a
new and superior technical constellation, which
enables a voice to function on two wave lengths
simultaneously.

Falsetto and the rest of the voice should
not only co-exist, they should be cross-ferti-
lized, so that they reinforce and refine each
other as much as the nature or structure of a
voice permits.

---

**Q.  How does one develop range?**
**A.  Range development results from tone develop-
ment. It is not a goal toward which we
should work separately. Before good, new
pitches can be produced, we must first turn
not-so-good tones---which are stumbling
blocks---into stepping-stones.**

---

The acquisition of additional range depends upon
preparation. Governed by the law of physical development, the process requires the incorporation of those elements that support growth.
Future pitches germinate from the body of the
present ones.

Range chasing, typified by the usual or unusual sounds emanating from some studios in our
most venerated music halls, is often a vain effort to carry too much too high. This results
more often in straining than training.

In the majority of cases, especially in male
voices, the heavy elements carry the burden.
These elements are impatiently driven to altitudes where they can no longer operate healthfully. Driving a voice upward against its will,
to take some extra steps, is like whipping a
horse to carry loads over high mountain passes,

where a pack mule should have been employed.

Increasing voice range means increasing the quantity of its pitches. The very aim for quantity has blinded many a vocalist to the true nature and order of range expansion. Healthful range extension comes out of the surplus of tone freedom and fullness that we must first build up on good present tones, which then spills over onto not-so-good tones, and then on to virgin territory.

To develop one's full potential range is a problem for many vocalists. A singer may spend sleepless nights over it. A typical example is the case of Enrico Caruso, who, while already established in Europe, cracked on many high tones and became the master of his top voice only after many years of study.

A fortunate voice student may find the solution to his range problem merely by working on his own courage. Students who are not aware of the range they possess or who do not have the confidence to produce all they have, can be shown how to do it quickly. They will discover that the pitch is not even as high as the fear was. Once they get over a feeling of newness when reaching there, they will laugh at their former obsession with being unable to make it. Eventually, they will forget that they had not been able to do it.

In some cases, a block in developing full potential voice range may occur because of psychological reasons. A female student may exclaim, "I hate to cope with the low Mama Bear parts of my voice." Or, the other way around: "My soprano bit gets on my nerves. Singing high reminds me of a warped Hollywood soubrette." Or, again, "I can't think happy and sing low," or "I think of death when I am singing low."

Not only one's singing voice, but the range of one's speaking voice, is affected by such choices, idiosyncrasies and aversions. For example, there is the person with an unconscious desire to remain a child. She will take refuge in vocal babyland, associated, of course, with a high speaking voice. On the other hand, there is the person who is afraid of sounding girlish. She will not allow herself that femininity. Just as a more masculine-minded female is accustomed to talking in the lower range and may at first be revolted by searching out the higher tones in her voice, so will a childlike person perhaps at first rebel against the use of low tones because of their masculine connotation.

The cure lies mainly in overcoming these misconceptions, biased views and unfortunate associations. Much depends upon the teacher's skill in manipulating the feeling of the student with respect to the sound she produces. The goal is to bring about a change in spirit and to create a new, accepting attitude within the student so that she is willing to utilize the existing, unexplored high and low range sections in her voice.

To deal with the psychic process and to revise conceptions is usually not as difficult as dealing with range limitations of a physical or structural nature. However, an organic inability to reach all the needed notes of the scale prevails in most voice students who have range problems. Because of the relative slowness with which the vocal organism grows and the muscles extend, no get-rich-quick scheme is possible. The student must find fulfillment in mostly unspectacular rewards of slow and patient practice. Each not-yet-possible link must gradually be established and equalized before the range chain is complete.

Unfortunately, the sense of highness is so often connected with strain in the voice, and a false idea that the voice is reaching its limit often has a very deep seed. The student admits: "When I am thinking of going high, I get nervous and tense," or "I can't go any higher unless I get a new throat." A step-by-step process is therefore required to eliminate anticipatory tension and the particular sense of wrong effort on high notes. Indeed, height as a fear factor is common---not only in voice.

Once tone freedom is established in the upper range, top tones tend to feel lower than before. This may at first startle a student. He exclaims, "Singing is not the physical effort I thought it was," or "The top and the bottom no longer seem so far apart," or "The keyboard seems to have come down." A temporary key uncertainty may then set in. This is not a bad fault. It is, in fact, a normal reaction to the change that has occurred. The student is not singing off key; he has no real pitch trouble. He merely thinks he is singing, for instance, the note D while he is really singing E. The student will so much welcome the feeling of "nothing to it" that he will gladly take into stride the trade involved in the learning process: the temporary loss of ability to guess accurately the pitch he is producing for the permanent gain of a greater degree of functional ease. (This goes to show that there can even be an advantage to a seeming disadvantage.) In time, the student will adjust to the difference in feeling, and key uncertainty will subside.

Voice students who have absolute pitch will be spared this uncertainty but will also be deprived of its advantage, the beneficial element of surprise. Their teachers cannot capitalize on this element because such students cannot be fooled as to pitch. This is a device frequently used in voice teaching to reduce the anxiety of a person facing the limits of his range.

The extension of voice range takes time. The impatient range chaser, unaware that time is on his side, makes time work against him. He wants to make every moment so valuable that the moments spent become valueless. He is always trying to get more work and range out of his voice than it is capable of, and he forever overextends himself.

How many ambitious contraltos do we know who hardly have the range for Carmen but take a crack at Amneris in Aida, then end up in tears, exclaiming, "I'll never make it"---which is, of course, very true.

Worse still, some beginners may be under the impression or may be told that they are baritones, so they buy vocal scores or sheet music and begin to sing the repertoire in the baritone key. When the music lies high, they sound as if they were tearing themselves apart. Even when they themselves do not realize strain, these beginners produce practically all top tones with a sort of strangulation quality, which is then often explained with the remark, "It was just a matter of thinking the high notes incorrectly," or "It happened only because the top notes were placed too far back instead of in front." But that is not where the trouble lies. The truth of the matter is simpler: The voice is just not naturally equipped to go that high. Therefore, it is not ready for baritone range, though it may show baritone promise in timbre, weight and size. Thus, a baritone he may be, but he just has not yet learned how to be one.

No concept, device or trick can correct these unfortunate high notes, for it is not a matter of correcting faulty technique or looking for error-correcting devices. The cause does not lie in a lack of knowledge about technique. It is rather a question of coping with inadequacy in the native equipment and overcoming vocal limitations. Constitutional and hereditary factors determine these limitations.

Unripe or muscularly prohibitive notes are not accessible to constructive work and do not respond to any direct intervention. They must, therefore, be temporarily declared "off limits." There is no use in trying for things that are beyond reach or stand no chance of success.

If we do not evade the challenge but go right after it and hit these high tones, we will

not ease the range problem but merely intensify
it into a crisis, such as hoarseness or
cracking. (This goes to show that vocal inaction
is sometimes better than action.)

    To gain more range one must first use less.
Demands put upon range must first be reduced
according to fitness. Only that part should be
used that can be produced with tone freedom.
Thereafter, beginners must be willing to undergo
the gradual training process and accept the
natural progression that "practicing up to it"
requires.

    Natural progression is, however, irregular
in its successions. Voice range consists of sections, not of one piece. In the average voice of
an untrained singer we can notice a tendency to
produce the tones until the voice reaches the
limit of a section. Then the voice suddenly
switches to something else---another section.
The singer remarks: "It jumps to a different
part of me." A lack of continuity in the vocal
line results.

    Voice range develops in these sections, and
certain sections of the range take longer to mature than others. In the course of a lesson, a
beginner may discover: "I seem to be in orbit
today," whereas in the next session he may complain: "I don't seem to be able to reach any
altitude today." But though his top notes may
not respond, the middle or lower tones may come
through more freely and fully than before. Particularly in the early stages of voice training,
we should follow the inclinations of the vocal
instrument, take whatever comes our way, and,
looking for "juicy bits" wherever they may appear in the range, establish them through use
and practice and build on them. Eventually,
these "bits" will extend so that the voice feels
more uniformly free and full throughout its
range.

    In addition to following the inclinations or
self-will of a voice, it is feasible to approach

the range problem in a more formalized and calculated way. Different notes work differently.
Different notes need different treatment. The
functional differences between the lower, the
middle and the upper vocal range must be recognized. The student must learn to hear and feel
what the vocal elements are that dominate one
vocal section as opposed to other sections, and
how part of these elements can be built up and
down to improve the continuity of the vocal
line.

The functional differences between the lower, the middle and the upper vocal range can be
exploited by means of vocal exercises. Working
from the bottom up will, generally speaking, encourage the more robust vocal elements (particularly when done in full voice). Conversely,
working from the top down will usually feed the
voice more lightness. In the choice of different
pitch successions or intervals, we can find effective means by which to develop vocal balancing factors. These will have a conditioning
influence on the weight of the voice and may
also improve our ability to link or tie on from
one range section to another.

Some beginners who do not realize that voice
range can be utilized in various ways for vocal
development resort to range chasing, because
they figure that running up and down the scale
is the only expansion the voice is capable of.

Most of us, at one time or another, have had
to cross a shallow stream. Those who got their
feet wet will well understand the comparison intended here. No two stones are quite the same.
Some may be well settled in the bed of the
stream. Others may be loose and ready to roll
the minute any weight is put upon them. It is
possible, of course, to cross the stream, if one
is resourceful and fortunate in carrying out the
idea of putting one's weight on the secure
stones and treading lightly on the shaky ones.
But what is to strengthen the shaky ones? Will

they ever be able to support us? To continue to
tread lightly and rapidly on the insecure stones
may not expose the weaknesses but will never
cure them, and the day will surely come when insecure stones will have to support weight. What
then? Attacking, sustaining and ending the tone
or tones in a phrase are demands for which a
voice brought up on scale running is unprepared. When such demands fall on weaker notes,
the singing will be shaky. The voice is apt to
slip. This is usually the time when a bag of
tricks is opened. One is advised that vocal
phrases relying on insecure notes are to be produced "lightly." One must not put too much
strain on the "weak sisters." Or a teacher will
perhaps try to make a student forget the technical problem entirely and, by overemphasizing expression, will seek in vain to maneuver him
across the stream via the crutch of "superemo-
tion."

Granted, at certain stages of vocal development, the superimposing of certain emotional and
mental attitudes in the form of suggestions such
as "get determined," "be more bored," "work under a fierce cloud" may produce results. The use
of these suggestions may put us into a different
mood and may exert a conditioning influence upon
our energy level. There are, of course, good or
positive influences, which help the individual
or turn her on. Conversely, there are bad or negative influences, which steer her in a wrong
direction and turn her off. What response a given stimulus will evoke is the question.

It is a well-known fact that every so often
someone will surprise us because of obvious
changes in voice, posture, expression, or similar characteristic. These changes are the result
of shifts in feeling. Each person has at his
disposal a certain number of such psychological
dynamics, and each person can shift with varying
degrees of ease from one state to another. The
states can be tested and their vocal worth can

be determined by means of comparison. Our task
is to dig out the arsenal of attitudes or
feelings and look for the ones most closely connected with vocal freedom and fullness. By
trying to isolate those factors, one student may
find out, "I seem to be best when I put myself
in a sort of sleeplike state." Still another
will say, "Laughing it out or crying it out"
seems to do the trick. Again, another student
will explain, "My telephone voice seems to get
me on the right track."[22] For the development
of the vocal mechanism, however, the use of such
attitudes and moods can be of only a general
value. They can merely serve as the means by
which an artist incites his tools. Hence, the
emotions and attitudes that can trigger the
voice into successful action (which will prove
lasting) belong to a very limited category. They
do not provide a base for the control of vocal
sound. Therefore, they cannot serve as a definite foundation upon which to build a vocal
technique. They cannot serve as a substitute for
the discipline and thoroughness of basic tone
study. Above all, they cannot replace the graded
basic tone exercises without which a "scale-
happy" voice suffers.

In later stages of development, a trick may
produce an effect but a trick cannot build. Before we start using tricks, a sturdy foundation
has to be laid that will support the demands of
maturity.

Scale running is a connecting and speeding
function. Before we can benefit from running and
connecting tones, we must first establish control over the right basic tone. Otherwise, instead of moving with freedom, fullness and flexibility from one note to another, we will be
doing the wrong thing: "up, down and fast."

Let us always remember: The vocal mechanism
that is not able to produce tones with freedom
cannot cope with other problems, such as adjusting to ever-changing pitch conditions in

scale work. Let us not put a strained framework to an additional task.

Let us repeat the principle for range development. Perfect strength where strength exists, and in that way develop a model strength. Then, infiltrate into weaker notes or into virgin territory, gradually.

When new tones are thin, they can be fattened up through continuous tone exercise. However, we must treat them gently. They will not fatten healthfully through forcing. When new tones are crude, they can be smoothed out and loosened up through a step-by-step process.

The difference between a range chaser and a nonchaser is simply this: Whereas the chaser, who persists in too much too soon, may never make it, the nonchaser, who approaches the range problem with patience and constructive, systematic work, sometimes persisting in the development of only a halftone at a time, has a fair chance of eventually succeeding.

---

**Q.   What is the best way to warm up the voice?**
**A.   The approach must be: Take what comes first. Harness it. Then add to it.**

---

It is a matter of courtesy---giving the voice a chance---treating your voice as you want it to treat you. Use it, but don't abuse it.

Forcing often begins with impatience. In waking up or warming up, gentleness and consideration are often forgotten in the daily drive for fast results and for volume. Many of us try to be too good and loud after too little warming up. The temptation sometimes exists to "grab the voice and kick it around." But a voice rebels against such rough treatment.

Frequently a voice feels unstretchable and needs considerable time until it gets used to being worked. Then, we must first settle for

less, then coax it, and sometimes work it in
small daily doses. It is indeed annoying when we
have to start at an almost nothing level. However, it is necessary to see first what the
vocal weather is like and then to accept in good
faith whatever condition exists and whatever
level of performance is available, in order to
rise above that level.

We must not forget that our energy level
varies. Sleep, climate, the digestive tract,
nervous system, and other factors will make for
daily change in our disposition. It is natural
that a vocalist will become aware of biological
and pyschological influences mainly in the organs concerned with voice production, as will a
dancer in the functions pertaining to dancing.[23]

We must learn to put up with a certain degree of inconsistency and fluctuation in physical development. Some rise and fall in vocal
efficiency is unavoidable. Vocal strength will
not establish itself uniformly all the time. The
voice does not work with equal strength and ease
each day. Tones that do come through best in the
beginning will vary.

Don't expect the operation of the voice to
start smoothly, and don't be discouraged when
the first tones produced are not so good. Think
of your television set. When you first turn it
on, the operation is sometimes rather poor. If
you just leave everything alone, the operation
picks up, and the performance improves by itself
as the set warms up. However, if you manipulate
it right from the start, you are apt to throw
the tuning out of kilter and the picture off
base.

After the warm-up, when the voice is not
quite what you think it should be, don't give up
by just saying to yourself, "I am in bad voice"
and leaving it at that. Don't settle for less
than you can try for. Pick up the challenge.
Practice, and do it genuinely, even if it is

less good. Use and trust your technical facilities. Try different ways to make it work. If you
work correctly, you may do especially well when
you are indisposed. The reason for this is often
largely psychological. The "I must be good"
pressure is off. You are not in conflict with
your self-expectation. You are acquitted of obligation and freed from self-blame. After all,
it's the cold's fault, you might say. As a result, you will drive yourself less. The instrument will respond favorably to a more indulgent
and kinder approach.

Of course, if you are really sick, you belong in bed. If you are forced to perform nevertheless, you must try to salvage from the impurity of the existing conditions whatever you
can, in the best way you can.

We cannot cure our disposition. But we can
learn how to deal with it and make the most of
it. We may be able to improve our functioning,
if we are clear about the proper strategy, if we
take up tasks in an appropriate order and stick
to that order.

The proper order for warming up as well as
for performing is: Test the instrument. See what
you have (that particular day and at that particular moment of the day). Never do more than you
have to, but use your voice and milk it. It will
gradually spread or extend by itself. In this
way, you will support nature. This keeps you
afloat under any and all conditions. However,
when you seek what isn't there and immediately
try for it, your approach will be negative; you
will be working against nature and you may never
make it.

Practice makes perfect. Don't wait to practice until the spirit moves you. It may not move
you often enough. Spasms of enthusiasm will not
suffice. Don't give in to the idea, "I feel so
uninspired today." Think of the French saying,
"The appetite comes with the eating." Stop for a
second after each exercise, to avoid piling one

exercise on top of another. Profit by the wait. A rest can give you a return of power.[24] Without a pause, you may "overheat" your tools. You can work only as much at a time as your equipment lets you. Like an athlete, you can overtrain. However, in one way or another, your constitution announces its needs and will rebel against the overuse. Remember, to practice well you must learn to set your own pace and know when to stop. To quote the German saying: "When it tastes best, stop eating."

If, as yet, you can't feel how to pace yourself, it's better to be too slow than too fast; it's better to do too little than too much, when you work on the voice by yourself. Rushing through a practice session is as bad as rushing through a meal.

Phlegm is the year-round bane of the vocalist. A certain amount you have to put up with. It's part of the game. Whenever it is not there, count your blessings, and take it as an exception. Whenever it is there, accept it as the rule. Phlegm may not hit you throughout the entire voice range but may appear or disappear on higher or lower range levels, much as clouds appear and disappear in various altitudes on the horizon. There is perhaps such a thing as "phlegm-producing weather." It is good to condition yourself to phlegm and to think of it as a protective film rather than a hostile element. Picasso regarded the dust that had accumulated in his studio as a protective element for his paintings and would not permit anyone to remove it. Through patient vocalizing, you can usually dislodge the phlegm and clear it away. If you don't mind speaking or singing a "duet" with your own phlegm, while warming up, you will usually come through more quickly, easily and healthfully than the eternal "throat clearer." When you clear your throat, you are cruel to it because you scratch it, and, as with scratching mosquito bites, the temptation is great but should be resisted lest you make things worse. Throat clearing is often a nervous habit.[25] Try to avoid it. Swallow instead.

There are phlegm-producing foods. Milk products, particularly when taken prior to performing, may have a coating influence on the voice. The type of nutrition as well as the amount to be consumed and the length of time before performing that it should be consumed are factors that may have to be closely watched by an artist. While a slim vocalist without a sufficient basis of food supply may complain, "I feel empty inside and can't give my all," stout people may feel burdened, inflexible and sluggish when eating much or shortly before performing.

Steam heat may have an unfortunate influence on the vocal tract. To avoid a dry feeling in nose, mouth, throat, make sure that a sufficient amount of moisture is present at all times in your living and sleeping quarters.

Instead of placing the voice early, which is easily overdone, just do it. Cut loose and forget it. Don't be too analytical for your own good. Don't let your mind get in your way. Don't encroach on your instincts: they may function better when left alone. Make the sounds spontaneously and allow the voice, first, to place itself.

Don't try forever to find meaning behind meaning. You may overprocess things and complicate them, and create pseudo problems. Your spontaneity will suffer. You may even lose the ability to make a simple statement. In this grand age of reason, if you try to figure out everything, you may end up with a patch of intellectualism that means little since it does not develop the skill for the act. So, try to be a doer and not an "intellectualizer."

Don't hack at problem tones; your ramming at them will only shatter them. First be intrigued by what you have rather than by what you don't have. Capitalize on the good tones. Repeat them. The less good tones will profit by this procedure. Until you are very highly developed, you will face problems. Almost everybody has some problems. People share different problems. This makes the solving of problems a little less tough.

Of course, you are nervous when performing. A little nervousness may even put you on your toes. Nervousness or stage fright affects you by degree. If stage fright makes you freeze up or greatly undermines your feeling of strength and control, you must study long enough to develop into a first-rate technician, before you are able to do a normal vocal job. Your technique will be the counterforce to anxiety. When your technique enters the stage of regularity and safety, your fright will adjust itself to something you can handle. Your self-confidence will grow with your technical security.

Don't concentrate on listening to your voice when performing; if you do, you may forget your purpose. You can't very well be an observer at the same time you are a doer. You hear your voice because you produce sound, but you should not make an effort to control the listening experience when you make sound. When you take children to the park, you watch them, but you restrain your gaze. In other words, you want the children to be safe but not to feel that they are being unduly observed, lest they become self-conscious.

Don't try too hard to recapture what you had last time or to imitate past performances. You may miss something new. Also, don't feel obliged to outdo yourself. Of course, most of us want to sound a little better than we think we are. (So many times, when you want to prove something, you disprove it.) Come to your work with an open mind. A fresh point of view at all times is desirable.

## Notes

[1]To "breathe in through the nose" is often prescribed for singers and speakers. It is true that the nostrils cleanse the breath, humidify it and favorably condition the temperature of the inhaled breath. However, these advantages are easily offset by the obligation or rigidity of "method-breathing" or by the taboo: "don't breathe in through the mouth." Moreover, the quantity of air that can enter through the nose at one time or that the nostrils can comfortably handle is often insufficient to fulfill the desired vocal purpose. Then, the nose breather may be compelled to force her intake. Sniffling or similar unfortunate noises may result. Additional unfortunate associations or reflexes, such as shoulder lifting, may also be engendered. From a practical standpoint and to avoid complications, it is advisable to use nose and/or mouth for breath intake, to have free choice and let the intake occur either way without prejudice.

[2]Allowing the voice to travel its own way, progressing toward freedom through improvisations and unorthodox musical advances rather than through fixed runs or scale work is a progressive technique in voice building. The desire of the voice to move is fulfilled in a more organic way through the creation of scales "as we go," rather than through predetermined ones. This special technique for free musical expression should serve mainly to explore fullness and "qualities" of tone. The travel must come from the function of the tone. Tone freedom, form, flow and substance provide resources from which to improvise, explore and expand. To go where the tone leads us rather than where fixed musical exercises tell us is the main purpose of a free run. Thus when we do a vocal exercise or produce a tone and feel the impulse to go on to

another note, we permit the voice to travel or run and play rather than forcing it to stay on one given note or exercise. A playful vocal technique is thus applied to a serious vocal purpose.

[3]Obvious examples of tightening ahead of time can be found in the cases of some dancers who begin a study of voice. When confronted with voice work, they often make unconscious efforts to help by contracting the pelvic region or the intestines. They thus produce body adjustments that are appropriate for dance but that make them tense and work against freedom in voice production. Other dancers "clamp" in an effort to keep the mouth closed in dancing. The effects of this habit may interfere with the proper use of the mouth and throat areas in voice production. Also, musical uncertainty or a fear of hitting a wrong note often leads to advanced tightening. This is particularly noticeable in some musically inexperienced actors and dancers trying to sing a song or without sufficient musical preparation.

[4]Some singers even go so far as to whisper all day long when they have to perform at night. They need not whisper and pamper themselves or act like invalids. They need not shout either; but simply act normally.

[5]The glottal stroke is sometimes depicted as the root of all vocal evil and then becomes a scapegoat, particularly in some speech methods and books on speech. Let us stress here that vocal faults manifest themselves in such varied conditions that the reduction of all vocal ills to a single one seems to be a gross exaggeration and oversimplification. Granted, glottal strokes may be contributing factors to the malfunctioning of a voice. This is particularly true in those extreme cases where the afflicted tone attack

sounds a bit as if someone were pulling too sharply on a harp. But to concentrate nine-tenths of one's attention on this subject is out of all proportion to its significance. In most cases the destiny of a voice is not bound up strongly with that solution.

[6]Mishaps affecting the horn section of an orchestra may sound similar and have an equally embarrassing effect.

[7]Quivering, wiggling or shaking of the jaw, tongue, uvula and Adam's apple is often particularly noticeable in coloratura sopranos. The TV camera in close-up shots reveals these movements very clearly.

[8]People who have a sensitive vasomotor system, producing almost uncontrollable contractions and dilations of superficial blood vessels, will be affected by a flushing of the face and should accept it as a natural condition and of no consequence.

[9]An extremely small mouth opening when speaking or singing is often typical of people who wear braces on their teeth. Vanity, or a fear of being seen with a corrective device, is often responsible for the acquisition of this habit. Even after the braces have been removed, a very small mouth opening is often retained and may very well interfere with the proper adjustment of the vocal instrument. A typical complaint of a voice student who tries to describe this condition is, "I feel as if my upper lip is stuck to my teeth." The effort to conceal protruding teeth and other dental problems may establish similar, unfortunate patterns of voice production. Psychological aspects, such as "I am foreign born and self-conscious about the way I speak," or a fear to open one's mouth because of some rather painful consequences in childhood,

may also be mentioned in this connection. Unfortunately, a person who is self-conscious in speech may also discover that she gets breathy to hide her inefficiency, thus admitting to another vocal fault.

10A deviated septum may cause a certain hollowness in vocal sound.

11Voice work may help to stimulate the circulation and dissipate the congestion of an affected resonance area. This shows that vocal technique can also have therapeutic value. The sound waves are a highly potent means to help relieve congestion because of their vibratory power, which may shake things loose and serve as a sort of "vibration massage" or treatment.

12It would be a pleasure to be able to report that humming can be recommended as a beneficial exercise for all. However, the reasons why this cannot be done are manifold. (1) Resonance cavities of a person may be congested. Thus, people who suffer from hay fever may be unable to hum or pronounce "M" and usually substitute a sort of "B" consonant instead. (2) An aversion to making any sound with a closed mouth may exist in some cases. (3) The student may discover, "There is not enough energy for me in the hum." (4) For one reason or another, or perhaps for no obvious reason at all, the hum may have an unfortunate influence upon sound quality or quantity. If so, the exercise may have to be classed unworkable simply because the defects overshadow the merits.

13Many can identify Tauber's voice immediately because of this distinctive demarcation. The predominance of such a characteristic may even tempt us to describe a whole voice in terms of its most telling feature. However, this does the voice an injustice. We should exercise care not to forget the many unique features each voice possesses. Only in caricature is a peculiarity that labels a voice overemphasized while other balancing functions, which contribute to the health and beauty of a voice, are left out.

14Because the vowel sounds in singing are interchangeable, phonetic explanations of the practice words are given in loose terms of singing rather than in the standard terms used in phonetic speech study.

15A detailed exposition or guide to the study of articulation is beyond the scope of this book.

16Unfortunately, in the study of speech as well as in singing, an overstretching of the faculties is often caused by dramatic intentions. In line reading, the young actress is perhaps told by her speech teacher how much she must do in one breath. (This is particularly true with the classics.) In a similar way, some vocal coaches and conductors, working on repertoire with young singers may be tempted to fix the length of a phrase to be produced in one breath. In both cases, arbitrary fixing is meant to serve the material of the playwright or composer rather than the organic needs of the student. The order in which we proceed should be first the organic and then the dramatic. Rather than laboring to sustain length or being made to pack into one breath as much text as possible, a beginner should be led to produce short phrases comfortably. As his capability in this grows, so will his skill in handling text. The main point is to stop striving before that becomes a strain and a last, gasping push or squeeze is made.

17A typical example of vocal weight mismatch can be found in present-day singing of Tristan and Isolde. Tristan is perhaps one of the

weightiest tenor parts in the entire opera literature. Most tenors today seem to lack the mere
technical ability to sing the notes of this
score. In particular, they lack the capacity
boldly to punch into the vocal music, as the nature of this towering Wagnerian work so often
requires. In many instances, therefore, Tristan
takes a lighter voice into the valley of vocal
death. As the opera progresses and the demands
of the vocal music become increasingly heroic
(especially in sections of the third act), the
lighter tenor voice tends to suffer from throat
strain and is apt to decline in tone purity as
well as carrying power to the point where it is
often not even achieving audibility. After
singing Tristan, it may take a tenor quite some
time until, in a lighter opera (if at all), he
regains some of his normal vocal properties. The
more strain brought to bear upon the voice, the
greater the reaction when the load is lifted.

[18]A sudden switch to pianissimo is sometimes
attempted by big-voiced singers (particularly
tenors) as an artistic feat or arty gesture.
Though some opera buffs seem to be greatly impressed when their hero suddenly sounds very
unheroic, in most cases the challenge exceeds
the critical limit, and the result is unreliable
and problematical. To do well what they set out
to do, such singers should learn first to sing
less loudly and then still less loudly until
they are able progressively to reduce volume to
the point where a soft tone emerges that is free
and floats and that does not sound choked off or
as though it had come from a moon voice.

[19]Of course, to be subtle and yet be heard is
a problem to many actors. Frequently it boils
down to a mere energy problem. An actor who has
deenergized his intimate speech (and perhaps his
acting too) to a subvocal level must learn to
reenergize it in order to meet the needs of a
performance level.

20Radical body reducing methods may cause a breath shortage and lack of general vocal strength, which are especially noticeable in singing. The area around the waist seems to be particularly affected, and a singer may put the matter bluntly by complaining, "It feels as if someone had hit me in the breadbasket," or "I feel like a deflated tire."

21It is easy to understand, therefore, why some of the singer's work plays free with score indications. Famous examples are the tenor arias from Carmen and Aida. Even in Caruso's recordings of both pieces, we find that he changed the demands of Bizet and Verdi for soft or piano tone to loud or forte on a high B flat. (Perhaps that was done much to the dismay of conductors engaged in a pianissimo hunt.)

22Because acting deals with so many emotional ranges, mental attitudes and mood values, the actor may discover that by exploring the variations in his emotional being, changes in his voice result. Some acting teachers who recognize the connection between emotional and vocal life use singing as an exercise in the course of developing acting techniques. When an acting student succeeds in freeing himself in the process of study, his voice will usually react favorably. This happens sometimes when an actor works on an exercise or scene by himself. In the presence of teacher or colleagues with whom he is at ease, he may do equally well, if not better. But with an increase of pressure, strangeness and hostility of an auditioning or performing situation, a hoped-for vocal outcome will not always be reached. As a matter of fact, in times of stress, and when the going gets rough, the first thing to go is usually the voice, unless an actor has an unusually good, natural voice or can depend on vocal technique. Similarly, an opera singer may, in a moment of vocal truth or greatness, suddenly improve her acting. Such an improvement should not blind the opera singer to the fact that she needs basic acting instruction. Unfortunately, many an actor suffers from oversimplification, thinking that when the acting is right, the voice will come "naturally." In most untrained voices, it comes "naturally bad."

[23]The female voice may suffer from a breath shortage before or during menstruation. The effects of menstrual tension are often not sufficiently recognized by performers. Even more important, premenstrual tension is often ignored. Most women realize that several days during the period may be difficult or uncomfortable, but few are aware of the more subtle problems before a period starts. This is the time when a vague depression or overall tenseness can show up as irregularity in breathing, timing and general performance stamina. The student complains, "I don't have the bottom of my stomach today." To combat these difficulties, a woman should make herself especially aware of the problem days, set them aside as such, and grant herself (and expect from others) automatic forgiveness for shortcomings at that time. If she can thus anticipate these problem days, she may be able to cushion them. Her main weapons are relaxation and an awareness that it will all blow over soon enough. It may also help her to adopt an attitude of, "There I go again," or "I won't take myself too seriously," or "I've got to get off my back." However, if she tries to fight it rather than accept it, matters will only get worse. This is not pampering. Anyone involved in the arts must be aware of the subtleties of the human condition and the inevitable effect of one's emotions on one's work.

A warning must be given to those vocalists who on occasion prove to be "emotional screamers." Many women encounter this difficulty in their daily lives, particularly during menopause, or even during or before the monthly period. At such times, one's general physical condition often causes a highly emotional state, which in turn may lead to an overloud use of the speaking voice and consequent abuse of both the speaking and singing voice. The problem is complicated by lack of awareness, both of the cause of this condition and of the resultant harmful vocal effects. At such times of physical unrest, a female artist should be on vocal guard and she should request that she be told by her family or friends when her speaking voice goes overboard.

[24]Prolonged vocal rest periods provide an opportunity for vocal self-repair and can restore the capacity of an abused voice to function normally again.

[25]So is smoking.

# IN CONCLUSION

Let us learn through practical application to be fundamental. We have more to learn, as we find our way to continual growth, through a process of exploration and elimination. To study the basic tone of the voice is the exercise and practice to break through, so that we can make the sounds we were built to make and are free to make. No matter how they vary, there are four essential qualities, (called the superior qualities), to be found in human tone: freedom, form, flexibility, vibrancy. They are the seeds that can grow and become manifest, if we know how to look for them and if the proper conditions are given for their development. This is the aim of basic tone study. In no one are these four qualities equally dormant, present or developed. Because of natural disposition, almost everybody adapts himself to the basic tone study by means of one or two of those four qualities, but almost always one or more lag behind. Such are the inferior qualities. Our motto should be: Build strength where strength exists. At first we may succeed on one note only. That note becomes our constant. It leads us on to others. It becomes

254

richer itself, because we can hear and feel the difference. Gradually we become familiar with the balance of body functions that produce this tone and with the sensations that accompany it. We know where we are and the direction to take. Our work is at a safe point.

Let us avoid the pitfalls of methods in our work on technique. Let us not generalize. Let us not join those who are out to satisfy dogma and who advocate fixed rules for breathing, vi-brating, resonating, registration, practice vowel, posture and so forth. It is not the me-thod or pet theory of a teacher, it is the sound of each voice whose needs must determine the me-thod for peak production.

Let us use an approach that is organic to the individual so that we need not apologize for exceptions. Differences and inequalities exist in equipment and talent. The essential simi-larity in voices is their ability to gain free-dom, flow, ring and roundness by training. The essential difference in voices is the degree to which each of the four exists as an inborn qua-lity and the extent to which each can be devel-oped through use and training.

Let us acquire now an awareness of our vocal possibilities in spite of our limitations. Our realistic attitude may help control our anxiety or frustration. If we have experienced spells of anxiety because of some vocal problem, our entire being has perhaps felt defeated. But yes-terday's frustration can become today's depres-sion, and today's depression may become tomor-row's boon. We may thus uncover for ourselves further evidence of a fundamental truth, which supports not only all art forms but, even more, the art of living in a complex civilization.

Let there be a distinct pleasure in knowing that, with an ever-increasing ability, we can use the voice throughout a wider range and with greater freedom and fullness than ever before, without abusing it---or, more important---

knowing that if and when we are abusing it, simple exercises can be depended upon to get it back into shape.

Let us consider that wise old dictum: "Know thyself," in all its connotations, when we judge the sum and substance of our progress.

Let us feel we can "lick" something. That, in turn, will seem to make us feel less heavy on the emotional side and contribute to our sense of well-being, both from artistic and human points of view.

# APPENDIX

Examples of practice words to choose from in
alphabetical order.

(See page 203)

AGENDA   ALIBI   ALONE   AMAZON   AMELIA   AMMONIA
AMNESIA   AMPHIBIOUS   ANALOGY   ANEMIA   ANGELA
ANITA   APOLOGY   AVENUE   AVOCADO   AVOW

BABY   BABYLONIAN   BALCONY   BALMY   BAMBOO   BANANA
BANJO   BAY   BAYONNE   BEAMY   BEATA   BEAUTIFY
BEAUTY   BECAUSE   BEE   BEELINE   BELAY   BELGIUM
BELIE   BELLBOY   BELOW   BENJAMIN   BEULAH
BIENNIAL   BIGAMY   BIOLOGY   BLOW   BLOW-OUT
BLUE-JAY   BODY   BOHEMIAN   BOLOGNA   BONANZA   BONY
BOTANY   BOUNTEOUS   BOW   BOWLING   BOY   BOYLIKE
BUFFALO   BULOVA   BUNGALOW   BY-LINE

CALEDONIAN   CALM   CALMLY   CAMEO   CAMOUFLAGE
CANADA   CANNONADE   CANOE   CANYON   CASUALLY
CATALOGUE   CAUSE   CAVALCADE   CELIA   CELLO
CHAMELEON   CHANCY   CHATTANOOGA   CHAUTAUQUA
CHEESY   CHEW   CHEWING   CHICAGO   CHINA   CHOOSY
CHOW   CHOWCHOW   CLAUDIA   CLAW   CLAY   CLAYEY
CLIENTELE   CLOUDY   CLOY   COALY   COCA-COLA
C.O.D.   COINCIDE   COLLOQUIAL   COLONY   COLUMBIA
COMA   COMEDY   COMELY   COMPANY   CONE   CONFUSE
CONGENIAL   CONGOLEUM   CONSOMME   COW   COWHIDE
COY   COZY   C.P.A.   CUBA   CUTIE   CYCLOPEDIA

D.A. DAILY DAISY DAKOTA DANIEL DAY DAYLIGHT
DENIAL DENY DIABOLIZE DIADEM DIAGNOSE
DIAGONAL DIAL DIALOGUE DIAMOND DIANA DIE
DIE-AWAY DILEMMA DINAH DIPLOMA DO DO-AWAY
DOE DOGMA DOMINO DONNA DOUGHBOY DOVELIKE
DOWDY DOWNLINE DOWNTOWN DUBIOUS DUEL
DUNGEON DUTY DYNAMITE DYNAMO

EASILY EGO EILEEN ELENA ELEVEN ELI ELIJAH
EMILY EMMANUEL EMPLOYEE ENCYCLOPEDIA ENJOY
ENVY EQUALIZE EUGENE EVA EVENTIDE EVIL-EYED
EYEBALL EYESHADE

FADEAWAY FALLACY FAMILY FAY F.B.I. FEE
FEEBLY FELLOW FELLOWMAN FELONY FIANCE
FIELD-DAY FINE FIVEFOLD FLAMBOYANT FLAMINGO
FLOW FLOW-IN FLOW-OUT FLUE FLUENCY FLY
FLY-AWAY FOAMY FOLIO FOLLOW FOLLOWING
FOUNTAIN FUME FUNNY FUNNYMAN

GALA GALA-DAY GALILEE GALVANIZE GAUDY
GEISHA GELATINE GENEVA GENIUS GENUINE
GEOLOGY GHOSTLY G.I. GIGOLO GLASSY
GLOBELIKE GLOOMY GLUE GLUEY G-MAN GO
GO-ALONG GOOFY GOWN GUILLOTINE GUMBO GUY
GYMNASIUM

HALLOWEEN HALLOWED HANDYMAN HELIOTYPE HEMAN
HIDEAWAY HIGHLAND HOBO HOLIDAY HOLLOW
HOLYOKE HOMELY HONEY HONEYMOON HOUSEHOLD
HOW HOWLING HUE HUGO HUMANIZE HYENA

I IDAHO IDEAL IDEALIZE IDEOLOGY IDOLIZE
ILLINOIS INDIA INDIANA INFLOW INSOMNIA
INVIOLATE IODINE IOTA I.O.U. IOWA I.Q.
ISAIAH ISLAND IVY

JAMAICA JANE JAVANESE JAW JAWLINE JEALOUSY
JELLY JENNY JEWEL JOAN JOE JOEL JOINING
JOLLY JOSEPHINE JOVIAL JOY JOYOUS JUBILEE
JUICY JULIA JUNE JUVENILE

KEYNOTE   KHAKI   KILLJOY   KIMONO   KNEELING   KNOW
KNOWINGLY   K.O.   KOWTOW

LADY   LADYLIKE   LADYLOVE   LAMA   LANDING
LANDLADY   LAUGHING   LAVA   LAW   LAYMAN   LAZY   LEE
LEEWAY   LEGION   LEMONADE   LENA   LENIENT   LEO
LEONA   LIAISON   LIE   LIE-LOW   LIE-ON   LIFE-BUOY
LIGHT-BLUE   LIGHTHOUSE   LIKELY   LILY   LIMA   LIME
LIMELIGHT   LIMOUSINE   LINOLEUM   LINOTYPE   LIONEL
LISA   LIVELY   LOCALIZE   LOIN   LONE   LONELY
LONESOME   LOOMING   LOUDLY   LOUISA   LOUISIANA
LOVE   LOVELY   LOW   LOWLAND   LOWNESS   LOYALTY
LULLABY   LUMBAGO   LYDIA

MADAM   MAGNOLIA   MAHOGANY   MAIDEN-LAND   MAINLAND
MAINLY   MAJESTY   MAMMALIAN   MANDALAY   MANDOLIN
MANUEL   MAYBE   MAYDAY   MEADOW   MEAN   MEANINGLY
MEANWHILE   MEDALLION   MEDIUM   MELANIE   MELLOW
MELODY   MIAMI   MIGHTILY   MIKADO   MILADY   MILLY
MILWAUKEE   MINE   MINIMUM   MINNIE   MOAN   MODELING
MOHAWK   MOLE-EYED   MOLLIFY   MONA   MONDAY   MONEY
MONGOLIAN   MONICA   MONOTONE   MONTANA   MONTEZUMA
MOODY   MOSQUITO   MOVIE   MOVIELAND   MOW   MOW-DOWN
MULE   MUMMY   MUSEUM   MUTINY

NAOMI   NAPOLEON   NAVY   NAVY-BLUE   NEEDY
NEGLIGEE   NEOPHYTE   NEPHEW   NEVADA   NEW
NEWFOUNDLAND   NEWLY   NIGHTGOWN   NIGHTINGALE
NINA   NINE   NINEFOLD   NO   NOAH   NOBLEMAN   NOBODY
NOISY   NO-MAN'S-LAND   NO-ONE   NOSTALGIA   NOSY
NOVELIZE   NOVOCAINE   NOW   NOWAY   NUCLEUS
NULLIFY   NYLON

OBLONG   OBVIOUS   O.D.   OILY   O.K.   OKLAHOMA
OLEO   OLYMPIAN   OMAHA   ONE   ONION   ONLY
ONTOLOGY   OOZY   OPENLY   OPHELIA   OUTFLOW   OUTLAW
OUTLINE   OWE

PACIFY   PALMY   PAMELA   PANAMA   PANTOMIME
PASADENA   PAULA   PAW   PAY   PAYMENT   PEA   PEELING
PEEWEE   PENALTY   PENDULUM   PENTAGON   PHENOMENON
PHILADELPHIA   PHILOSOPHY   PHOBIA   PHOTO

PHOTOPHOBIA  PHYSIOLOGY  PIANO  PIANOLA  PIE
PILE  PILLOW  PILOT  PINE  PINE-CONE  PLASMA
PLATEAU  PLAY  PLAYBOY  PLAYLAND  PLEA  PLEADING
PLEBEIAN  PLENTY  PLIANCY  PLOW  PLOWBOY  P.M.
PNEUMONIA  POISON  POLE  POLICY  POLIO  PONY
POSY  POTATO  PSEUDO  PSYCHO  PSYCHOANALYZE
PSYCHOLOGY  PUNY

QUALIFY  QUALITY  QUEENLY  QUIETLY  QUININE
QUOTA

SABINA  SADIE  SAGA  SALAMI  SALOME  SAMUEL
SAN-DIEGO  SAW  SAWBONE  SAXOPHONE  SAY  SAY-SO
SCANDALIZE  SCANDINAVIA  SCHEDULE  SCHOOLBOY
SEA  SEA-LANE  SEA-LION  SEASONING  SEMICOLON
SEVEN  SHADOW  SHADOWY  SHAH  SHALLOW  SHEILA
SHINING  SHOE  SHOVEL  SHOW  SHOWY  SHY  SIAMESE
SIGH  SIGHING  SKYLINE  SLAYING  SLOWLY  SLY
SMELLY  SMILE  SMOKY  SNOW  SNOWBOUND  SO
SO-AND-SO  SOAPY  SOCIALITE  SODA  SOLELY  SOLO
SOLOMON  SOMEONE  SONATA  SONIA  SON-IN-LAW
SONNY-BOY  SOPHIE  SOUPY  SPEEDILY  SPELLBOUND
SPOOKY  SPY  STADIUM  STAGY  STAMINA  STONY
STOWAWAY  STUDIO  SUE  SUNDAY  SUNDOWN  SWALLOW
SYLVIA  SYMPHONY

TABU  TANGO  TAPIOCA  TEA  TEA-GOWN  TELEPHONE
TIDY  TILING  TIMPANO  T.N.T.  TOE  TOLEDO
TOMATO  TOMBOY  TOO  TOOLING  TOTEM-POLE  TOW
TOWLINE  TOY  TOYLAND  TUBA  T.V.  TWENTY-ONE
TWILIGHT  TYMPANY

U-BOAT  UNA  UNALIKE  UNEMPLOYED  UNGODLY  UNIFY
UNION  UNITY  UNKNOWN  UNLOYAL  UNVEILING
UNYIELDING  USUALLY  UTICA  UTOPIA

VACUUM  VALENTINE  VALUE  VANITY  VASELINE
VEILING  VELVETY  VENUS  VETO  VIA  VIEW  VIEWY
VIOLA  VIOLATE  VIOLIN  VISA  VOCALIZE  VODKA
VOLCANO  VOW

WANTON   WAVY   WELCOME   WELL-DONE   WHOLESALE
WILLOW   WINE   WISE-GUY   WOE   WOO   WOOING
WYOMING

YAWN   YAWNING   YEA   YELLOW   YEOMAN   YOGI
YOLANDA   YOWLING   YULETIDE

ZION   ZOO   ZULU

---

## Note

---

The practice session should have enjoyable and
purposeful meaning to each student. On the one
hand, there is the person who has no problems
here. He loves to make sound, whips up a sen-
suous excitement through the act of making
sound, similar to the musician who plays his
instrument for the sheer joy of the tones he
produces or the dancer whose pleasure is "moving
through space." There are, however, people who
are inhibited or lack the urge to sing: they
find it difficult to let go with a full release
of vocal sound. Particularly, the actor who
sounds pale and "speechy" in his singing may
well benefit by putting "more purpose" behind
the singing exercise. He can create situations
for himself which serve as stimulants and moti-
vations. When these situations are of a very
personal nature, students are for the most part
reluctant to discuss them. However, a situation
can be of a general nature---for example, "I am
calling to a person who is quite remote from
me." The image of communication and distance is
thus used for the sake of vocal projection.
    Sometimes the speaking voice of an actor is
strong and colorful but his singing voice sounds
weak and pale. Advice such as, "Say it rather
than sing it" may then help the actor to overcome the further hurdle of being withdrawn and
"song-shy." A speaking image, when applied to
singing, may unlock the chain and induce the

actor to sound off in singing, also. Additional helpful images may be found in the form of vocal parodies. Good parodies come very close to the truth. Also, parodies relieve us of the burden of taking ourselves too seriously. When we feel less anxious about what comes out vocally, we fulfill our work-task in a more carefree manner. This can bring us out of ourselves. Because we want to sound as though we are just making a joke, we lose the fear of making fools of ourselves. The latter problem is one of those ghosts that haunt people who would like to take off in song but don't dare because they consider singing too far out of their reach. Under the disguise of a vocal funnyman who, for example, gives an imitation of the "grand manner of singing," some vocal beginners seem able to muster up courage and are apt to produce sound more freely and fully than when they are their own singing selves.

Just as some actors have problems with singing, so some singers have difficulties projecting speech. Most of us remember the famous opera singer who, having accepted a lead in a Broadway musical, found that throughout the run of the show the eight performances per week presented many more problems to his speaking than to his singing voice.

In order to overcome such vocal difficulties, a gradual and systematic vocal process may have to take place, the purpose of which is to transfer the strong points of the singing to the weaker function, the speaking. The steps involved are: first, singing exercises with tones, syllables and words; then, chanting exercises with syllables and words; thereafter, sing-song, melodramatic and exaggerated speaking exercises; finally, normal speaking and reading exercises. The task is to carry the same vocal material through different stages of vocal preparation and, as far as possible, to maintain tonal freedom and fullness throughout the related but

varying modes of vocal utterance. The same
pattern, the same key words, are thus used to
bring out the singing side of speaking and the
speaking side of singing, in order to bridge the
gap between the two.

In doing reading exercises, it is advisable
not to use the lines of a play the artist may
have to perform lest his performance becomes
self-conscious or too voicy.

# INDEX

265